The Wealth Inequality Reader

2nd Edition

Edited by Dollars & Sense and United for a Fair Economy

Preface by Jesse Jackson Jr.

DOLLARS & SENSE — ECONOMIC AFFAIRS BUREAU
BOSTON, MASSACHUSETTS

THE WEALTH INEQUALITY READER

Edited by Chuck Collins, Daniel Fireside, Amy Gluckman, Betsy Leondar-Wright, Meizhu Lui, James McBride, Amy Offner, Smriti Rao, Adria Scharf.

ISBN: 978-1-878585-69-1

Published by:

Dollars & Sense
Economic Affairs Bureau
29 Winter Street
Boston, MA 02108
617-447-2177
dollarsandsense.org

Cover: David Gerratt
Section Illustrations: Nick Thorkelson
Production: Noel Cunningham
Manufactured by Vision Lithographics
Printed in the United States

CONTENTS

SECTION III   THE CONSEQUENCES OF INEQUALITY

SECTION IV   STRATEGIES FOR CHANGE

SECTION V LOOKING FORWARD

APPENDIX

PREFACE

BY JESSE JACKSON JR.

Wealth does matter.

It's the difference between being a tenant and a homeowner, a sharecropper and a shareholder.

It's the difference between buying a soda, wearing sneakers, or eating a hamburger—and owning Coca-Cola, Nike, or McDonalds.

It's what divides consumers standing in check-out lines from stakeholders who have a voice in the future of the economy.

As *The Wealth Inequality Reader* chronicles, our country's disparities of wealth and power are now at their greatest point since the 1920s. The richest 1% of the population now owns almost 35% of all the private wealth in America, more than the bottom 90% of the population combined.

The racial wealth divide is even more dramatic, underscoring how the legacy of discrimination in lending practices, business ownership, and employment has thwarted wealth-building opportunities for people of color. In 2001, the typical black household had a net worth of just $19,000, including home equity, compared with $121,000 for whites. Blacks had 16% of the median wealth of whites, up from 5% in 1989. This is progress, but at this rate it will take until 2099 to reach parity in median wealth.

The growth in wealth inequality is the result of two and a half decades of government policies tilted in favor of large asset owners at the expense of wage earners. Tax policy, trade policy, monetary policy, government regulations, and other rules have reflected this pro-investor bias. Under President George W. Bush, pro-rich policies have gotten worse, as Congress and the president funnel tax giveaways to their wealthy friends and donors.

It hasn't always been like this. Throughout U.S. history, our government has helped expand the wealth and security of many of its citizens. For example, after the Civil War, the government gave millions of acres of land to homesteaders. Then, in the two decades after World War II, massive government scholarships for higher education, and subsidies for small business development and affordable housing, greatly expanded the white middle class. These scholarships and subsidies, plus federally insured low-interest mortgages to homebuyers, enabled millions to get on board the wealth-building train. Unfortunately, discrimination in federal policies left red, brown, and black people standing at the train station during both historical periods.

We must work to overcome the perpetuation of wealth inequality. The accumulated advantages and disadvantages of wealth inequality are like sediment. The opportunities for those with wealth build up, layer upon layer, from the previous generation's wealth, education, and opportunity. And the accumulated disadvantages of having no wealth and savings deepen the hole of discrimination, poverty, debt, and blocked opportunity.

Inclusion is the key to economic growth. If people have adequate incomes and access to capital, they can buy homes and increase their stake in society. Instead of redlining low-income communities, let's green-line America and make the grass grow in scorched areas.

We know from research that the wealth of a child's parents has an enormous influence on his or her economic prospects. Only a bold approach to wealth building will dramatically reduce the number of "asset-less" households and create wealth-building opportunities for all those who have been left out.

Our challenge is to level the playing field, expand the marketplace, embrace the assurances of the American dream, and allow all to realize life, liberty, and the pursuit of happiness.

Jesse Jackson Jr. represents the 2nd Congressional District of Illinois in the U.S. House of Representatives. He is co-author of A More Perfect Union: Advancing New American Rights (Welcome Rain Publishers, 2001).

INTRODUCTION

The United States entered the new millennium with the most unequal distribution of wealth since the eve of the Great Depression. This sorry fact forms the kernel for *The Wealth Inequality Reader*. The authors here—sociologists, economists and activists—analyze the issue of wealth inequality through multiple entry points and a range of disciplines.

Most discussions of economic inequality focus on income, not wealth, for the simple reason that data on income are more readily available. But wealth has its own dynamic, and its distribution has unique causes and consequences. More than income, wealth both tells of the past and foretells the future. A family's wealth today reflects the asset-building opportunities open not only to this generation, but to parents, grandparents, and great-grandparents. Likewise, parents use their wealth to position their children for future economic success in countless ways—moving into an excellent school district or giving an adult child money for a down payment, for example—that are out of reach for those who may earn a middle-class income but have few assets.

Given the country's severe and growing wealth gap, asset-building as a solution to poverty has recently come into vogue (although its chief policy incarnation, a matched savings plan known as an Individual Development Account (IDA), has yet to become more than a minor pilot program). This approach is in line with the individualist ethos that reigns in U.S. politics. This volume describes IDAs and a range of other policies that can help individuals accumulate assets. But more important, several of the authors here argue that the wealth gap cannot be addressed unless our commonwealth of shared public assets, which form the foundation of individual wealth, are expanded and shared.

Section I documents the worsening landscape of wealth inequality. Here are just a few items:

- In just 15 years, from 1992 to 2007, the average net worth of the wealthiest 400 Americans more than tripled in real terms, from $937 million to $3.85 billion.
- The racial wealth divide persists: In 2004, the median family net worth of Blacks was $20,400, only 14.5 percent of the median white net worth of $140,700. The median net worth for Latino families was $27,100.
- The U.S. savings rate has plummeted from 11.2 percent in 1982 to *negative* 1.1 percent in 2006.
- Households headed by single men are far better off (median net worth $46,990) than households headed by single women (median net worth $27,850).

Although systematic data are scarce for many other parts of the world, the trend in the United States is clear: wealth is becoming more and more concentrated. Recent fluctuations in the stock market have both added to and diminished the share of total wealth owned by the top 1% of American households. But the sub-prime mortgage meltdown is putting the wealth of many average Americans—whose home is their single largest asset—at risk. There is every reason to believe that wealth concentration will continue to grow, given the current direction of so many of the political-economic vectors that shape wealth distribution.

Why is the wealth gap in the United States widening now? It's not hard to see (and Section II fills in the details). For nearly 30 years following World War II, both the state and organized labor acted as counterweights to the power of corporations. Building on the legacy of the New Deal years, a range of government policies and a relatively stable business-labor compact moderated the excesses of the market, and as a result, a broad swath of Americans shared, at least to a degree, in the prosperity of the time.

But since the mid-1970s, determined efforts by conservatives and corporations have succeeded in dismantling parts of the New Deal legacy and crushing the labor movement. These efforts have both contributed to and benefited from the country's history of race and discrimination. Playing "the race card" has been a key piece of the GOP's strategy for enlisting low– and moderate-income white voters against their own economic interests; meantime, conservative economic policies worsen the racial wealth gap, an artifact of centuries of slavery and post-slavery discrimination.

The consequences of the growing wealth gap are dissected in Section III. As we noted, inequality is usually conceptualized in terms of income. But wealth inequality matters at least as much as, if not more than, income inequality. For one thing, incomes are volatile, subject to the vicissitudes of the domestic business cycle and deepening global competition. In contrast, assets like a home, land, or savings offer a more stable form of security and allow families to survive financial setbacks without seeing their standard of living permanently undermined. Ownership and control of assets may be particularly important to members of historically disadvantaged groups; for example, a study in India has shown that women who own land or a house in their own names are, other things equal, far less likely to be victims of domestic violence.

Furthermore, wealth inequality is self-reinforcing and worsens over time absent proactive efforts at redistribution. Wealth allows parents to give their children a wide range of advantages that position them to build even greater wealth as adults.

Extreme concentrations of wealth do not only hurt those far down the economic ladder. Concentrated wealth distorts democracy by giving a small elite both the motive and the means to buy the policies they want from contribution-hungry politicians. Concentrated wealth bites the hand that feeds it, too: evidence suggests that extreme inequality actually undermines economic growth. And concentrated wealth spawns a culture of excessive consumption that subverts all of the nonmaterial values people find difficult enough to sustain in a modern capitalist economy.

While the picture up to this point may seem dismal, we need only look back to find the cause for optimism. Throughout U.S. history, periods of excessive wealth polarization have been followed by mass movements for economic reform. The Gilded Age was followed by populism and progressivism; the 1929 crash was followed by poor people's movements and the New Deal. These movements for change succeeded, however unevenly, in moving the country's capitalist economy to a new equilibrium in which working people and the middle class had access to a larger morsel of the ownership pie than they otherwise would have (although, to be clear, wealth has never been divided near equitably, even in the country's most egalitarian eras).

Likewise, today, a movement to restructure the economy and reorient government policies so that wealth will be more widely shared is beginning to grow. "Movements" might be a more appropriate term: countless activists, scholars, unions—and a few politicians and business leaders—are engaging this issue from many angles. Sections IV and V sketch out some of these potential solutions, from the nuts and bolts of specific asset-building programs to visionary proposals for institutionalizing an overall more equitable distribution of wealt—for example, by collecting rents and fees from private interests who use common assets like the sky and the airwaves, then paying those revenues out to all.

For those who believe that two human beings can vary so widely in merit—however merit is defined—that one of them deserves to possess billions of dollars and a surfeit of mansions and jets while the other deserves to sleep on a sewer grate, the authors here will have little to say. But for anyone who is convinced that inherent in any definition of a healthy and just society are some limits to the unequal distribution of wealth, this volume provides a roadmap through—and, we hope, beyond—the current political economy of wealth inequality.

Wealth Inequality by the Numbers

N ot since the Gilded Age has this country seen such a yawning gap between the very rich and those with little wealth. Global wealth disparities are even larger. The following pages capture this polarization with facts and figures on the distribution of wealth in the United States and, to the extent possible, worldwide.

THE WEALTH PIE

The wealthiest 1% of households owns more than a third of the nation's household wealth. The next tier, those in the 95th through 98th percentiles, claims another 24%. While the top 5% holds well over half of the wealth pie, the bottom 50% makes do with the crumbs—holding a meager 2.5% of total net worth.

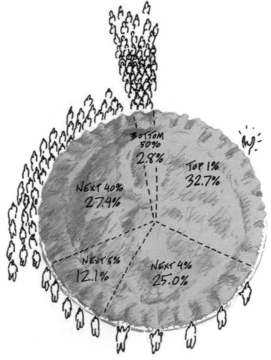

Source: Arthur B. Kennickell, "Currents and Undercurrents", January 2006

WHAT IS WEALTH?

A family's wealth, or net worth, is defined as the sum of its assets minus its debts. In other words, wealth is "what you own" minus "what you owe." *Assets* are all resources that a household holds in store—the bank of reserves a family has available to invest in its members and their futures. Many assets grow in value and generate interest income. Just as important, asset wealth provides a cushion, protecting families from the vicissitudes of the business cycle, as wealth assets may be drawn down during periods of crisis (a job loss, for example). *Financial assets* include savings, bonds, certificates of deposit, stocks, mutual fund investments, retirement pensions, and the like. *Nonfinancial assets* may include homes, other real estate, vehicles, ownership in a privately held business, and all sorts of other property—from rare baseball card collections to jewelry or hobby equipment. *Debts* are liabilities—credit card balances, mortgages, and other loans—that are owed.

One way to think about wealth, as distinct from income, is to picture it as a pool of resources—much like a pond. Income, by contrast, is more like a stream or a river that flows. Most adults receive an income stream of paychecks, entitlement payments like Social Security, child support, or pensions. This cash flow is normally spent on housing, health care, food, clothing, consumer goods, entertainment, and miscellaneous expenses. If any trickle of income remains, it is set aside as savings—becoming wealth. People with large "ponds" of wealth typically receive streams of income in the form of interest, dividends, or rent from those assets. The very wealthy have "lakes" of assets that spring substantial rivers of income.

Looking at information about wealth can tell us a lot about people's lives, and it can tell us things that income statistics fail to reveal. The bottom quartile of U.S. families has a mean net worth of $0—an average family in the bottom quartile carries a debt burden equal to all of its assets combined. From this, we can surmise that such a family most likely does not own a home, or if they do, all of its value

Different researchers use slightly different definitions of wealth. For example, some exclude those retirement pensions that an individual cannot currently access, while others include the estimated present value of pensions. And some scholars consider automobiles a form of wealth, whereas others exclude the value of automobiles from their calculations.

Data on wealth is far scarcer than data on income. The primary source of information on private wealth in the United States is the Federal Reserve's triennial Survey of Consumer Finances, which collects household-level data on assets, liabilities, income, use of financial services, and other household financial behavior.

has been mortgaged or its market value has declined. If such a family owns any asset, it is probably a car that they had to borrow money to purchase. By contrast, a family in the second or third wealth quartile is likely to own a home as its largest asset. Families in the top quartile probably own not just one or more homes, but also stocks and other financial assets.

While private wealth is an important source of security in our society, *social wealth* can reduce and even eliminate the need for substantial individual or household wealth. For instance, an adequate social safety net that includes income support and health care would reduce the need for individual savings to ensure basic economic security.

THE SUPER-RICH

Over a 30-year period beginning in 1970, the richest 1% (as ranked by income) accrued a mounting share of the nation's private wealth. Throughout the 1990s, the top percentile held a larger concentration of total household wealth than at any time since the 1920s. Its wealth share declined somewhat during the 2001 recession, thanks to falling corporate share prices, but began rising again in 2004 to 34.3%.

PERCENTAGE OF WEALTH OWNED BY THE TOP 1%

Illustrations in this section by Nick Thorkelson

The past two decades have been kind to the super-rich. Since 1992, the average wealth held by the nation's wealthiest 400 people more than quadrupled, rising

THE WEALTHIEST 400 PEOPLE IN THE UNITED STATES

Wealth by Rank and Average Wealth (in millions of 2004 dollars), 1992-2007

Wealth by Rank in the *Forbes* 400	1992	1995	1999	2000	2001	2002	2005	2007
1st	7,746	17,002	89,716	64,318	54,000	42,361	51,000	59,000
10th	4,303	4,940	17,943	17,356	17,500	11,723	15,400	17,000
50th	1,537	2,068	4,222	4,798	3,900	3,152	4,200	6,300
100th	984	1,034	2,533	2,654	2,000	1,773	2,500	3,500
400th	326	391	660	740	600	542	900	1,300
Avg. Wealth	937	1,025	2,731	3,057	2,366	2,148	2,813	3,850
Number of billionaires	92	107	278	301	266	205	374	400

Source: Calculated from *Forbes* 400.

HOUSEHOLDS WITH NET WORTH EQUAL TO OR EXCEEDING $10 MILLION

The number of households with $10 million or more has grown more than five fold since 1983 (from 66,500 to 344,800).

2001: 338,400

2004: 344,800

1998: 239,900

1995: 190,400

1983: 66,500

1989: 64,900

1992: 41,600

Source: Edward N. Wolff, "Recent Trends in Household Wealth in the United States", June 2007.

THE WEALTHLESS

The 1980s and 1990s were supposed to be economic good times, but the share of Americans with no wealth at all was larger in 2004 than it had been in 1983. The late-1990s economy gave a small boost to those at the bottom, but it didn't make up for the losses of the previous 15 years. The result: even after the 1990s—the most fabulous decade of economic growth in recent U.S. history—over a quarter of American households had less than $5,000 in assets.

HOUSEHOLDS WITH LITTLE OR NO NET WORTH, 1983–2004

	Percentage of Households with Zero or Negative Net Worth	Percentage of Households with Net Worth Less Than $5,000[a]
1983	15.5%	25.4%
1989	17.9%	27.6%
1992	18.0%	27.2%
1995	18.5%	27.8%
1998	18.0%	27.2%
2001	17.6%	26.6%
2004	17.0%	26.8%

a. Constant 1995 Dollars

Source: Edward N. Wolff, "Recent Trends in Household Wealth in the United States", June 2007. Studies of wealth ownership define wealth differently. Because Wolff subtracts the value of automobiles, his figures show a higher percentage of the population with little or no wealth than studies that include cars as wealth.

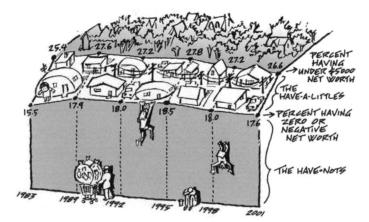

CLASS MOBILITY

LIKE PARENT, LIKE CHILD

In the United States, a sure way to secure a high income is to be born to parents with high incomes. Only 7.3% of children born to parents with incomes in the top 20% grow up to have incomes in the bottom 20%, no matter how lazy or incompetent they might be. Likewise, just 6.3% of children with parents in the bottom income quintile earn incomes in the top 20% as adults. So much for the myth of meritocracy.

If anything, these figures actually overstate the degree of income mobility in the United States. This is because it takes much more significant increases in income to enter the top quintile from the others than it takes to move up one, two, or even three quintiles from the bottom. In 2006, for example, the mean household income of the lowest quintile was $11,352 (2006 dollars), compared to $28,777 for the second quintile (a difference of $17,425). By contrast, the mean household income of the top quintile was $111,536, compared to $58,163 for the next highest quintile (a difference of $53,373—a much larger distance to travel). Although a large percentage of children born to parents in the bottom 20% move up a few quintiles as adults, their mobility is less striking than the *lack* of mobility into the top quintile.

Figures on mobility by wealth don't exist, but if they did, they'd probably paint an even bleaker picture.

CHANCE OF CHILD ATTAINING INCOME LEVEL AS ADULT, BY PARENTAL INCOME

Parents' Income Quintile	Child's Income Quintile as Adult		
	Top 20%	Middle 20%	Bottom 20%
Top 20%	37.3%	18.4%	7.3%
Middle 20%	17.3%	25.0%	15.3%
Bottom 20%	6.3%	16.5%	42.3%

Source: Thomas Hertz, "Rags, Riches and Race."

Note: These figures are based on total family income for black and white participants in the Panel Study of Income Dynamics who were born between 1942 and 1972, observed as children in their households of origin, and later as adults (26 or older) in their own households.

THE OWNING CLASS

While upwards of 90% of people in the United States make their living by work-ing for a wage or salary, a small number gain their incomes from the ownership of property. These large-scale property owners may have jobs (usually high-paying ones), but they do not *have* to work for a living. They own businesses, which yield profits; stocks, which yield dividends; real estate, which yields rent; and money, which yields interest. Unlike the houses and cars that are most Americans' primary assets, these forms of wealth typically accumulate income; they also give their own-ers, in varying ways and degrees, some control over the nation's economy.

Some of the 90% also own these kinds of property: a triple-decker or a small stock portfolio, perhaps. But ownership of income-accumulating property is even more highly concentrated than ownership of wealth overall. The income from such property is considerable—nearly $3 trillion in the United States in 2003, or over one-quarter of gross national income (even by the most conservative estimate). This is the tribute the owning class extracts each year from society's total production.

Profits and other private property income have ranged between one-fourth and one-third of U.S. national income over the last 45 years. This variation may not seem like much, but when the private-property share of national income declined sharp-ly in the mid-1960s, as a result of high employment and rising worker militancy,

PRIVATE PROPERTY INCOME (PROFITS, INTEREST, RENT, ETC., BEFORE TAXES) AS A PERCENTAGE OF NATIONAL INCOME, 1959-2003

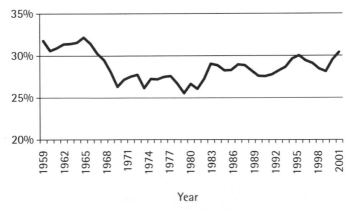

Year

Source: U.S. Dept. of Commerce, Bureau of Economic Analysis, National Income and Product Accounts, Table 1.10 Gross Domestic Income by Type of Income. Percentages equal "Net operating surplus, private enterprises" divided by the sum of itself and "Compensation of employees, paid."

U.S. capitalism went into crisis. The "recovery" beginning in the early 1980s coincided with property ownership garnering an increasing share of national income, as attacks on unions and social welfare programs eroded workers' bargaining power. In short, capitalism "functions" as long as the owning class can take a satisfactory cut of the national income.

THE STOCK OWNERSHIP PIE

If the distribution of wealth overall in the United States is very skewed, the distribution of financial assets such as stocks and bonds is far more so. A home is the single largest asset for most American families who have any wealth at all; most other kinds of assets are heavily concentrated in the hands of the wealthiest few percent of families. The chart shows the distribution of the nation's publicly traded stock that is directly held—in other words, outside of a managed account such as a mutual fund. The richest 1% of families owns over half of all directly held stock; the bottom 50% owns one-half of one percent. Assets not directly held—those in IRAs, 401(k)s, mutual funds, and similar accounts—are more equally distributed—among the wealthier half of the population. But the bottom 50% owns almost none of those assets either: only 0.7% of the value of mutual funds and 3.4% of the value of retirement accounts such as 401(k)s.

SHARE OF STOCK OWNED, BY WEALTH CLASS (2004)

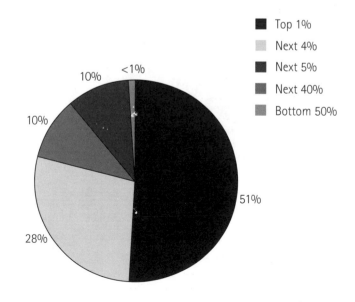

Source: Kennickell, "Currents and Undercurrents", January 2006.

THE RACIAL WEALTH GAP

The United States has a racial wealth gap that far exceeds its racial income gap. This wealth gap persists even during periods of economic growth. In the 1990s boom, the wealth of families of color (nonwhite and Latino) actually fell, although this drop was reversed in the 2000s. This intransigent wealth gap is the product of a long history of discrimination in the United States, and is perpetuated by family inheritance patterns that pass accumulated advantages and disadvantages from one generation to the next. The median net worth of families of color is just a fraction of white families', and racial wealth disparities are found across all categories of asset ownership.

WEALTH VS. INCOME BY RACE, 1995-2004

		1995	1998	2001	2004	$ change
Median Net Worth	Families of color	$19,500	$19,300	$19,100	$24,800	$5,300
	White families	$94,300	$111,000	$129,600	$140,700	$46,400
Median Income	Families of color	$24,400	$27,000	$27,400	$29,800	$5,400
	White families	$40,700	$44,200	$48,200	$49,400	$8,700

* 2006 Dollars
Source: Brian K. Bucks, Arthur B. Kennickell, and Kevin B. Moore, "Recent Changes in U.S. Family Finances" (February 2006)

THE RACIAL WEALTH GAP IN 2001 (IN 2000 DOLLARS)

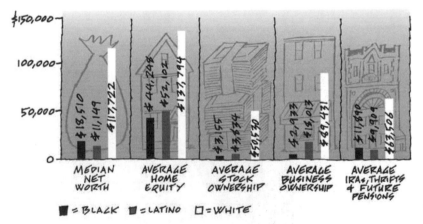

WOMEN'S WEALTH

WOMEN AND WEALTH IN THE UNITED STATES

Women own less wealth than men, but the gender wealth gap may be shrinking. So suggest the most recent data on wealth ownership in the United States. Virtually all data on asset ownership is by household and does not distinguish among people living in the household. So, the only gender comparison that typically can be made is between single women and single men.

According to the most recent Survey of Consumer Finances, there is still a dramatic gap overall between the net worth of households headed by single females and those headed by single males: the median net worth of the latter is 69% higher. Data on young baby boomers—those born between 1957 and 1964—from the National Longitudinal Survey of Youth, however, show a much smaller gap between these two groups. As young adults born after 1964 have relatively little wealth at all, this snapshot of the young boomers does suggest a promising trend.

MEDIAN NET WORTH AND FINANCIAL ASSETS OF ALL HOUSEHOLDS (2001)

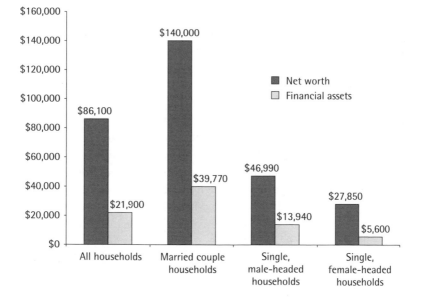

Source: Jeanne M. Hogarth and Chris E. Anguelov, "Descriptive Statistics on Levels of Net Worth." Data from 2001 Survey of Consumer Finances.

MEDIAN NET WORTH OF YOUNG BABY BOOMERS (2000)

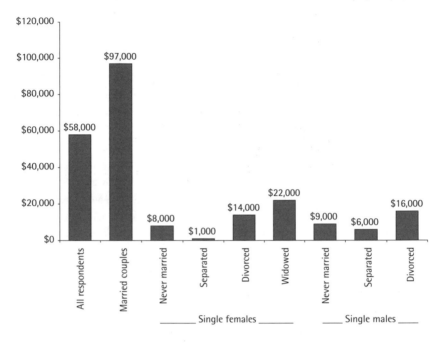

Source: Lisa A. Keister and Alexis Yamokoski, "Single Females and Wealth." Data from the National Longitudinal Survey of Youth, 1979 Cohort. The sample contained too few widowers to include.

GENDER AND PROPERTY RIGHTS

Around the world, women continue to face discriminatory laws and customs that restrict their rights to own and inherit property, whether land, houses, or financial assets. In the United States, a woman's right to own and control property was intially defined by the common law doctrines of *couverture* and *jure uxoris*: a woman's legal identity—and hence her right to own and control property—was "suspended" upon marriage. In the second half of the 19th century, state statutes began giving married women property rights, but custom continued to limit those rights well into the 20th century. Likewise, many countries in the global South have passed laws or constitutional provisions giving women equal rights to own and control property, but customary practices continue to restrict the exercise of these rights.

WORLD WIDE WEALTH

Data on wealth ownership and its distribution are scarce compared to data on income. This is particularly true on an international scale: only a handful of countries systematically collect information on individual or household wealth holdings. In the absence of such data, two World Bank economists have estimated the per capita wealth in different world regions using national-level data. They derive total wealth by adding the monetary values of a nation's natural resources (for example, oil, timber, and cropland), its produced assets (for example, goods and factories), and its "human resources" (the wealth inhering in people's projected lifetime productivity, computed as a function of GNP with some adjustments). The authors acknowledge that these are rough, preliminary estimates.

Poor countries tend to have lower per-capita natural resource wealth than rich countries. But it's notable that the natural resource gap is much smaller than the gap in the other components of wealth (the Middle East excepted). This suggests that a country's natural endowments are less important than how it deploys them and how the international rules governing trade and financial transactions shape its economy.

GLOBAL WEALTH DISTRIBUTION (2000)

	Population Share	Wealth Per Adult	Wealth Share
North America	6.1%	$190,653	34.3%
Latin American & Caribbean	8.2%	$18,163	4.4%
Europe	14.9%	$67,232	29.5%
Asia: China	22.8%	$3,885	2.6%
Asia: India	15.4%	$1,989	0.9%
Asia: High Income	4.5%	$172,414	22.9%
Asia: Other	17.4%	$5,952	3.1%
Africa	10.2%	$3,558	1.1%
Oceania	.6%	$72,874	1.2%

Source: James B. Davies, Susanna Sandstrom, Anthony Shorrocks, Edward N. Wolff. "The World Distribution of Household Wealth", (December 2006).

CONCENTRATED CORPORATE OWNERSHIP IN EAST ASIA

In several East Asian countries, vast wealth—in particular, the ownership of publicly held corporations—is concentrated in the hands of just a few families: the Suhartos in Indonesia and the Ayalas in the Philippines, for example. The figure shows the results of an analysis of the ownership of almost 3,000 companies as of December 1996. Notably, Japan stands out for its far lower concentration of ownership than the other countries studied—a result in part of land reform and related policies implemented by the Allied occupying forces following World War II.

The authors, economists at the World Bank and the Chinese University of Hong Kong, also discovered that greater wealth concentration was correlated with more dysfunctional legal and regulatory systems. This, in turn, may have contributed to the late-1990s East Asian financial crisis. "In some East Asian economies," they conclude, "successful legal and regulatory reform may require changes in ownership structures and concentration of wealth."

SHARE OF TOTAL MARKET CAPITALIZATION CONTROLLED BY THE WEALTHIEST FAMILIES

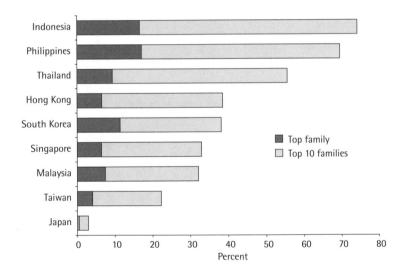

Source: Stijn Claessens, Simeon Djankov, and Larry H. P. Lang, "Who Controls East Asian Corporations."

There's more than one way to measure poverty, and the government's method of drawing the poverty line has provoked criticism from the left as well as the right. What does "living in poverty" really mean?

MEASURES OF POVERTY

BY ELLEN FRANK

Each February, the Census Bureau publishes the federal poverty thresholds—the income levels for different sized households below which a household is defined as living "in poverty." Each August, the bureau reports how many families, children, adults, and senior citizens fell below the poverty threshold in the prior year. As of 2004, the federal poverty thresholds were as follows:

Household Size	Federal Poverty Threshold
1 person	$10,210
2 people	$13,690
3 people	$17,170
4 people	$20,650
5 or more	Add $3,480 per person

Using these income levels, the Census Bureau reported that 12.3% percent of U.S. residents and 17.4% of U.S. children lived in poverty in 2004. Black Americans experience poverty at nearly double these rates: 24.3% of all Blacks and 33.4% of Black children live in households with incomes below the poverty line.

The poverty threshold concept was originally devised by Social Security analyst Mollie Orshansky in 1963. Orshansky estimated the cost of an "economy food plan" designed by the Department of Agriculture for "emergency use when funds are low." Working from 1955 data showing that families of three or more spent one-third of their income on food, Orshansky multiplied the food budget by three to calculate the poverty line. Since the early 1960s, the Census Bureau has simply recalculated Orshansky's original figures to account for inflation.

The poverty line is widely regarded as far too low for a household to survive on in most parts of the United States. For one thing, as antipoverty advocates point out, since 1955 the proportion of family budgets devoted to food has fallen from

19

one-third to one-fifth. Families expend far more on nonfood necessities such as child care, health care, transportation, and utilities today than they did 50 years ago, for obvious reasons: mothers entering the work force, suburbanization and greater dependence on the auto, and soaring health care costs, for example. Were Orshansky formulating a poverty threshold more recently, then, she would likely have multiplied a basic food budget by five rather than by three.

Furthermore, costs—particularly for housing and energy—vary widely across the country, so that an income that might be barely adequate in Mississippi is wholly inadequate in Massachusetts. Yet federal poverty figures make no adjustment for regional differences in costs.

A number of state-level organizations now publish their own estimates of what it takes to support a family in their area, in conjunction with the national training and advocacy group Wider Opportunities for Women. Using local data on housing costs, health care premiums, taxes, and child care costs as well as food, transportation and other necessities, these "self-sufficiency standards" estimate that a two-parent two-child family needs between $40,000 and $50,000 a year, depending on the region, to cover basic needs.

State and federal officials often implicitly recognize that official poverty thresholds are unrealistically low by setting income eligibility criteria for antipoverty programs higher than the poverty level. Households with incomes of 125%, 150%, or even 185% of the federal poverty line are eligible for a number of federal and state programs. In addition, the Census Bureau publishes figures on the number of households with incomes below 200% of the federal poverty line—a level many social scientists call "near poor" or "working poor."

Poverty calculations also have critics on the right. Conservative critics contend that the official poverty rate overstates poverty in the United States. While the Census Bureau's poverty-rate calculations include Social Security benefits, public assistance, unemployment and workers' compensation, SSI (disability) payments, and other forms of cash income, they exclude noncash benefits from state and federal antipoverty programs like Food Stamps, Medicaid, and housing subsidies. If the market value of these benefits were counted in family income, fewer families would count as "poor." On the other hand, by not counting such benefits, policy makers have a better grasp of the numbers of Americans in need of such transfer programs.

Source: For background information on poverty thresholds and poverty rate calculations, see <aspe.hhs.gov/poverty/papers/hptgssiv.htm>. Self-sufficiency standards for different states can be found at <www.sixstrategies.org/states/states.cfm>. In addition, the Economic Policy Institute has calculated family budgets for the 435 metropolitan areas: <www.epi.org/content.cfm/datazone_fambud_budget>.

Illness and medical bills trigger about half of all personal bankruptcies, and private insurance offers little protection. Kayty Himmelstein examines data on the causes of bankruptcy, and finds that a one-size-fits-all approach punishes "frivolous" spenders and families down on their luck with the same indifferent hand.

ILL AND INSOLVENT

BY KAYTY HIMMELSTEIN

I n spring 2005, Congress voted overwhelmingly to pass the Bankruptcy Abuse Prevention and Consumer Protection Act, which makes it harder for people to declare bankruptcy. President Bush hurriedly added his signature on April 20, 2005 saying, "America is a nation of personal responsibility where people are expected to meet their obligations." The law, a gift to the banking and credit card industries, imposes new restrictions on bankruptcy filing, including rigid rules for setting repayment schedules, mandatory credit counseling, and a predetermined formula (dubbed a "means test") that takes away judges' discretion in determining whether a person may file for bankruptcy at all.

The means test provision has alarmed legal scholars because it does not allow judges to take individual circumstances into consideration. As Harvard Law School Professor Elizabeth Warren testified to the Senate Judiciary Committee, "The means test as written … treats all families alike. … If Congress is determined to sort the good from the bad, then begin by sorting those who have been laid low by medical debts, those who lost their jobs, those whose breadwinners have been called to active duty and sent to Iraq, those who are caring for elderly parents and sick children from those few who overspend on frivolous purchases."

The new rule is especially worrisome in light of a recent study that found health care costs contributed to about half of America's 1.5 million bankruptcy filings in 2001. The study was coauthored by Elizabeth Warren, David Himmelstein, Deborah Thorne, and Steffie Woolhandler, and published in February 2006 on the website of the journal *Health Affairs*. The authors surveyed 1,771 people who filed for personal bankruptcy, conducting interviews with 931 of them. Nearly half (46.2%) of those surveyed met the authors' criteria for "major medical bankruptcy," and more than half (54.5%) met their broader criteria for "any medical bankruptcy" (see figure). Assuming the data are representative, 1.9 to 2.2 million Americans (filers and dependents) experienced some type of medical bankruptcy in 2001.

CAUSES OF BANKRUPTCY, 2001

Specific reason cited by debtor	Percent of bankruptcies	Number of debtors and dependents in affected U.S. families annually[a]
Illness or injury	28.3	1,039,880
Uncovered medical bills exceeding $1,000 in 2 years before filing	27.0	1,150,302
Debtor or spouse lost at least 2 weeks of work-related income because of illness/injury	21.3	825,113
Mortgaged home to pay medical bills	2.0[b]	
Birth/addition of new family member	7.7	421,256
Death in family	7.6	281,309
Alcohol or drug addiction	2.5	109,180
Uncontrolled gambling	1.2	39,566
Major medical cause (illness or injury listed as specific reason; uncovered medical bills exceeding $1,000; lost at least 2 weeks of work-related income because of illness/injury; or mortgaged home to pay medical bills)	46.2	1,850,098
Any medical cause (any of the above)	54.5	2,227,000

a Extrapolation based on number of bankruptcy filings during 2001 and household size of debtors citing each cause.

b Percentage based on homeowners rather than all debtors.

These are not by and large the uninsured. Three-fourths of medical debtors interviewed had health insurance at the onset of the illness. Many, however, faced lapses in coverage. One-third of those who had private insurance at first lost their coverage during the course of the illness. These gaps in coverage, tied primarily to unaffordable premiums and loss of employment, left debtors with enormous out-of-pocket expenses. Patients who lost private insurance racked up medical costs averaging $18,005 from hospital bills, prescription medicines, and doctor visits. Some who kept their insurance sunk into debt nonetheless, thanks to copayments and deductibles. In sum, private health insurance offers surprisingly little protection from bankruptcy, given involuntary interruptions in coverage and privately borne costs.

Illness triggered financial problems both directly, through medical costs, and indirectly, through lost income. Three-fifths (59.9%) of families bankrupted by medical problems said that bills from medical-care providers contributed to bankruptcy; 47.6% cited drug costs. Thirty-five percent had to curtail employment because of an illness, often to care for someone else. In the interviews, filers described the compounding effects of direct medical costs and indirect employment-related costs—for example, when an illness caused a job loss, which led to the loss of employment-based health coverage, or when parents of chronically ill children had to take time off from work, only to find that the simultaneous costs of the child's medical care and the loss of their income proved catastrophic.

The congressional debate over the bankruptcy bill focused on debtors who cheat the bankruptcy system and pass costs on to more responsible consumers, but the *Health Affairs* study paints a different picture. It shows that about half of those who file for bankruptcy do so because they or their family members have fallen ill or become injured in the context of a shredded health safety net. The new bankruptcy law wrongly treats all debtors as careless spendthrifts. It will make it far more difficult for hundreds of thousands forced by circumstance into overwhelming medical debt to regain their financial footing.

Source: "Illness and Injury as Contributors to Bankruptcy," *Health Affairs Web Exclusive* (2005); authors' analysis of data from the Consumer Bankruptcy Project.

From *Dollars & Sense* magazine, May/June 2005.

During the recent economic recovery, the unemployment rate for African Americans continued to rise, even though the overall number of jobs increased. Dena Libner looks at some contributing factors, including racial discrimination as well as the influx of immigrant labor.

UNEQUAL RECOVERY

BY DENA LIBNER

The last economic recovery was also called many things, especially "jobless" and "wageless." But the recovery has also been exceedingly unequal. Although the recession ended in late 2001, and despite overall job growth and improvements in the white unemployment rate, the black unemployment rate has been worsening. The trend has caught economists by surprise.

African-American employment is generally more "elastic," or responsive to changes in the business cycle, than white employment; it falls sooner than white unemployment during recessions, but rises more quickly during recoveries. Not so this time.

Whites enjoyed a 0.4 percentage point decrease in unemployment over the first 13 quarters of the last recovery (the fourth quarter of 2001 through the first quarter of 2005) while African Americans faced a 0.8 percentage point *increase* in unemployment. During the equivalent period of the 1990s recovery, the African-American unemployment rate improved by 0.6 percentage points (falling 50% more than white unemployment), according to analysis by Economic Policy Institute senior economist Jared Bernstein (see Figure 1).

In many other respects, the recent recession and recent recovery are comparable to the early 1990s. Both decades' recessions were at least partly the result of falling investor and consumer confidence brought on by wars in the Middle East. Both recoveries were "jobless"; GDP growth was not matched by strong growth in employment.

Given the parallels, what explains today's post-recession rise in African-American unemployment? No consensus explanation has emerged, but several factors likely contribute.

First, racial discrimination, a persistent feature of labor markets, may actually intensify in slack labor markets. Research conducted by economist William M. Rodgers suggests that discrimination may decline during boom periods, and, he

FIGURE 1

QUARTERLY CHANGE IN UNEMPLOYMENT

Last Recovery and the Early 1990s Recovery by Race

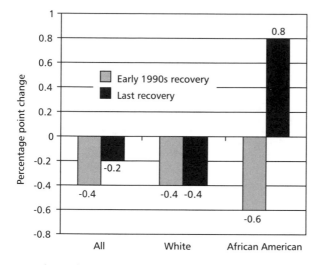

Source: Analysis of Bureau of Labor Statistics data by Economic Policy Institute senior economist Jared Bernstein.

speculates, the reverse may also hold. When there are many unemployed workers vying for a job, employers can indulge their personal preferences or prejudices. Conversely, when job markets are tight, employers cannot afford to keep their biases in play. "It makes sense that, in a period of slow job growth, workers are hired not just for their skill but also because of their race," Rodgers says.

Another culprit is the extremely weak demand for labor. Although the early 1990s and most recent recoveries are both described as "jobless," the recent one was extra "jobless." In 1994, the economy generated 321,080 jobs per month on average, according to the Bureau of Labor Statistics. In comparison, the 2004 average of 182,830 jobs per month was positively tepid. The recession that began in 2001 resulted in the loss of 2.7 million jobs. Only 3.1 million jobs have been added since, so the net job creation since 2001 is 400,000 jobs—less than the number of new workers entering the labor force. "There is a job deficit in the millions relative to what you would expect at this stage, and that wasn't the case three years into the last recovery," notes Bernstein.

Rodgers adds, "At least 150,000 new jobs must be created per month just to absorb the labor market's natural population growth. Average monthly job growth well in excess of 150,000 new jobs is needed before displaced workers, particularly African Americans, are re-employed." For instance, the 110,000 jobs created in March 2005 was not enough to absorb even the natural growth of the work

FIGURE 2

CHANGES IN EMPLOYMENT RATES BY RACE

First Four Years of Last Business Cycle and Previous Cycle

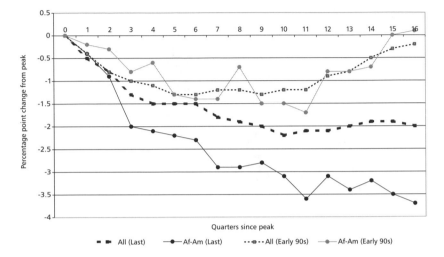

Source: Analysis of Bureau of Labor Statistics data by Economic Policy Institute senior econo-mist Jared Bernstein.

force, let alone make a dent in national unemployment (or African-American un-employment.)

In the early 1990s, the African-American employment rate tracked the overall employment rate (see the top lines of Figure 2). In the last recovery, the African-American employment rate was significantly outperformed by the (weak) overall employment rate. (The employment rate—also called the employment-to-population ratio—is the percentage of working-age people who have jobs.)

The influx of immigrants may also play a role. During the 1990s, the immigrant population grew by 11.3 million—faster than at any other time in history. In the context of weak overall job growth and the contraction of the manufacturing sec-tor, competition from immigrants for scarce jobs in the service, office, and clerical occupations may have compounded African Americans' already fragile employment situation. Steven A. Camarota, director of research at the Center for Immigration Studies, points out that "between March of 2000 and March of 2004, the number of adults working actually increased, but all of the net change went to immigrant workers." During that period, Camarota continues, the number of unemployed adult natives increased by 2.3 million, while the number of employed adult im-migrants increased by 2.3 million.

One thing is certain. The black unemployment rate hit a staggering 10.6% in the first quarter of 2005, up from 9.8% in 2001, widening the already dramatic gap with the white unemployment rate (which hovers at 4.4%). With more than one in 10 African Americans unemployed today, many who experienced some degree of economic opportunity and mobility in the 1990s are finding themselves losing ground—well into what was supposed to be a recovery.

Sources: Jared Bernstein, "African Americans in the current recovery," Economic Snapshots. The Economic Policy Institute, April 6, 2005 <www.epinet.org>; Steven A. Camarota, "A Jobless Recovery? Immigrant Gains and Native Losses," Center for Immigration Studies, October 2004 <www.cis.org>.

From *Dollars & Sense* magazine, May/June 2005.

SECTION II

The Causes of Inequality

Capitalist economies are characterized by an almost inexorable tendency toward ever-increasing levels of inequality. Government intervention in the form of regulation, taxation, and redistribution may partially counterbalance that tendency, but in recent decades, the U.S. political system has shifted in the opposite direction, to rig the economic game in favor of corporations and the very rich, at the cost of everyone else. Here are the seven recent government rule changes that have most exacerbated the wealth and income divide.

THE VISIBLE HAND

Seven Government Actions That Have Worsened Inequality

BY CHUCK COLLINS

A primary reason that U.S. wealth inequality has accelerated in the last two decades is that power has shifted in our democracy. Corporations, investors, and campaign donors have gained power while main street business, wage earners, and voters have lost power. As political influence has shifted, the rules governing the economy have changed to benefit asset-owners and large corporations at the expense of wage-earners.

These rule changes—the visible hand of government—have worsened the wealth and income divide, putting a heavy thumb on the scale in favor of the rich and powerful. Rules governing taxes, trade, wages, spending priorities, and monetary policy have all changed, and in each case, the government has acted on behalf of corporations and the rich to rig who wins and who loses in the economy.

Of course, the U.S. economy has always been governed by rules that created inequality, from regulations protecting private property, to labor laws stacked against workers, to state taxes that fall disproportionately on the poor. Government actions can either mitigate or exacerbate inequality, and in recent years, hundreds of deliberate public policy choices have made it much worse. Here are seven nominations for the public policy hall of shame.

1. THE PLUMMETING MINIMUM WAGE

Decent wages are a prerequisite for individual wealth accumulation: workers cannot save money when their wages barely pay for basic necessities. Today, even when they earn a decent wage, most Americans are not able to save much of anything. And it's much worse for those at the bottom. The U.S. minimum wage has plummeted in value over the last 35 years, and today leaves families below the federal poverty line.

Over 2.1 million workers earn today's minimum wage of $5.15 per hour. In 1968, the minimum wage of $1.60—or $7.07 in today's dollars—was 86% of the amount needed to bring a family of four to the federal poverty line. But today the minimum wage is only 61% of that benchmark. A full-time worker earning today's minimum wage has an annual income of just $10,712. And Congress has not raised the minimum wage since 1996.

It didn't have to be this way. While the minimum wage has been falling, worker productivity has skyrocketed, reducing costs for employers and increasing their profits. If worker wages overall had shared in the productivity gains since the late 1970s, they would be 33% higher in real terms than they are today.

2. TAXING WAGES, NOT WEALTH

Over the last 30 years, the federal government has shifted the tax burden off wealth and onto wages. Since 1980, the payroll tax rate—the main tax on work income—has jumped 25%. In the same period, top tax rates on investment income fell by 31% and taxes on large inheritances have been cut by 79%. This shift means that a person who derives millions of dollars solely in dividend income from investments now pays a marginal tax rate of just 15%, down from 28% in 1997. Compare that with a schoolteacher earning an adjusted gross income of $28,400. The teacher pays a payroll tax rate of 15.3% plus a marginal income tax rate of 28% for a total marginal rate of over 43%!

One policy exacerbating this shift was the 1997 Tax Reform Act, signed into law by President Clinton, which reduced capital gains tax rates from 28% to 20%. The 1997 capital gains provision was wrapped in pretty packaging, including expanded child and education credits for the middle class, and it didn't get much attention. But it was a centerpiece of the right-wing tax program. The 2003 Bush tax cut further reduced the capital gains rate to 15% and cut taxes on dividend income, delivering windfalls for the wealthy.

At the same time that the tax burden has been shifted from wealth to wages, the sheer size of recent tax cuts threatens the social programs many wage-earners depend on. The 2001 and 2003 federal tax cuts, which the Bush administration's 2005 budget proposes to make permanent, guarantee further cuts to social spending. The 2001 tax cut was the largest income tax rollback in two decades, and the 2003 cut reduced dividend and capital gains taxes while accelerating the 2001 rate cut for the top income brackets. These tax cuts, which mainly benefit the rich, will cost at least $824.1 billion between 2001 and 2010; if extended, they will cost $5.9 trillion over the next 75 years, according to William G. Gale and Peter R. Orszag of the Brookings Institution. Revenue losses of this magnitude can be sustained only by cutting social programs.

3. STACKING LABOR LAWS AGAINST WORKERS

Collective action is the most effective means that workers have to win a larger share of the economic pie. But U.S. workers face repressive labor laws that make many forms of collective action difficult or even illegal.

Workers who want to organize a union in the United States must overcome obstacles unheard of in Canada and Western Europe. Canadian workers simply need to present signatures showing that a majority of workers wish to form a union. But in the United States, the 1935 National Labor Relations Act, which governs union organizing in most sectors of the economy, requires workers to complete a lengthy election process during which employers can run intimidating anti-union campaigns. Employers force workers to attend meetings, individually and in groups, in which supervisors spread misinformation about unions. They routinely challenge election bids on frivolous grounds, delaying elections and vote-counting for months and years. And employers illegally fire worker organizers in 25% of unionization drives. Workers who seek reinstatement after being illegally fired face years of hearings before the National Labor Relations Board.

Workers who win union representation face other legal obstacles. When protesting their employer, for instance, they cannot conduct "secondary boycotts," or protests targeting firms that do business with their employer. Moreover, U.S. labor law makes it very difficult for workers to strike. Employers can permanently replace workers who strike for "economic" reasons—like wanting higher wages. The 1947 Taft-Hartley Act banned "sympathy strikes" in which workers striking at one employer could be joined by those at other companies and in other sectors of the economy. Taft-Hartley also gave the president the right to end strikes by executive order.

Unions and legal scholars have proposed labor law reforms for decades, but have been thwarted by both Democrats and Republicans in Congress. Union certification procedures have not changed even as employers' anti-union campaigns have grown more virulent. Congress has taken no action on proposals to ban strikebreakers and permanent replacements, or to lift restrictions on secondary boycotts. The legislative record on workers' substantive demands has also been dismal. Congress and state legislatures could have passed laws to raise workplace standards, require minimum benefits, and limit the use of contract or temporary labor. Instead, Congress has passed laws to reclassify jobs in ways that disqualify workers from receiving overtime pay, reducing the paychecks and clout of millions of workers.

4. SHREDDING THE SAFETY NET

The U.S. safety net has historically been much thinner than those in other industrialized nations. Yet, over the last 20 years, state and federal governments have slashed public programs that historically worked to narrow economic inequalities. Cuts in social spending increase Americans' reliance on unequal personal income and savings, and guarantee a growing divide between rich and poor.

In 1996, President Clinton and a Republican Congress ended "welfare as we knew it" by abolishing Aid to Families with Dependent Children (AFDC) and replacing it with Temporary Assistance to Needy Families (TANF). Unlike AFDC, a federal entitlement that provided a guaranteed minimum benefit, TANF includes strict work requirements, a five-year lifetime limit on assistance, and sanctions that can push people off the rolls. TANF is administered by the states with little federal oversight, allowing for inequities in benefit provisions.

Federal Pell grants, created in 1972 to provide aid to working-class college students, are much less generous than they used to be. Whereas the maximum Pell grant in 1975–76 covered 84% of the average cost of attending a four-year public institution, today it covers just 39% of that cost.

In 2004, the Department of Housing and Urban Development (HUD) changed the formulas it uses to finance the Section 8 housing voucher program. Section 8 vouchers help 2 million poor, elderly, and disabled Americans pay their rent and were originally lauded by conservatives as a market-based alternative to public housing. The new HUD formulas mean that the state housing authorities that administer the vouchers received $183 million less than they expected, even though Congress had already appropriated the funds. The new policy wasn't announced until April 23, 2004, but HUD made it effective retroactive to January 1, meaning that local housing authorities have to make up for funds they had already spent. In order to fill the budget gap, housing agencies across the country are being forced to take harmful steps including prohibiting eligible new families from receiving vouchers, reducing the maximum rent that a voucher will cover, and withdrawing newly issued vouchers from families that are still looking for an apartment. The Bush administration's proposed 2005 budget includes $1 billion in cuts for Section 8 housing vouchers, or 5.5% of the program's total funding.

5. LETTING EXECUTIVE PAY SKYROCKET

In 1992, President Clinton was elected calling for reform of executive compensation laws. At the time, corporations deducted the entire value of their bloated CEO pay packages as a tax-reducing business expense. Some salary expense is obviously a business expense, but corporations were using these excessive pay packages to shrink their tax liabilities on paper while bestowing largess on a privileged few. Clinton proposed limiting the "tax deductibility of excessive compensation" to $1 million. This still would have allowed corporations to take tremendous tax deductions, but it would have been a step in the right direction.

However, the final bill that passed was amended to exempt pay packages where compensation was judged to be "performance based." As a result, corporate boards today simply pass resolutions stating that their executive compensation pay packages are "performance based," and circumvent the law's intent. Apparently, it doesn't matter if that performance was abysmal. Safeway CEO Steven Burd cashed out $13 million in stock options in 2003 even as the company lost $169.8 million in net revenue. Imagine if a law with teeth had been in place during the late 1990s, when average executive compensation grew to more than 500 times average worker pay.

6. CHANGING THE RULES ON INVESTMENT AND TRADING

The recent stock market and accounting scandals have had a crushing effect on small stockholders and pension plans but put billions into the pockets of insider investors in America's largest corporations. The scandals were made possible by rule changes and "reforms" that took the few remaining teeth out of the regulatory process. In 1999, Congress repealed the 1933 Glass-Steagall Act, a banking law that prohibited mergers between banks, insurance companies, and securities trading firms. The New Deal-era law was designed to guard against the conflicts of interest that had led to a series of corporate abuses in the 1920s. The finance, insurance, and real estate sectors spent $200 million in campaign contributions, according to the Center for Responsive Politics, to remove this reform. Glass-Steagall was replaced by the Financial Modernization Act, which created a new kind of corporation—the financial holding company—that could bring together any number of these formerly separate financial institutions in a single corporation.

By removing the barriers between banks and securities firms, Congress ushered in a new wave of speculative mega-mergers. Firms such as Citigroup, J.P. Morgan Chase and others took advantage of the new rules by forming mega-conglomerates that financed Enron and other disasters.

Repealing Glass-Steagall also exposed small investors to new risks. Glass-Steagall had required banks to maintain a firewall between investment bankers (who facilitate deals between banks and corporations) and brokers (who buy and sell securities for investors). Eliminating this firewall gave brokers incentives to lie to investors about the quality of securities in order to promote deals that the bankers were pushing. In one case uncovered by New York State Attorney General Eliot Spitzer, Citigroup CEO Sandy Weill was on AT&T's board of directors when he sent an e-mail to Citigroup analyst Jack Grubman asking him to upgrade AT&T's investment rating as a personal favor. Grubman upped the company's rating just before Citigroup secured a deal to manage the AT&T wireless division's initial public offering. Soon after the IPO, Grubman downgraded AT&T's stock, and the price plummeted. Citigroup reaped over $40 million in fees from managing the IPO, while investors were duped out of millions more.

In 2000, Congress passed the Commodity Futures Modernization Act to deregulate derivative investments, which are highly speculative investment vehicles. Sen. Phil Gramm (R-Texas) attached the act to an omnibus bill immediately after the 2000 Supreme Court decision in favor of Bush's selection. The bill included the infamous "Enron exclusion" that exempted Enron's online energy-trading floor from public oversight, creating the conditions in which Enron was able to manipulate California's electricity market. This law also exempted over-the-counter derivatives from regulation, helping to pave the way for the 2001 Wall Street fiascos. It specifically included an exception for the trading of energy derivatives, a provision strongly supported by Gramm, whose wife Wendy had deregulated energy swaps in 1993 as chairman of the Commodity Futures Trading Commission and then joined Enron's board of directors. These changes helped produce the corporate meltdowns that looted employees and investors alike, fueling wealth inequality.

Finally, thanks to a little-known 1995 rule change, shareholders and pensioners who saw their wealth vanish in the post-1990s corporate debacles found that they had little recourse against corporate malfeasance. This was because the 1995 Private Securities Litigation Reform Act had raised hurdles for investors attempting to file securities-fraud lawsuits in federal court. Investors fleeced by companies like World Com have been thwarted in their efforts to recoup their loses.

7. LETTING CORPORATE ACCOUNTING GO WILD

For years, shady corporate accounting left workers' savings and pensions dangerously exposed. The SEC and Congress failed to enact meaningful safeguards, and small investors were left holding the bag when disaster finally struck. Throughout the 1990s, the Financial Accounting Standards Board (FASB) and Securities and Exchange (SEC) Chairman Arthur Leavitt considered a number of reforms to make accounting more transparent and reduce opportunities for corporate manipulation. Leavitt proposed several reforms, including one which would have required companies to treat stock options as expenses. The SEC also proposed a rule requiring auditors to be independent of the companies they audited, as many were not. For instance, a number of accounting firms conducting corporate audits also maintained lucrative consulting contracts with the same firms. Knowing that they might lose consulting revenue if their audits weren't rosy enough, accounting firms had strong incentives to cook the books.

These proposals weathered an onslaught of industry and political attacks during the 1990s. Legislators led by Sen. Joseph Leiberman (D-Conn.), representing Connecticut's insurance industry, intervened to stop the SEC from implementing rules requiring auditor independence. When President Bush came into office, he appointed Harvey Pitt, the former chief lobbyist for the accounting industry, to replace Leavitt—a way of preventing further reforms. Rule changes were thwarted until corporate fraud scandals created a tremendous public backlash. Even then, Congress enacted only modest reforms such as the Sarbanes-Oxley Public Company Accounting and Investor Protection Act of 2002. While this law mandated some restrictions on certain non-auditing services that auditors can provide for their clients, it left in place the cozy auditor-client relationships that encouraged auditors to approve the shady accounting practices of Enron and WorldCom. In the end, even these weak reforms came too late to protect the millions of working Americans who saw their pensions and savings vanish, nor did it insure that similar scandals would be prevented from happening in the future.

Today, economic inequality in the United States is more extreme than at any time since the 1920s. Left to its own devices, the underlying tendency of the U.S. private sector is toward ever-increasing levels of inequality. This tendency must be counteracted by the visible hand of progressive government policies. But the rule changes and policy choices described here have taken the country in exactly the wrong direction. It doesn't have to be that way. We could have public policy that restores the lost purchasing power of the minimum wage; insists that the rich pay their fair share in taxes by blocking the repeal of the estate tax and reinstituting the lost progressivity of the income tax; patches the holes in the social safety net by returning non-defense discretionary spending to its level at the beginning of the Reagan administration (5.2% of GDP); enforces labor laws that oversee an orderly process of helping workers gain a voice in their work life; and reregulates financial markets and large corporations as opposed to celebrating corporate recklessness. These measures would go a long way toward counteracting the two-decade trend of widening inequality of the U.S. economy.

Wealth doesn't just reside in individual bank accounts, but in public programs that take care of people when they are elderly or fall on hard times. During the 1930s and 1960s, new public initiatives began providing Americans with greatly expanded social wealth. Whereas Americans had previously depended on unequal private resources to finance their retirement and health care, and to support themselves during periods of unemployment, programs like Social Security, Medicare, Medicaid, and unemployment insurance created a safety net available to all.

Today, however, federal tax cuts are threatening to bankrupt these programs. Paul Krugman explains that the 2001–2003 tax cuts can only be sustained by shredding the federal safety net. And that's exactly the point. Krugman notes that conservatives have always opposed initiatives that promote social, rather than individual, wealth, and he argues that they pushed through the recent tax cuts precisely to starve these programs out of existence.

THE TAX-CUT CON

BY PAUL KRUGMAN

B ruce Tinsley's comic strip, "Mallard Fillmore," is, he says, "for the average person out there: the forgotten American taxpayer who's sick of the liberal media." In June 2003, that forgotten taxpayer made an appearance in the strip, attacking his TV set with a baseball bat and yelling: "I can't afford to send my kids to college, or even take 'em out of their substandard public school, because the federal, state and local governments take more than 50% of my income in taxes. And then the guy on the news asks with a straight face whether or not we can 'afford' tax cuts."

Nobody likes paying taxes, and no doubt some Americans are as angry about their taxes as Tinsley's imaginary character. But most Americans also care a lot about the things taxes pay for.

All politicians say they're for public education; almost all of them also say they support a strong national defense, maintaining Social Security and, if anything, expanding the coverage of Medicare. When the "guy on the news" asks whether we can afford a tax cut, he's asking whether, after yet another tax cut goes through, there will be enough money to pay for those things. And the answer is no.

But it's very difficult to get that answer across in modern American politics, which has been dominated for 25 years by a crusade against taxes.

I don't use the word "crusade" lightly. The advocates of tax cuts are relentless, even fanatical. An indication of the movement's fervor—and of its political power—came during the Iraq war. War is expensive and is almost always accompanied by tax increases. But not in 2003. "Nothing is more important in the face of a war," declared Tom DeLay, the House majority leader, "than cutting taxes." And sure enough, taxes were cut, not just in a time of war but also in the face of record budget deficits.

A result of the tax-cut crusade is that there is now a fundamental mismatch between the benefits Americans expect to receive from the government and the revenues government collect. This mismatch is already having profound effects at the state and local levels: teachers and policemen are being laid off and children are being denied health insurance. The federal government can mask its problems for a while by running huge budget deficits, but it, too, will eventually have to decide whether to cut services or raise taxes. And we are not talking about minor policy adjustments. If taxes stay as low as they are now, government as we know it cannot be maintained. In particular, Social Security will have to become far less generous; Medicare will no longer be able to guarantee comprehensive medical care to older Americans; Medicaid will no longer provide basic medical care to the poor.

How did we reach this point? What are the origins of the antitax crusade? And where is it taking us?

SUPPLY-SIDERS, STARVE-THE-BEASTERS, AND LUCKY DUCKIES

It is often hard to pin down what antitax crusaders are trying to achieve. The reason is not, or not only, that they are disingenuous about their motives—though as we will see, disingenuity has become a hallmark of the movement in recent years. Rather, the fuzziness comes from the fact that today's antitax movement moves back and forth between two doctrines. Both doctrines favor the same thing: big tax cuts for people with high incomes. But they favor it for different reasons.

One of those doctrines has become famous under the name "supply-side economics." It's the view that the government can cut taxes without severe cuts in public spending. The other doctrine is often referred to as "starving the beast," a phrase coined by David Stockman, Ronald Reagan's budget director. It's the view that taxes should be cut precisely in order to force severe cuts in public spending. Supply-side economics is the friendly, attractive face of the tax-cut movement. But starve-the-beast is where the power lies.

The starting point of supply-side economics is an assertion that no economist would dispute: taxes reduce the incentive to work, save and invest. A businessman who knows that 70 cents of every extra dollar he makes will go to the IRS is less willing to make the effort to earn that extra dollar than if he knows that the IRS will take only 35 cents. So reducing tax rates will, other things being the same, spur the economy.

This much isn't controversial. But the government must pay its bills. So the standard view of economists is that if you want to reduce the burden of taxes, you must explain what government programs you want to cut as part of the deal. There's no free lunch.

What the supply-siders argued, however, was that there was a free lunch. Cutting marginal rates, they insisted, would lead to such a large increase in gross domestic product that it wouldn't be necessary to come up with offsetting spending cuts. What supply-side economists say, in other words, is, "Don't worry, be happy and cut taxes." And when they say cut taxes, they mean taxes on the affluent: reducing the top marginal rate means that the biggest tax cuts go to people in the highest tax brackets.

The other camp in the tax-cut crusade actually welcomes the revenue losses from tax cuts. Its most visible spokesman today is Grover Norquist, president of Americans for Tax Reform, who once told National Public Radio: "I don't want to abolish government. I simply want to reduce it to the size where I can drag it into the bathroom and drown it in the bathtub." And the way to get it down to that size is to starve it of revenue. "The goal is reducing the size and scope of government by draining its lifeblood," Norquist told *U.S. News & World Report*.

What does "reducing the size and scope of government" mean? Tax-cut proponents are usually vague about the details. But the Heritage Foundation, ideological headquarters for the movement, has made it pretty clear. Edwin Feulner, the foundation's president, uses "New Deal" and "Great Society" as terms of abuse, implying that he and his organization want to do away with the institutions Franklin Roosevelt and Lyndon Johnson created. That means Social Security, Medicare, Medicaid—most of what gives citizens of the United States a safety net against economic misfortune.

The starve-the-beast doctrine is now firmly within the conservative mainstream. George W. Bush himself seemed to endorse the doctrine as the budget surplus evaporated: in August 2001 he called the disappearing surplus "incredibly positive news" because it would put Congress in a "fiscal straitjacket."

Like supply-siders, starve-the-beasters favor tax cuts mainly for people with high incomes. That is partly because, like supply-siders, they emphasize the incentive effects of cutting the top marginal rate; they just don't believe that those incentive effects are big enough that tax cuts pay for themselves. But they have another reason for cutting taxes mainly on the rich, which has become known as the "lucky ducky" argument.

Here's how the argument runs: to starve the beast, you must not only deny funds to the government; you must make voters hate the government. There's a danger that working-class families might see government as their friend: because their incomes are low, they don't pay much in taxes, while they benefit from public spending. So in starving the beast, you must take care not to cut taxes on these "lucky duckies." (Yes, that's what the *Wall Street Journal* called them in a famous editorial.) In fact, if possible, you must raise taxes on working-class Americans in order, as the *Journal* said, to get their "blood boiling with tax rage."

So the tax-cut crusade has two faces. Smiling supply-siders say that tax cuts are all gain, no pain; scowling starve-the-beasters believe that inflicting pain is not just necessary but also desirable. Is the alliance between these two groups a marriage of convenience? Not exactly. It would be more accurate to say that the starve-the-beasters hired the supply-siders—indeed, created them—because they found their naive optimism useful.

A look at who the supply-siders are and how they came to prominence tells the story. The supply-side movement likes to present itself as a school of economic thought like Keynesianism or monetarism—that is, as a set of scholarly ideas that made their way, as such ideas do, into political discussion. But the reality is quite different. Supply-side economics was a political doctrine from Day 1; it emerged in the pages of political magazines, not professional economics journals.

That is not to deny that many professional economists favor tax cuts. But they almost always turn out to be starve-the-beasters, not supply-siders. And they often secretly—or sometimes not so secretly—hold supply-siders in contempt. N. Gregory Mankiw, now chairman of George W. Bush's Council of Economic Advisers, is definitely a friend to tax cuts; but in the first edition of his economic-principles textbook, he described Ronald Reagan's supply-side advisers as "charlatans and cranks."

It is not that the professionals refuse to consider supply-side ideas; rather, they have looked at them and found them wanting. A conspicuous example came earlier this year when the Congressional Budget Office tried to evaluate the growth effects of the Bush administration's proposed tax cuts. The budget office's new head, Douglas Holtz-Eakin, is a conservative economist who was handpicked for his job by the administration. But his conclusion was that unless the revenue losses from the proposed tax cuts were offset by spending cuts, the resulting deficits would be a drag on growth, quite likely to outweigh any supply-side effects.

But if the professionals regard the supply-siders with disdain, who employs these people? The answer is that since the 1970s almost all of the prominent supply-siders have been aides to conservative politicians, writers at conservative publications like National Review, fellows at conservative policy centers like Heritage or economists at private companies with strong Republican connections. Loosely speaking, that is, supply-siders work for the vast right-wing conspiracy. What gives supply-side economics influence is its connection with a powerful network of institutions that want to shrink the government and see tax cuts as a way to achieve that goal.

Supply-side economics is a feel-good cover story for a political movement with a much harder-nosed agenda.

A PLANNED CRISIS

Right now, much of the public discussion of the Bush tax cuts focuses on their short-run impact. Critics say that the 2.7 million jobs lost since March 2001 prove that the administration's policies have failed, while the administration says that things would have been even worse without the tax cuts and that a solid recovery is just around the corner.

But this is the wrong debate. Even in the short run, the right question to ask isn't whether the tax cuts were better than nothing; they probably were. The right question is whether some other economic-stimulus plan could have achieved better results at a lower budget cost. And it is hard to deny that, on a jobs-per-dollar basis, the Bush tax cuts have been extremely ineffective. According to the Congressional Budget Office, half of this year's $400 billion budget deficit is due to Bush tax cuts. Now $200 billion is a lot of money; it is equivalent to the salaries of four million average workers. Even the administration doesn't claim its policies have created four million jobs. Surely some other policy—aid to state and local governments, tax breaks for the poor and middle class rather than the rich, maybe even WPA-style public works—would have been more successful at getting the country back to work.

Meanwhile, the tax cuts are designed to remain in place even after the economy has recovered. Where will they leave us?

Here's the basic fact: partly, though not entirely, as a result of the tax cuts of the last three years, the government of the United States faces a fundamental fiscal shortfall. That is, the revenue it collects falls well short of the sums it needs to pay for existing programs. Even the U.S. government must, eventually, pay its bills, so something will have to give.

The numbers tell the tale. This year and next, the federal government will run budget deficits of more than $400 billion. Deficits may fall a bit, at least as a share of gross domestic product, when the economy recovers. But the relief will be modest and temporary. As Peter Fisher, undersecretary of the treasury for domestic finance, puts it, the federal government is "a gigantic insurance company with a sideline business in defense and homeland security." And about a decade from now, this insurance company's policyholders will begin making a lot of claims. As the baby boomers retire, spending on Social Security benefits and Medicare will steadily rise, as will spending on Medicaid (because of rising medical costs). Eventually, unless there are sharp cuts in benefits, these three programs alone will consume a larger share of GDP than the federal government currently collects in taxes.

Alan Auerbach, William Gale and Peter Orszag, fiscal experts at the Brookings Institution, have estimated the size of the "fiscal gap"—the increase in revenues or reduction in spending that would be needed to make the nation's finances sustainable in the long run. If you define the long run as 75 years, this gap turns out to be 4.5% of GDP. Or to put it another way, the gap is equal to 30% of what the federal government spends on all domestic programs. Of that gap, about 60% is the result of the Bush tax cuts. We would have faced a serious fiscal problem even if those tax cuts had never happened. But we face a much nastier problem now that they are in place.

And more broadly, the tax-cut crusade will make it very hard for any future politicians to raise taxes.

So how will this gap be closed? The crucial point is that it cannot be closed without either fundamentally redefining the role of government or sharply raising taxes.

Politicians will, of course, promise to eliminate wasteful spending. But take out Social Security, Medicare, defense, Medicaid, government pensions, homeland security, interest on the public debt and veterans' benefits—none of them what people who complain about waste usually have in mind—and you are left with spending equal to about 3% of gross domestic product. And most of that goes for courts, highways, education and other useful things. Any savings from elimination of waste and fraud will amount to little more than a rounding-off error.

So let's put a few things back on the table. Let's assume that interest on the public debt will be paid, that spending on defense and homeland security will not be compromised and that the regular operations of government will continue to be financed. What we are left with, then, are the New Deal and Great Society programs: Social Security, Medicare, Medicaid and unemployment insurance. And to close the fiscal gap, spending on these programs would have to be cut by around 40%.

It's impossible to know how such spending cuts might unfold, but cuts of that magnitude would require drastic changes in the system. It goes almost without saying that the age at which Americans become eligible for retirement benefits would rise, that Social Security payments would fall sharply compared with average incomes, that Medicare patients would be forced to pay much more of their expenses out of pocket—or do without. And that would be only a start.

All this sounds politically impossible. In fact, politicians of both parties have been scrambling to expand, not reduce, Medicare benefits by adding prescription drug coverage. It's hard to imagine a situation under which the entitlement programs would be rolled back sufficiently to close the fiscal gap.

Yet closing the fiscal gap by raising taxes would mean rolling back all of the Bush tax cuts, and then some. And that also sounds politically impossible.

For the time being, there is a third alternative: borrow the difference between what we insist on spending and what we're willing to collect in taxes. That works as long as lenders believe that someday, somehow, we're going to get our fiscal act together. But this can't go on indefinitely.

Eventually—I think within a decade, though not everyone agrees—the bond market will tell us that we have to make a choice.

IN SHORT, EVERYTHING IS GOING ACCORDING TO PLAN

For the looming fiscal crisis doesn't represent a defeat for the leaders of the tax-cut crusade or a miscalculation on their part. Some supporters of President Bush may have really believed that his tax cuts were consistent with his promises to protect Social Security and expand Medicare; some people may still believe that the wondrous supply-side effects of tax cuts will make the budget deficit disappear. But for starve-the-beast tax-cutters, the coming crunch is exactly what they had in mind.

WHAT KIND OF COUNTRY?

The astonishing political success of the antitax crusade has, more or less deliberately, set the United States up for a fiscal crisis. How we respond to that crisis will determine what kind of country we become.

If Grover Norquist is right—and he has been right about a lot—the coming crisis will allow conservatives to move the nation a long way back toward the kind of limited government we had before Franklin Roosevelt. Lack of revenue, he says, will make it possible for conservative politicians—in the name of fiscal necessity—to dismantle immensely popular government programs that would otherwise have been untouchable.

In Norquist's vision, America a couple of decades from now will be a place in which elderly people make up a disproportionate share of the poor, as they did before Social Security. It will also be a country in which even middle-class elderly Americans are, in many cases, unable to afford expensive medical procedures or prescription drugs and in which poor Americans generally go without even basic health care. And it may well be a place in which only those who can afford expensive private schools can give their children a decent education.

But that's a choice, not a necessity. The tax-cut crusade has created a situation in which something must give. But what gives—whether we decide that the New Deal and the Great Society must go or that taxes aren't such a bad thing after all—is up to us. The American people must decide what kind of a country we want to be.

Excerpted from the New York Times Magazine, *September 14, 2003.*

African Americans and other minorities hold far less wealth than whites. But why should the wealth gap be so large, greater even than the racial income gap? It turns out that government has played a central role. Throughout U.S. history, countless specific laws, policies, rules, and court decisions have made it more difficult for nonwhites to build wealth, and transferred wealth they did own to whites.

DOUBLY DIVIDED

The Racial Wealth Gap

BY MEIZHU LUI

Race—constructed from a European vantage point—has always been a basis on which U.S. society metes out access to wealth and power. Both in times when the overall wealth gap has grown and in times when a rising tide has managed to lift both rich and poor boats, a pernicious wealth gap between whites and nonwhite minorities has persisted.

Let's cut the cake by race. If you lined up all African-American families by the amount of assets they owned minus their debts and then looked at the family in the middle, that median family in 2001 had a net worth of $10,700 (excluding the value of automobiles). Line up all whites, and *that* median family had a net worth of $106,400, almost 10 times more. Less than half of African-American families own their own homes, while three out of four white families do. Latinos are even less wealthy: the median Latino family in 2001 had only $3,000 in assets, and less than half own their own homes.

We do not know how much Native Americans have in assets because so little data has been collected, but their poverty rate is 26% compared to 8% for whites, even though more than half own their own homes. Nor is much information collected about Asian Americans. What we do know is that their poverty rate is 13%, and that 60% of Asian Americans own their own homes, compared to 77% of whites.

Almost 40 years after the passage of the 20th century's major civil rights legislation, huge wealth disparities persist. However, the myth that the playing field was leveled by those laws is widespread. For anyone who accepts the myth, it follows that if families of color are not on an economic par with whites today, the problem must lie with *them*.

But the racial wealth gap has nothing to do with individual behaviors or cultural deficits. Throughout U.S. history, deliberate government policies transferred wealth from nonwhites to whites—essentially, affirmative action for whites. The specific mechanisms of the transfer have varied, as have the processes by which people have been put into racial categories in the first place. But a brief review of American history, viewed through the lens of wealth, reveals a consistent pattern of race-based obstacles that have prevented Native Americans, African Americans, Latinos, and Asians from building wealth at all comparable to whites.

NATIVE AMERICANS: IN THE U.S. GOVERNMENT WE "TRUST"?

When European settlers came to what would become the United States, Indian tribes in general did not consider land to be a source of individual wealth. It was a resource to be worshipped, treasured, and used to preserve all forms of life. Unfortunately for them, that concept of common ownership and the way of life they had built around it would clash mightily with the idea that parcels of land should be owned by individuals and used to generate private profit.

After the American Revolution, the official position of the new U.S. government was that Indian tribes had the same status as foreign nations and that good relations with them should be maintained. However, as European immigration increased and westward expansion continued, the settlers increasingly coveted Indian land. The federal government pressured Native Americans to sign one treaty after another giving over land: In the United States' first century, over 400 Indian treaties were signed. Indians were forcibly removed, first from the south and then from the west, sometimes into reservations.

Eventually, the Indians' last large territory, the Great Plains, was essentially handed over to whites. In one of the clearest instances of land expropriation, the 1862 Homestead Act transferred a vast amount of land from Indian tribes to white homesteaders by giving any white family 160 acres of land for free if they would farm it for five years. Of course, this massive land transfer was not accomplished without violence. General William Tecumseh Sherman, of Civil War fame, wrote: "The more [Indians] we can kill this year, the less will have to be killed the next year, for the more I see of these Indians, the more convinced I am that they all have to be killed or be maintained as a species of paupers." (Ironically, the Homestead Act is often cited as a model government program that supported asset-building.)

Out of the many treaties came the legal concept of the U.S. government's "trust responsibility" for the Native nations, similar to the relationship of a legal guardian to a child. In exchange for land, the government was to provide for the needs of the Native peoples. Money from the sale of land or natural resources was to be placed in a trust fund and managed in the best interests of the Indian tribes. The government's mismanagement of Indian assets was pervasive; yet, by law, Indian tribes could not fire the designated manager and hire a better or more honest one.

The Dawes Act of 1887 was designed to pressure Indians to assimilate into white culture: to adopt a sedentary life style and end their tradition of collective land ownership. The law broke up reservation land into individual plots and forced Indians to attempt to farm "western" style; "surplus" land was sold to whites. Under this scheme, millions more acres were transferred from Native Americans to whites.

After 1953, the U.S. government terminated the trust status of the tribes. While the stated purpose was to free Indians from government control, the new policy exacted a price: the loss of tribally held land that was still the basis of some tribes' existence. This blow reduced the remaining self-sufficient tribes to poverty and broke up tribal governments.

Thus, over a 200-year period, U.S. government policies transferred Native Americans' wealth—primarily land and natural resources—into the pockets of white individuals. This expropriation of vast tracts played a foundational role in the creation of the U.S. economy. Only in recent years, through the effective use of lawsuits to resurrect tribal rights assigned under the old treaties, have some tribes succeeded in building substantial pools of wealth, primarily from gaming businesses. This new-found casino wealth, though, cannot make up for the decimation of Native peoples or the destruction of traditional Native economies. Native Americans on average continue to suffer disproportionate poverty.

AFRICAN AMERICANS: SLAVES DON'T OWN, THEY ARE OWNED

From the earliest years of European settlement until the 1860s, African Americans were assets to be tallied in the financial records of their owners. They could be bought and sold, they created more wealth for their owners in the form of children, they had no rights even over their own bodies, and they worked without receiving any wages. Slaves and their labor became the basis of wealth creation for plantation owners, people who owned and operated slave ships, and companies that insured them. This was the most fundamental of wealth divides in American history.

At the end of the Civil War, there was an opportunity to create a new starting line. In the first few years, the Freedmen's Bureau and the occupying Union army actually began to distribute land to newly freed slaves: the famous "40 acres and a mule," a modest enough way to begin. But the Freedmen's Bureau was disbanded after only seven years, and the overwhelming majority of land that freed slaves had been allotted was returned to its former white owners. Unable to get a foothold as self-employed farmers, African Americans were forced to accept sharecropping arrangements. While sharecroppers kept some part of the fruits of their labor as in-kind income, the system kept them perpetually in debt and unable to accumulate any assets.

In 1883, the Supreme Court overturned the Civil Rights Act of 1875, which had given blacks the right to protect themselves and their property. By 1900, the Southern states had passed laws that kept African Americans separate and unequal, at the bottom of the economy. They began migrating to the North and West in search of opportunity.

Amazingly, some African-American families did prosper as farmers and businesspeople in the early 20th century. Some African-American communities thrived, even establishing their own banks to build savings and investment within the community. However, there was particular resentment against successful African Americans, and they were often targets of the vigilante violence common in this period. State and local governments helped vigilantes destroy their homes, run them out of town, and lynch those "uppity" enough to resist, and the federal government turned a blind eye. Sometimes entire black communities were targeted. For example, the African American business district in north Tulsa, known as the "Black Wall Street" for its size and success, was torched on the night of June 21, 1921 by white rioters, who destroyed as many as 600 black-owned businesses.

The Depression wiped out black progress, which did not resume at all until the New Deal period. Even then, African Americans were often barred from the new asset-building programs that benefited whites. Under Social Security, workers paid into the system and were guaranteed money in retirement. However, domestic and agricultural work—two of the most significant black occupations—were excluded from the program. Unemployment insurance and the minimum wage didn't apply to domestic workers or farm workers either. Other programs were also tilted toward white people. The Home Owners' Loan Corporation was created in 1933 to help homeowners avoid foreclosure, but not a single loan went to a black homeowner.

Following World War II, a number of new programs provided a ladder into the middle class—for whites. The GI Bill of Rights and low-interest home mortgages provided tax-funded support for higher education and for homeownership, two keys to family wealth building. The GI Bill provided little benefit to black veterans, however, because a recipient had to be accepted into a college—and many colleges did not accept African-American students. Likewise, housing discrimination meant that homeownership opportunities were greater for white families; subsidized mortgages were often simply denied for home purchases in black neighborhoods.

In *The Cost of Being African American*, sociologist Thomas Shapiro shows how, because of this history, even black families whose incomes are equal to whites' generally have unequal economic standing. Whites are more likely to have parents who benefited from the land grants of the Homestead Act, who have Social Security or retirement benefits, or who own their own homes. With their far greater average assets, whites can transfer advantage from parents to children in the form of college

TULSA HISTORICAL SOCIETY

Thirty-five blocks in Greenwood, a prosperous African-American business district in Tulsa, were destroyed by white rioters on June 1, 1921.

tuition payments, down payments on homes, or simply self-sufficient parents who do not need their children to support them in old age.

These are the invisible underpinnings of the black-white wealth gap: wealth legally but inhumanely created from the unpaid labor of blacks, the use of violence—often backed up by government power—to stop black wealth-creating activities, tax-funded asset building programs closed to blacks even as they, too, paid taxes. The playing field is not level today. For example, recent studies demonstrate that blatant race discrimination in hiring persists. But even if the playing field were level, the black/white wealth gap would still be with us.

LATINOS: IN THE UNITED STATES' BACK YARD

At the time of the American Revolution, Spain, not England, was the largest colonial landowner on the American continents. Unlike the English, the Spanish intermarried widely with the indigenous populations. In the 20th century, their descendents came to be identified as a distinct, nonwhite group. (In the 1800's, Mexicans were generally considered white.) Today, Latinos come from many countries with varied histories, but the relationship of Mexicans to the United States is the longest, and people of Mexican descent are still the largest Latino group in the United States (67% in 2002).

Mexico won its independence from Spain in 1821. Three years later, the Monroe Doctrine promised the newly independent nations of Latin America "protection" from interference by European powers. However, this doctrine allowed the United States itself to intervene in the affairs of the entire hemisphere. Ever since, this paternalistic relationship (reminiscent of the "trust" relationship with Native tribes) has meant U.S. political and economic dominance in Mexico and Central and South America, causing the "push and pull" of the people of those countries into and out of the United States.

Mexicans and Anglos fought together to free Texas from Mexican rule, creating the Lone Star Republic of Texas, which was then annexed to the United States in 1845. Three years later, the United States went to war against Mexico to gain more territory and continue fulfilling its "manifest destiny"—its God-given right—to expand "from sea to shining sea." Mexico lost the war and was forced to accept the 1848 Treaty of Guadalupe Hidalgo, which gave the United States half of Mexico's land. While individual Mexican landowners were at first assured that they would maintain ownership, the United States did not keep that promise, and the treaty ushered in a huge transfer of land from Mexicans to Anglos. For the first time in these areas, racial categories were used to determine who could obtain land. The English language was also used to establish Anglo dominance; legal papers in English proving land ownership were required, and many Spanish speakers suffered as a result.

In the twentieth century, government policy continued to reinforce a wealth gap between Mexicans and whites. The first U.S.-Mexico border patrol was set up in 1924, and deportations of Mexicans became commonplace. Like African Americans, Latino workers were disproportionately represented in the occupations not covered by the Social Security Act. During World War II, when U.S. farms needed more agricultural workers, the federal government established the Bracero program, under which Mexican workers were brought into the United States to work for subminimum wages and few benefits, then kicked out when their labor was no longer needed. Even today, Mexicans continue to be used as "guest"—or really, reserve—workers to create profits for U.S. agribusiness.

The North American Free Trade Agreement, along with the proposed Central American Free Trade Agreement and Free Trade Agreement of the Americas, is the newest incarnation of the Monroe Doctrine. Trade and immigration policies are still being used to maintain U.S. control over the resources in its "back yard," and at the same time to deny those it is "protecting" the enjoyment of the benefits to be found in papa's "front yard."

ASIAN AMERICANS: PERPETUAL FOREIGNERS

The first Asian immigrants, the Chinese, came to the United States at the same time and for the same reason as the Irish: to escape economic distress at home and take advantage of economic opportunity in America. Like European immigrants, the Chinese came voluntarily, paying their own passage, ready and willing to seize the opportunity to build economic success in a new land. Chinese and Irish immigrants arrived in large numbers in the same decade, but their economic trajectories later diverged.

The major reason is race. While the Irish, caricatured as apes in early cartoons, were soon able to become citizens, the Naturalization Act of 1790 limited eligibility for citizenship to "whites." Asians did not know if they were white or not—but they wanted to be! The rights and benefits of "whiteness" were obvious. Other Americans didn't know whether or not they were white, either. Lawsuits filed first by Chinese, then by Japanese, Indian (South Asian), and Filipino immigrants all claimed that they should be granted "white" status. The outcomes were confusing; for example, South Asians, classified as Caucasian, were at first deemed white. Then, in later cases, courts decided that while they were Caucasian, they were not white.

A series of laws limited the right of Asians to create wealth. Chinese immigrants were drawn into the Gold Rush; the Foreign Miners Tax, however, was designed to push them out of the mining industry. The tax provided 25% of California's annual state budget in the 1860s, but the government jobs and services the tax underwrote went exclusively to whites—one of the first tax-based racial transfers of wealth. And with the passage of the Chinese Exclusion Acts in 1882, the Chinese became the first nationality to be denied the right to join this immigrant nation; the numbers of Chinese-American citizens thus remained small until the 1960s.

The next wave of Asians came from Japan. Excellent farmers, the Japanese bought land and created successful businesses. Resentment led to the passage of the 1924 Alien Land Act, which prohibited noncitizens from owning land. Japanese Americans then found other ways to create wealth, including nurseries and the cut flower business. In 1941, they had $140 million of business wealth.

World War II would change all that. In 1942, the Roosevelt administration forced Japanese Americans, foreign-born and citizen alike, to relocate to internment camps in the inland Western states. They had a week to dispose of their assets. Most had to sell their homes and businesses to whites at fire sale prices—an enormous transfer of wealth. In 1988, a successful suit for reparations gave the survivors of the camps $20,000 each, a mere fraction of the wealth that was lost.

Today, Asians are the group that as a whole has moved closest to economic parity with whites. (There are major variations in status between different Asian nationalities, however, and grouping them masks serious problems facing some groups.) While Asian immigrants have high poverty rates, American-born Asians have moved into professional positions, and the median income of Asians is now higher than that of whites. However, glass ceilings still persist, and as Wen Ho Lee, the Chinese-American nuclear scientist who was falsely accused of espionage in 2002, found out, Asians are still defined by race and branded as perpetual foreigners.

The divergent histories of the Irish and the Chinese in the United States illustrate the powerful role of race in the long-term accumulation of wealth. Irish-Americans faced plenty of discrimination in the labor market: consider the "No Irish Need Apply" signs that were once common in Boston storefronts. But they never faced legal prohibitions on asset ownership and citizenship as Chinese immigrants did, or the expropriation of property as the Japanese did. Today, people of Irish ancestry have attained widespread material prosperity and access to political power, and some of the wealthiest and most powerful men in business and politics are of Irish descent. Meantime, the wealth and power of the Chinese are still marginal.

* * * * *

Throughout history, federal policies—from constructing racial categories, to erecting barriers to asset building by nonwhites, to overseeing transfers of wealth from nonwhites to whites—have created the basis for the current racial wealth divide. If the gap is to be closed, government policies will have to play an important role.

It's long past time to close the gap.

* * * * *

The concept of meritocracy, in which opportunities and wealth are bestowed upon those who most deserve them, seems foundational in a democracy. But according to Harvard law professor Lani Guinier, there are fundamental flaws in how we define and measure "merit." Guinier says the current system undervalues the "merit" of poor people and people of color.

THE MERITOCRACY MYTH

A *Dollars & Sense* interview with Lani Guinier

BY REBECCA PARISH

Lani Guinier became a household name in 1993 when Bill Clinton appointed her to head the Civil Rights Division of the Justice Department and then, under pressure from conservatives, withdrew her nomination without a confirmation hearing. Guinier is currently the Bennett Boskey Professor of Law at Harvard University where, in 1998, she became the first black woman to be tenured at the law school.

Guinier has authored and co-authored numerous books including, most recently, *The Miner's Canary: Enlisting Race, Resisting Power, Transforming Democracy* (2002, with Gerald Torres); and *Who's Qualified?: A New Democracy Forum on Creating Equal Opportunity in School and Jobs* (2001).

Guinier's latest book is *Meritocracy Inc.: How Wealth Became Merit*, Class Became Race, and College Education Became a Gift from the Poor to the Rich, published in 2007. This past summer, she offered a glimpse of her latest book in this interview with D&S intern Rebecca Parrish.

Rebecca Parrish: What is meritocracy? What is the difference between the conventional understanding and the way you are using the term in Meritocracy, Inc.?

Lani Guinier: The conventional understanding of meritocracy is that it is a system for awarding or allocating scarce resources to those who most deserve them.

The idea behind meritocracy is that people should achieve status or realize the promise of upward mobility based on their individual talent or individual effort. It is conceived as a repudiation of systems like aristocracy where individuals inherit their social status.

I am arguing that many of the criteria we associate with individual talent and effort do not measure the individual in isolation but rather parallel the phenomena associated with aristocracy; what we're calling individual talent is actually a function of that individual's social position or opportunities gained by virtue of family and ancestry. So, although the system we call "meritocracy" is presumed to be more democratic and egalitarian than aristocracy, it is in fact reproducing that which it was intended to dislodge.

Michael Young, a British sociologist, created the term in 1958 when he wrote a science fiction novel called *The Rise of Meritocracy*. The book was a satire in which he depicted a society where people in power could legitimate their status using "merit" as the justificatory terminology and in which others could be determined not simply to have been poor or left out but to be deservingly disenfranchised.

RP: How did you become interested in studying meritocracy in the first place?

LG: I became interested in the 1990s as a result of looking at the performance of women in law school. A student and I became interested in the disparity between the grades that men and women at an Ivy League law school were receiving. Working with Michelle Fein and Jean Belan, we found that male and female students were coming in with basically the same credentials. The minor difference was that the women tended to have entered with slightly higher undergraduate grades and the men with higher LSATs.

The assumption at that time was that incoming credentials predicted how you would perform. Relying on things like the LSAT allowed law school officials to say they were determining admission based on merit. So several colleagues told me to look at the LSAT scores because they were confident that I might find something to explain the significant differences in performance. But we found that, surprisingly, the LSAT was actually a very poor predictor of performance for both men and women, that this "objective" marker which determined who could even gain access was actually not accomplishing its ostensible mandate.

I then became interested in studying meritocracy because of the attacks poor and working class whites were waging against Affirmative Action. People were arguing that they were rejected from positions because less qualified people of color were taking their spots. I began to question what determines who is qualified. Then, the more research I did, the more I discovered that these so-called markers of merit did not actually correlate with future performance in college but rather correlated more with an applicant's parents' and even grandparents' wealth. Schools were substituting markers of wealth for merit.

RP: As a theorist of democracy, how do you approach issues of educational equity and achievement differently from other scholars? Are current educational institutions democratic?

LG: My approach builds on and borrows from work of many other scholars. It perhaps expands on it or shifts emphasis. For example, many people defend Affirmative Action on grounds that there are multiple measures of merit and that bringing diverse students to the school would benefit the learning environment. The problem with this argument is that it pits diversity as a counterpoint to merit. And, the argument is not strong enough to counter the belief in "merit" as an egalitarian and democratic way to allocate scarce resources. I am arguing that there are fundamental flaws in the over-reliance on these supposedly objective indicators of merit. This approach positions poor people and people of color as the problem rather than problematizing the ways we measure merit in the first place.

RP: Can you talk about the Harvard and Michigan studies?

LG: Harvard University did a study based on thirty Harvard graduates over a thirty-year period. They wanted to know which students were most likely to exemplify the things that Harvard values most: doing well financially, having a satisfying career and contributing to society (especially in the form of donating to Harvard). The two variables that most predicted which students would achieve these criteria were low SAT scores and a blue-collar background.

That study was followed by one at the University of Michigan Law School that found that those most likely to do well financially, maintain a satisfying career, and contribute to society, were black and Latino students who were admitted pursuant to Affirmative Action. Conversely, those with the highest LSAT scores were the least likely to mentor younger attorneys, do pro-bono work, sit on community boards, etc.

So, the use of these so called "measures of merit" like standardized tests is backfiring on our institutions of higher learning and blocking the road to a more democratic society.

RP: You refer to college education as a gift from poor to rich.

LG: Anthony Carnevaly made that statement when he was the vice president of the Educational Testing Service. He did a study of 146 of the most selective colleges and universities and found that 74% of students came from the top 25% of the socio-economic spectrum. Only 3% came from the lowest quartile and 10% (which is 3% plus 7%) came from the bottom half. So that means that 50% of people in the country are providing substantial state and federal taxes to both public and private institutions even though they are among those least well off and are being excluded from the opportunity.

RP: In *Meritocracy Inc.*, you'll be exploring the relationship between class and race in structuring US society. What insights can you offer into their relationship? How can we think about class and race in our efforts to democratize higher education?

LG: The argument I'm making is that in many ways race is being used as a stand in for class. I am not saying that race and class are coterminous but that people look at race and see race because it is highly visible but they don't see class.

RP: Can you give some examples?

LG: In Arkansas in 1957 whites rioted as Central High School in Little Rock was de-segregated by nine carefully-chosen middle-class black students. The rage and hate on people's faces was broadcast on national television and President Eisenhower had to send in the National Guard to ensure that blacks could get an education. What most people don't know is that at same time as the leaders of city of Little Rock planned the desegregation of Central High, they built and opened a new high school located in an area where the sons and daughters of the doctors and lawyers lived.

Blacks were coming in at the same time that upper-class whites were exiting and this was part of what provoked the intense backlash; there was the sense among the working-class whites who remained that their chances for upward mobility were lost because they could no longer fraternize with the middle and upper class. Previously, there were only two high schools in Little Rock, one white and one black. So Central High was segregated by race and integrated by class. Now Central was integrated by race and segregated by class.

Beth Roy did interviews with white graduates of Central High thirty years later [for her book *Bitters in the Honey*] and determined that many of them still blame blacks for the failure of themselves and their children to gain a secure toehold in a middle class lifestyle. They think that the American Dream owed them individual opportunity through its promise that if you work hard and play by the rules you will succeed. The problem with the American Dream is that it offers no explanation for failure other than that you deserve your lot in life and that if you fail there must be something wrong with you. Many people are perfectly willing to believe that success is individual but don't want to think about failure as individual and no one wants to believe that they deserve to fail. So they find a scapegoat and blacks were an easy scapegoat in this case. Even thirty years later, the white graduates of Central High claimed that blacks stole the American Dream.

While the integration of Central was hyper-visible, the building of Hall High was kept under wraps—most people still don't know about it. Wealthier whites were able to get away with building Hall High because blacks were used as a scapegoat.

RP: You and Gerald Torres wrote about the Texas Ten Percent Plan in *The Miner's Canary*. How does that relate to this?

LG: Sheryl Hopwood was a white working-class woman who applied to the University of Texas Law School and was denied admission. In 1996, she sued the university for racial discrimination, arguing that less qualified blacks and Latinos had taken her spot. Thirty-nine years after Central, she sued in the district court and then in the Fifth Circuit and won, but the problem with the court's analysis was that they did not look behind the school's claim that all slots, except for those bestowed through Affirmative Action, were distributed based on merit.

It actually turns out that the school's own formula for determining merit disadvantaged Sheryl Hopwood. She went to a community college and the University of Texas Law weighted her LSAT scores with those of other applicants from her school and graduating year. Because her community college drew from a working class population, Hopwood's own LSAT score was negatively weighted. So Hopwood's chance of attending the University of Texas was diminished because of class status not because of her race.

After the ruling in Hopwood's favor, a group of legislators and concerned citizens determined that the University of Texas would not return to its segregationist roots. They started investigating the population of the University of Texas graduate school and found that 75% students admitted according to "merit" were coming from only 10% of high schools in the state. These schools tended to be suburban, white, and middle or upper class. Their logic was that if the University of Texas is supposed to be a flagship school and a place from which the state's leaders would be drawn, then 10% of students from each high school in the state should be automatically eligible for access. So the Texas Ten Percent Plan was passed by the legislature and Governor Bush signed it into law.

It all started with concern about racial diversity but it was discovered that class was also at the core. The law ultimately passed because a conservative republican legislator voted for the law when he learned that not one of his constituents, who were white and poor or working class, had been admitted in the previous cycle. So, "meritocratic" standards were keeping out poor and working class whites, especially the rural poor. Many people worried that if SAT scores were eliminated as marker, then grades would go down. However, those who've come in based on the Ten Percent plan have had higher freshman year grades.

RP: You've said before that race is being used as a decoy.

LG: Race was being used as a decoy for class, leading working-class and poor whites to challenge Affirmative Action, and to challenge the integration of Central High School. In fact, meritocratic standards, which favor the wealthy, have kept them out. Too often, poor and working class whites are willing to throw their lot in with upper class and middle class whites because class is obscured while race is quite visible. People think that if anyone can succeed, if these other whites can succeed, then they can too because merit claims to be about the individual operating without regard to background conditions.

RP: So what are the background conditions of students of color attending elite universities?

LG: Many students admitted through Affirmative Action are not that different from those admitted through conventional standards of merit because schools are so committed to the annual issue of *U.S. News and World Report* that ranks educational institutions according to the their students' standardized test scores.

In Ivy League schools, a large percentage of Latinos and blacks are foreign-born and don't identify with communities of color who are born in the United States. I'm not arguing that international students should not have access to US institutions. It is significant, however, that in the '70s and '80s, blacks and Latinos entering through Affirmative Action were coming in from poor U.S. communities and were passionate about returning to those communities and lifting as they climbed. Currently, schools are more concerned about admitting people that have high SAT scores who will boost their status than recruiting leaders. Education is changing from an opportunity for students to explore and grow to institutions that are consumed with rankings. Education is becoming about providing credentials to obtain high-paying jobs rather than training people for a thriving democracy.

From *Dollars & Sense* magazine, January/February 2006.

The United States' growing wealth gap reflects the fact that, for about three decades now, government policies have channeled the gains from the country's expanding economy and increasing productivity more and more toward a small elite. How did policies that disadvantage the majority of Americans ever get adopted in the first place? United for a Fair Economy's Chuck Collins dissects one explanation: the right built public-policy advocacy organizations designed to bring about long-term shifts in public opinion, and then gave them the resources to do it.

THE RIGHT-WING IDEA MACHINE

Moving an Economic Agenda

BY CHUCK COLLINS

For decades, right-wing conservatives have advanced an economic agenda that has worsened America's wealth divide: tax cuts for the rich, weaer labor rights, privatization of public services, corporate-driven global trade agreements, and the rest of the familiar litany. What is striking is that a small number of conservative foundations and nonprofit policy organizations have promoted—and with great success—a public policy agenda that runs counter to the interests of the vast majority of Americans. Those who support moving the United States away from a wealth-gap agenda and toward a wealth-broadening agenda can learn a great deal from how it was done. The lessons for progressive forces are clear: think big, get the message right, fund movement-building, dig in for the long term, and build power.

"DEATH TAX" DECEPTION

The battle over the federal estate tax, the United States' only tax on accumulated wealth, offers a telling case study. Today, over 60% of Americans support abolishing this tax. How do you convince the majority of Americans that it is in their interest to abolish a tax that only multimillionaires and billionaires pay?

The short answer is that the right-wing infrastructure, which has been so effective in the battle of ideas over three decades, was fully deployed to shift public opinion and get the tax repealed.

In March 2001, a new group, "Disabled Americans for Death Tax Relief," placed a full-page ad in newspapers around the country. The ad claimed that there are "2.5 million disabled people who are family members of millionaires." It argued that the estate tax deprives these people of the inheritance they need: "Some of us who would receive this wealth are in wheelchairs. Some are deaf and blind. Some are on respirators. Others require medication or nursing services. In order to live a full life, these Americans may require medical help, nursing and living assistance far beyond that which is covered by medical insurance." Claiming her group had attracted 1,000 members in just two weeks, Erin O'Leary, the group's photogenic leader, held a Capitol Hill press conference, followed by appearances on "Hardball" with Chris Matthews, the "O'Reilly Factor," and "Special Report" with Brit Hume.

Groups claiming to represent other alleged victims of the estate tax—for example, African-American, Hispanic, and women small business owners—sprang up as well, generating plenty of press.

Small farmers were another group of alleged victims. Time and again, repeal backers claimed the estate tax was costing many working farmers their farms. When Congress passed legislation to repeal the tax in 2000, it delivered the bill to the White House on a tractor to symbolize the pain they claim the tax causes farmers.

Repeal backers like to describe their movement as "grassroots," a mad-as-hell uprising by all of the ordinary Americans the estate tax supposedly injures. Peek behind the curtain, though, and you find a well-funded public relations, lobbying, media, and research apparatus led by sophisticated operatives, many with deep connections to the Republican Party. The "Disabled Americans" group was the creation of conservative communications maven Craig Shirley, whose public relations firm represents the National Rifle Association, the Heritage Foundation, and the Republican National Committee. It's impossible to evaluate the 1,000-members claim (a query to the group went unanswered), but O'Leary's is the only name that appears anywhere on the group's website.

The pro-repeal American Farm Bureau Foundation, when challenged, could not produce one actual example of a farm that was lost because of the estate tax, according to the *New York Times*. The group sent an urgent memo to its affiliates in 2001, stating "it is crucial for us to be able to provide Congress with examples of farmers and ranchers who have lost farms ... due to the death tax," but even this plea produced no real farm-loss stories. Other front groups advertising themselves as grassroots supporters of estate tax repeal included the Small Business Survival Coalition, United Seniors Association, and Americans for Job Security. All of these groups have articulated a single, carefully-crafted message; for example, they always called the estate tax a "death tax," a moniker that Republican pollster Frank Luntz urged repeal backers to use as a rhetorical centerpiece of the repeal campaign.

BEHIND THE CURTAIN

If the campaign to repeal the estate tax was not a genuine outpouring of grassroots concern, then where did it come from? In the early 1990s, a group including the heirs to the Mars and Gallo family fortunes embarked on a long-term effort to eliminate the tax. They enlisted the help of Patricia Soldano, an Orange County, Calif., advisor to wealthy families. She formed a lobbying organization called the Policy and Taxation Group to provide an "outlet" for wealthy families "interested in communicating

RIGHT-WING ECONOMIC POLICY ADVOCACY: THE TOP FIVE

The Heritage Foundation was founded in 1973 by beer magnate Joseph Coors and new right institution-builder Paul Weyrich. Heritage is the grand dame of conservative think tanks, with an annual budget over $50 million and more than 200 employees. It came to prominence with the 1980 election of Ronald Reagan, whose policy agenda it played a significant role in shaping. Heritage not only conducts research, but, as any journalist can testify, also has a sophisticated capacity to package and disseminate its ideology. For example, the foundation issues daily briefs, via fax broadcast and email, on a variety of policy issues. Among the conservative donors who also serve on Heritage's board are banking scion Richard Mellon Scaife, beer magnate Joseph Coors, and Jay van Andel, the founder of Amway and a major funder of initiatives to privatize education.

Americans for Tax Reform was founded by conservative activist Grover Norquist in the mid-1980s, based inside the Reagan White House as an in-house operation to build support for the 1986 tax reform bill. It is now an independent organization that is propelled by Norquist's strong movement-building orientation. Its policy focus is on federal and state tax cuts. The group's financial backing comes largely from corporations in the tobacco, gambling, and alcohol industries. Americans for Tax Reform has links to hundreds of local anti-tax committees and organizations.

The **Cato Institute** was founded in 1977 by libertarian businessmen Charles Koch and Edward Crane. It has an annual budget of over $17 million and a staff of 90, plus more than 75 adjunct scholars and research fellows. With its libertarian orientation, Cato sometimes clashes with other conservative advocacy groups, and has

their concerns to members of Congress." Soldano channeled funds to congressional backers of repeal and hired the powerful lobbying firm Patton Boggs.

By the mid-1990s, Soldano's outfit and other early pro-repeal groups had joined together with a veritable industry of think tanks, lobbying firms, and interest groups in Washington, D.C., to form a powerful "death tax elimination" lobby.

Conservative think tanks, including the Heritage Foundation and the libertarian National Center for Policy Analysis, produced policy backgrounders criticizing the estate tax, and generated the requisite op-eds and TV appearances as well. The antigovernment group Citizens for a Sound Economy encouraged its members to lobby their senators and representatives against the tax.

campaigned with progressive groups on issues like civil liberties and corporate welfare. But as a major advocate of shrinking the federal government and privatizing public services such as Social Security, Cato is solidly in the aid-the-rich camp on key economic issues. The organization's funding comes from the usual conservative foundations and a large number of corporations including Philip Morris, Viacom International, and Chase Manhattan Bank.

Citizens for a Sound Economy was founded in 1984 by multimillionaire Libertarian Party vice-presidential candidate David Koch. Its primary focus is on free markets and limited government, but the group also works to oppose environmental and corporate regulation. CSE functions as a field operation for the conservative economic movement, claiming 280,000 members and chapters in 23 states. The bulk of the group's financial support comes from corporations that want to advance specific policy agendas, which has gained it a reputation as a corporate shill. For instance, in 1998 CSE received over $700,000 in contributions from the Florida sugar industry, which was fighting federal efforts to restore the Everglades at the time.

The **Club for Growth** was founded in 1999 by Stephen Moore, the former director of fiscal policy at the Cato Institute. It functions as a sort of EMILY's list for economic conservatives, bundling donations from wealthy Wall Street financiers and executives. The organization also runs a 527 committee that runs issue ads (527 committees are groups permitted to use unlimited soft-money contributions for political activities but not to directly support a candidate) and a traditional Political Action Committee to contribute to candidates. It works to maintain ideological discipline within the Republican party, running far-right candidates against moderate Republicans who stray from its anti-tax and limited government orthodoxy. In April 2004, a Club for Growth-backed challenger was narrowly defeated in his bid to unseat longtime incumbent Senator Arlen Specter (R-Pa.).

Other groups involved in the anti-estate tax crusade include the private campaign organization Club for Growth; the political arm of the libertarian Cato Institute; the American Conservative Union; Grover Norquist's Americans for Tax Reform; and the 60 Plus Association, a self-styled conservative alternative to the American Association of Retired Persons. At the center of the lobbying effort is the National Federation of Independent Businesses (NFIB), a business trade association and one of the most influential organizations in Washington.

The combined efforts of these groups succeeded in getting estate tax repeal included in the 2001 Bush tax cut. What would have seemed unthinkable a decade earlier is now a fact of public policy.

WHO PAID THE PIPER?

It takes money to whip up "grassroots" political organizations where none exist, to place full-page newspaper ads, to conduct research, and to lobby. But the funding that underwrites right-wing public policy advocacy is largely hidden. Corporations are an important source of funds, but they don't have to disclose the bulk of their philanthropic giving.

The strategic role of conservative grantmaking foundations is more visible, though, thanks to research by the National Committee for Responsive Philanthropy. The committee's 2004 report, "Axis of Ideology: Conservative Foundations and Public Policy," discloses that right-wing foundations like the David H. Koch Charitable Trust, the Linde and Harry Bradley Foundation, the Carthage Foundation (one of the Scaife Foundations), the John M. Olin Foundation, and the Claude R. Lamb Charitable Trust don't have the net worth or grantmaking dollars of the giants such as the Ford Foundation, which are all centrist or liberal; however, they spend their money in a more focused way. For example, these foundations specifically support public policy advocacy, directing over a fifth of their resources to it. Their advocacy includes Social Security privatization, free-trade agreements, tax cuts, corporate deregulation and weakening of labor laws. Liberal and centrist foundations tend to shy away from policy advocacy, focusing their funding instead on provision of basic services.

Right-wing nonprofits and the foundations that fund them are networked in a way that centralizes their efforts and leverages their resources. The 20 largest right-wing foundations donated over 80% of the $250 million that conservative foundations allocated to public policy advocacy between 1999 and 2001. And 20 nonprofit organizations—key groups that set the conservative agenda through research and market and lobby for that agenda—received over half of these allocations.

Conservative foundations are also strategic about *how* they fund the groups they fund. While liberal foundations tend to fund "projects," the leading-edge conservative foundations fund movement infrastructure. While liberal foundations rarely provide multiyear support that would enable grantees to build up permanent capacity, conservative foundations often provide long-term general support, in some cases over decades. While only 27% of grants from liberal and centrist foundations are for general operating support, almost 80% of conservative foundation grants are of this kind.

Progressive infrastructure is outgunned on almost every front. But there are efforts underway to change this. The National Committee on Responsive Philanthropy has stimulated discussion within the funding community about applying some of the lessons of right-wing grantmaking. Some liberal funders, recognizing the need for a message-oriented progressive think tank, ponied up $10 million in 2003 to launch the Center for American Progress.

Today, conservatives are harvesting the fruits of several decades of investment in shaping public attitudes and promoting right-wing ideas and policies. Ideas that were once considered marginal, such as privatizing Social Security, providing vouchers for private education, and eliminating the progressive income tax, are now at the center of policy debates. If progressive forces can build and fund an equally effective infrastructure, the wealth-broadening agenda will have a fighting chance.

Like nobility in feudal times, shareholders claim wealth they do little to create. Marjorie Kelly questions our assumptions about the rights of the corporate stockholder, and asks why employees, by contrast, have no claim on corporate wealth, no voting rights, and no say in corporate governance.

A LEGITIMATE MANDATE?

Maximizing Returns to Shareholders

BY MARJORIE KELLY

Where does wealth come from? More precisely, where does the wealth of major public corporations come from? Who creates it?

To judge by the current arrangement in corporate America, one might suppose capital creates wealth—which is odd, because a pile of capital sitting there creates nothing. Yet capital-providers (stockholders) lay claim to most wealth that public corporations generate. They also claim the more fundamental right to have corporations managed on their behalf.

Corporations are believed to exist for one purpose alone: to maximize returns to shareholders. This principle is reinforced by CEOs, the *Wall Street Journal,* business schools, and the courts. It is the law of the land—much as the divine right of kings was once the law of the land. Indeed, "maximizing returns to shareholders" is universally accepted as a kind of divine, unchallengeable mandate.

It is not in the least controversial. Though it should be.

What do shareholders contribute to justify the extraordinary allegiance they receive? They take risk, we're told. They put their money on the line, so corporations might grow and prosper.

Let's test the truth of this with a little quiz:

Stockholders fund major public corporations—*True or False?*

False. Or, actually, a tiny bit true—but for the most part, massively false.

What's intriguing is that we speak as though it were entirely true: "I have invested in AT&T," we say—imagining AT&T as a steward of our money, with a fiduciary responsibility to take care of it.

In fact, "investing" dollars don't go to AT&T but to other speculators. Equity "investments" reach a public corporation only when new common stock is sold—which for major corporations is a rare event. Among the Dow Jones Industrials, only a handful have sold any new common stock in 30 years. Many have sold none in 50 years.

The stock market works like a used car market, as accounting professor Ralph Estes observes in *Tyranny of the Bottom Line.* When you buy a 1989 Ford Escort, the money doesn't go to Ford. It goes to the previous owner. Ford gets the buyer's money only when it sells a new car.

Similarly, companies get stockholders' money only when they sell new common stock—which mature companies rarely do. According to figures from the Federal Reserve and the Securities and Exchange Commission, about 99% of the stock out there is "used stock." That is, 99 out of 100 "invested" dollars are trading in the purely speculative market, and never reach corporations.

Public corporations do have the ability to sell new stock. And they do need capital (funds beyond revenue) to operate—for inventory, expansion, and so forth. But they get very little of this capital from stockholders.

In 1993, for example, corporations needed $555 billion in capital. According to the Federal Reserve, sales of common stock contributed 4% of that. I used this fact in a pull-quote for a magazine article once, and the designer changed it to 40%, assuming it was a typo. It's not.

Well, yes, critics will say—that's recently. But stockholders did fund corporations in the past. Again, only a tiny bit true. Take the steel industry. An accounting study by Eldon Hendriksen examined capital expenditures in that industry from 1900 to 1953, and found that issues of common stock provided only 5% of capital. That was over the entire first half of the 20th century, when industry was growing by leaps and bounds.

So, what do stockholders contribute, to justify the extraordinary allegiance they receive? Very little. And that's my point.

Equity capital is provided by stockholders when a company goes public, and in occasional secondary offerings later. But in the life of most major companies today, issuance of common stock represents a distant, long-ago source of funds, and a minor one at that. What's odd is that it entitles holders to extract most of the corporation's wealth, forever.

Equity investors essentially install a pipeline, and dictate that the corporation's sole purpose is to funnel wealth into it. The pipeline is never to be tampered with—

and no one else is to be granted significant access (except executives, whose function is to keep it flowing).

The truth is, the commotion on Wall Street is not about funding corporations. It's about extracting from them.

The productive risk in building businesses is borne by entrepreneurs and their initial venture investors, who do contribute real investing dollars, to create real wealth. Those who buy stock at sixth or seventh hand, or 1,000th hand, also take a risk—but it is a risk speculators take among themselves, trying to outwit one another like gamblers.

It has little to do with corporations, except this: Public companies are required to provide new chips for the gaming table, into infinity.

It's odd. And it's connected to a second oddity—that we believe stockholders are the corporation. When we say "a corporation did well," we mean its shareholders did well. The company's local community might be devastated by plant closings, its groundwater contaminated with pollutants. Employees might be shouldering a crushing workload, doing without raises for years on end. Still we will say, "the corporation did well."

One does not see rising employee income as a measure of corporate success. Indeed, gains to employees are losses to the corporation. And this betrays an unconscious bias: that employees are not really part of the corporation. They have no claim on wealth they create, no say in governance, and no vote for the board of directors. They're not citizens of corporate society, but subjects. Investors, on the other hand, may never set foot inside "their" companies, may not know where they're located or what they produce. Yet corporations exist to enrich investors alone. In the corporate society, only those who own stock can vote—like America until the mid-1800s, when only those who owned land could vote. Employees are disenfranchised.

We think of this as the natural law of the free market. It's more accurately the result of the existing corporate governance structure, which violates free-market principles. In a free market, everyone scrambles to get what they can, and they keep what they earn. In the construct of the corporation, one group gets what another earns.

The oddity of it all is veiled by the incantation of a single, magical word: "ownership." Because we say stockholders "own" corporations, they are permitted to contribute very little, and take quite a lot.

What an extraordinary word. One is tempted to recall [Greek poet] Lycophron's comment, during an early Athenian slave uprising against the aristocracy. "The splendour of noble birth is imaginary," he said, "and its prerogatives are based upon a mere word."

"The feminization of poverty," "the gender gap"—these terms have helped put women's economic status onto the agenda in both rich and poor countries. We know that in the United States, the racial wealth gap outpaces the racial income gap in both magnitude and, very likely, effects. Is the same true for gender? Here, Dollars & Sense co-editor Amy Gluckman reviews what we know about women and wealth ownership, in the United States and globally.

WOMEN AND WEALTH

A Primer

BY AMY GLUCKMAN

Put "wealth" and "women" into the same sentence, and contradictory images jump to mind: from Cleopatra, Marie Antoinette ("let them eat cake"), or Oprah to an anonymous Asian, Latin American, or African woman lugging buckets or bales along a rugged path. Each of these images bears some truth: women's relationship with wealth is not a simple one. Women have, historically, held every possible juxtaposition with wealth and property. They have been property themselves, essentially sold in marriage, and in some instances inherited upon a husband's death by his brother or other male relative. They have almost universally faced restricted rights to own, control, and inherit property compared to men. Yet women have also been fabulously wealthy, and in not insignificant numbers— sometimes benefiting from family-owned wealth, occasionally wealthy in their own right. Today, according to a recent report in Datamonitor, more than half of Britain's millionaires are women.

Furthermore, women's access to wealth is always conditioned by race, ethnicity, class, and all of the other parameters that shape the distribution of wealth in any society. Her gender is never the sole factor that shapes a woman's acquisition or use of property.

Marriage in particular has acted as a double-edged sword for women. On one hand, marriage typically gives a woman access to a man's income and wealth, affording her a higher standard of living than most social orders would have allowed her to achieve on her own. On the other hand, women have widely lost rights to own, control, and inherit wealth when they married. And when divorced or widowed, women have sometimes lost the access that marriage afforded them to their husbands' property without gaining any renewed rights to the property of their natal families.

Discriminatory laws and customs in many parts of the world have broken down, although it's sobering to remember how recent this change has been. In the United States, the first state to enact a comprehensive law removing restrictions on property ownership by married women was New York, in 1848. (Mississippi passed a limited statute in 1839. In a clear illustration of the complicated nexus of race, class, and gender that always shapes wealth ownership, the Mississippi law was primarily focused on giving married women the right to own slaves; the law was likely intended to offer plantation owners a way to avoid having their slaves seized to pay the husband's debts.) Other states were still passing similar laws up to 1900, and discrimination on the basis of sex and marital status in granting credit was made illegal at the federal level only in 1974. And of course, custom and economic institutions continued to discriminate against women in the ownership and control of property, access to credit in their own names, and related matters long after laws had been changed.

Around the world, many countries have only recently granted women—or married women in particular—property rights. A 2000 U.N. report lists Bolivia, the Dominican Republic, Eritrea, Malaysia, Nepal, Uganda, Tanzania, and Zimbabwe among countries that have recently passed laws recognizing women's ownership of land, for example. Many countries still lack statutes giving women an express right to own land or other wealth in their own names (see the map on pages 18–19).

FREE BUT NOT EQUAL

Even with the right to own wealth, women have not necessarily had the means to accumulate any. Among the factors key to building assets are income, education, and inheritance—and, of course, in each of these, women face obstacles, whether customary or legal.

In the rich countries, women today have largely the same educational attainment as men—up to, but not including, the highest levels. In the United States, for example, more girls than boys graduate from high school, and more women than men are enrolled in bachelor's degree programs. But there are still far more men than women who hold advanced degrees, especially in lucrative fields such as engineering, business, law, and medicine. Women workers remain concentrated in female-dominated occupations that continue to pay less than male-dominated occupations requiring the same degree of skill, preparation, and responsibility. This is a key reason for the persistent gender pay gap. The median income of U.S. men working full-time, year-round was $38,275 in 2001; the equivalent figure for women was $29,215, or only 76% of men's pay.

Women in the global South continue to face far larger education and income gaps, although with great variation among countries. For example, Yemen, Pakistan, and Niger all have female-male adult literacy ratios under 60%, while Jordan, Sri Lanka, and Cameroon all have ratios of 95% or above. Income data disaggregated by sex is not available for many countries, according the most recent U.N. Human Development Report. But the report's rough estimates show a substantial gender gap in income in every country. And in many developing countries, women continue to hold only limited rights to inherit property.

Plenty of factors account for women's lack of wealth accumulation across the globe, but working too little is certainly not one of them. Women work longer hours every day than men in most countries, according to time-use studies assembled by the United Nations. The unequal work burden is most pronounced in rural areas, where women typically work 20% more minutes a day than men. Environmental problems in many countries have exacerbated women's work burden; a Population Reference Bureau report notes that "Given the variety of women's daily interactions with the environment to meet household needs, they are often most keenly affected by its degradation. In the Sudan, deforestation in the last decade has led to a quadrupling of women's time spent gathering fuelwood. Because girls are often responsible for collecting water and fuelwood, water scarcity and deforestation also contribute to higher school dropout rates for girls."

WOMEN'S WEALTH HOLDINGS: WHAT WE KNOW

Today's wealth distribution reflects the accumulation of assets over years, even generations. So it will take time before the uneven but dramatic changes in women's status over the past few decades will show up in the wealth statistics. Given that, what is the distribution of wealth by gender today?

The first thing to note is that we really don't know what it is, for a number of reasons. First, data on personal wealth are scarce. Most countries do not systematically collect data on wealth ownership. Among the few countries that do are the United States, Sweden, Germany, and Britain.

Where data *are* regularly collected, the unit is typically the household, not the individual. Thus the assets of most married couples are assigned to both wife and husband equally in wealth surveys, obscuring any differences in the two spouses' authority to manage or benefit from those assets or to retain them if the marriage ends. This leaves gender comparisons possible only between unmarried men and unmarried women, a minority of the adult population.

In many countries, property ownership is governed by customary or informal rules rather than legal title. The term "ownership" itself is a simplification; ownership is really a bundle of rights that don't necessarily reside in the same person. In statutory systems and particularly in customary systems, women may have limited ownership rights; for example, a woman may have the right to use a piece of property but not to transfer or bequeath it. This limits the value of any simple, quantitative snapshot of wealth distribution by gender. Instead, a complex qualitative portrait is necessary.

Given all of these limitations, what *do* we know?

In the United States, the significant gap is between married and unmarried people. Married-couple households have median net worth far more than two times that of households headed by unmarried adults (see "Women and Wealth in the United States," page 16). However, there is also a gender gap between unmarried men and unmarried women. The median net worth of single female-headed households in 2001 was $28,000; of single male-headed households, $47,000. And this gap has to be viewed in relation to the greater financial responsibilities of single women: a greater portion of single-female headed households include children under 18. There is also a vast wealth gap between white women and women of color: the median net worth of households headed by single white women was $56,590 in 2001; of households headed by single African-American women, $5,700; and of households headed by single Hispanic women, $3,900.

The young baby-boomer cohort, looked at separately, shows nearly no wealth gap between unmarried men and women (see page 17). This suggests that women are catching up—at least in a rich country like the United States. This is not surprising, as women are moving toward parity with men in several of the factors correlated with higher net worth, such as education and income. However, the income gap has long been smaller between young women and men than between older women and men, at least in part because the workforce participation of women—who typically bear greater parenting responsibilities than men—becomes more uneven over time. As the young boomers age, how much the wealth gap is really shrinking will become more clear.

For the global South, systematic personal wealth data simply do not exist. But it's possible to assess some of the factors that are shaping the distribution of wealth by gender in poor and middle-income nations. The transition to formal systems of property ownership has had complex effects in many poor, predominantly rural countries. In theory, holding legal title to land can benefit small farmers—many of whom around the world are women. With a legal title, a farmer can use the land as collateral and thereby gain access to credit; she can also more confidently invest in improvements. However, in the process of formalizing land titles, governments have often taken land that was customarily under a woman's control and given the title to it to a man. Likewise, land reform programs have often bypassed women. Women were "left out of the agrarian reforms of the 1960s and 1970s" in Latin America, according to a U.N. report, because household heads, to whom land titles were given, were simply assumed to be men. Women do 60% to 80% of the agricultural labor throughout the developing world, but are not nearly as likely to be actual landowners: the percentage of agricultural landowners who are women ranges from 3% in Bangladesh to 57% in Namibia, and their average holdings are smaller than men's.

Lacking formal title to land, women have very limited access to agricultural credit. The same is true outside of agriculture: of the 300 million low-income self-employed women in the global South, hardly any have access to credit (aside from money-lenders, who typically charge exorbitant interest rates that can range up to 100% a month). Microcredit programs have sprung up in many countries and are making a dent in this problem, but just a dent. Although it's now worth some $2.5 billion, the microcredit sector reaches only an estimated 3% of those across the global South (both women and men) who could benefit from it.

Liberalization and structural adjustment policies pressed on third world governments have been hard on women's economic status. Consider the case of Mexico where, following the introduction of economic liberalization in the mid-1980s, growth has been slow for everyone. But women have suffered disproportionately. With the opening of lots of export-oriented *maquiladoras*, women's share of industrial jobs grew. But women's industrial wages fell from 80% of men's in 1984 to 57% of men's in 1992. At the same time, the bland term "structural adjustment" means, in practice, often-huge cutbacks in public services such as health care, education, and aid to the poor. Women (and children) are typically more dependent on these programs than men, and so suffer more when they are cut.

WHAT IS WEALTH GOOD FOR?
Does it matter if women have less wealth and less capacity to acquire and control assets than men? Most adult women across the globe are married, and for most married women, these forms of gender-specific discrimination do not prevent them from enjoying a family standard of living underwritten by their husbands' income and wealth. But a woman's ability to own property in her own name turns out to be more important than it might appear. Women with property are less vulnerable to all of life's vicissitudes. Owning property can protect women affected by HIV/AIDS from destitution, for example; the International Center for Research on Women is currently documenting this association.

And asset ownership changes the balance of power between women and men. In a study of 500 urban and rural women in Kerala, India, Pradeep Panda of the Centre for Development Studies, Trivandrum, and Bina Agarwal of the Institute of Economic Growth, Delhi, found that women who are wealthless are considerably more vulnerable to domestic violence than women who own property. The study's remarkable results are worth quoting at length:

The study's findings did, bear out the fact that ownership of immovable property by women is associated with a dramatically lower incidence of both physical and psychological harassment, as well as long-term and current violence. For example, as many as 49% of the women who owned neither land nor house suffered long-term physical violence, compared with 18% and 10% respectively of those who owned either land or a house, and 7% of those who owned both.

The effect of property ownership on psychological violence is even more dramatic. While 84% of property-less women suffered abuse, the figure was much lower (16%) for women who owned both land and a house.

The ownership of property also offers women the option of leaving an abusive environment—of the 179 women experiencing long-term physical violence, 43 left home. The percentage of women leaving home was much higher among the propertied (71%) than among those without property (19%). Moreover, of the women who left home, although 24 returned, 88% of the returning women were property-less. Few propertied women returned.

So, not only are propertied women less likely to experience marital violence, they are also able to escape further violence. Hence, property ownership serves both as a deterrent and as an exit option for abused women.

Interestingly, while a fair proportion of women (propertied and property-less) faced dowry demands, only 3% of propertied women faced dowry-related beatings by their in-laws and husbands, compared to 44% of property-less women. This suggests another form in which the ownership of personal property lessens the incidence of domestic crimes against women.

The protective impact of house or land ownership on reducing a woman's risk of violence emerged as significant even after such factors as household economic status, a woman's age, duration of marriage, childlessness, educational and employment levels of both husband and wife, spousal gaps in education or employment, the husband's alcohol consumption, childhood exposure to violence and social support from parents and neighbours were controlled.

In contrast to a woman's property ownership status, there seems to be no clear relationship between risk of violence and employment status, except if the woman has a regular job. This reduces the risk only of long-term physical violence. Employment does not offer the same protection to women as does property ownership. ... Land access enhances a woman's livelihood options and gives her a sense of empowerment.

It has long been a shibboleth in the U.S. women's movement that all women can face domestic violence regardless of their economic circumstances. But owning and controlling some wealth surely offers women in rich countries the same kinds of protection the Kerala study revealed: a stronger position in the marital power dynamic, and the ability to exit. And owning some property no doubt underwrites a woman's ability to struggle against patriarchal institutions in other ways too, at least on an individual level, and to achieve her own potential. Virginia Woolf wrote a century ago that a woman who wanted to create needed a modest (unearned) income and a room of her own; Woolf's vision is no less true today.

But today most women around the world still don't have the modest unearned income or the room of their own—and not only because of their gender. What then would a progressive feminist agenda around wealth look like? Of course, it would address all of the remaining customs, statutes, and institutional barriers that limit women's economic rights relative to men's. But it would also seek to reorient all economic institutions toward the provision of social forms of wealth and the deconcentration of private wealth. Only a dual agenda like this can offer any hope—for achieving either gender equity *or* a decent standard of living—to a majority of the world's women.

A society's system of property rights underlies its distribution of wealth. It sets the rules that determine how ownership is defined, what benefits accrue to those defined as owners, and at what cost to the larger social good.

PROPERTY

Who Has a Right to What and Why?

BY ARTHUR MACEWAN

In 1948, siblings Joseph and Agnes Waschak purchased a home in Taylor, Pennsylvania, in the midst of coal mining country. Within a few years, hydrogen sulfide fumes and other gases from the nearby mines and mine waste turned the Waschaks' white house black and stained all the internal fixtures yellowish-brown or black. The Waschaks filed suit for damages. According to evidence presented in the subsequent court case, the Waschaks and other area residents who were forced to breathe the gases "suffered from headaches, throat irritation, inability to sleep, coughing, light-headedness, nausea and stomach ailments."

Eric Freyfogle describes the *Waschak v. Moffat* case in his book *The Land We Share: Private Property and the Common Good* as an illustration of how changing concepts of property relate to the preservation of the natural environment. Eventually, the case worked its way up to the Pennsylvania Supreme Court. *Waschak v. Moffat* was not simply an instance of citizens challenging property owners, but of one set of property owners positioned against another. On one side were the Waschaks and others who claimed that the actions of the coal companies constituted a nuisance that prevented them from fully using their property; on the other side were the coal companies who wanted to use their mines as they saw fit. The court had to decide not *whether* property rights would prevail, but *which* set of property rights had priority.

In 1954, the court ruled that a nuisance existed only when the actions involved were intentional or the result of negligence. The coal companies, the court maintained, intended no harm and were not negligent because they were following standard practices in the mining industry. The Waschaks lost.

Four decades later, concepts of property rights and priorities had changed, as illustrated by a 1998 case in Iowa, *Borman v. Board of Supervisors,* also described by

Freyfogle. In this case, the landowning plaintiffs wanted to prevent another landowner from developing a "Confined Animal Feeding Operation" (CAFO) that would involve thousands of animals generating large amounts of waste, odors, and other damage to the surrounding properties. Again, the dispute was between the conflicting rights of two sets of property owners.

The Iowa Supreme Court ruled in favor of the plaintiffs, agreeing that the nuisance that would be created by the CAFO would be an illegitimate interference with their property rights. The court did not deny that its ruling limited the property rights of the CAFO planners, but it gave priority to the rights of the plaintiffs. Moreover, the court ruled that the CAFO planners were not due any compensation by the state, even though it was preventing them from using their land as they chose and thereby reducing the value of that property.

What changed between 1954 and 1998? Many things were different, of course, including the fact that the earlier case was in one state and the later case in another. But the most important difference was that society's views on environmental issues had changed, evolving along with the development of a broad social movement to protect the environment. As a result, concepts regarding property rights changed. What had earlier been seen as legitimate action by a property owner was, by the end of century, viewed as an illegitimate degradation of the environment.

Property rights, it turns out, are not fixed. They change. They are a product of society and of social decisions. As society changes, so too do property rights. And the changes in property rights are contested, subject to political power and social struggle.

WHY DO WE PROTECT PRIVATE PROPERTY?

Although we often take property rights for granted, as though they are based on some absolute standard, in reality they are both changing and ambiguous. Moreover, many widely accepted ideas about property rights start to fall apart when we ask: Why do we protect private property?

For example, suppose a family has a deed on a particular field. Why do we as a society say that another family cannot come along, take part of that field, and sow and reap their own crops? Does it make any difference if the family with the deed has never used the field for any productive purpose, but has simply let it sit idle?

Or, for another example, suppose a pharmaceutical company develops a new antibiotic. Why do we allow that company the right to take out a patent and then prevent other firms or individuals from producing and selling that same antibiotic? Does it make any difference if the antibiotic is one that would save the lives of many people were it more readily available—that is, available at a lower price than the company charges?

Or, for still another example, what if a man owns a large house in the suburbs, an extensive apartment in the city, a ski lodge in the mountains, a beach house at the shore, two or three other homes at convenient sites, three yachts, a jet plane, and seven cars? Why do we prevent a poor man who has nothing—no home, no car, and certainly no yacht or jet plane—from occupying one of these many homes?

Perhaps the most common argument in favor of our protection of private property is the claim: We protect private property because it works to do so. That is, secure property rights are viewed as a basis for a stable and prosperous society. If people do not know that their accumulated wealth—held in the form of cash, land, houses, or factories—will be protected by society, they will see little point in trying to accumulate. According to the argument, if the pharmaceutical company cannot be assured of the profit from its patent, it will have no incentive to finance the research that leads to the drug's development. And if the state did not protect people's wealth, society could be in a continual state of instability and conflict.

As a defense of private property rights, however, this it-works-to-do-so argument is incomplete, as the *Waschak* and *Borman* cases illustrate, because it does not tell us what to do when property rights come into conflict with one another. This defense of property rights is also flawed because it is too vague, failing to provide a sufficiently clear statement of what things can legitimately be held as private property. Can air or water or people be held as private property? Can a patent be held forever?

What's more, the argument puts defenders of property rights in a precarious position because it implicitly concedes that private property rights exist in order to serve the larger good of society. If we determine that the larger good of society dictates a change in property rights—new restrictions on the use of property, for example— then the it-works-to-do-so argument provides no defense.

In many instances, property owners have claimed that environmental regulations infringe on their property rights. Property owners who are prevented from establishing a CAFO as in the Borman case, from filling wet-lands, from building along fragile coast lines, or from destroying the habitat of an endangered species argue that government regulation is, in effect, taking away their property because it is reducing the value of that property. And they demand payment for this "taking." Such a claim loses its ideological and legal force, however, in a world where property rights change, where they are a creation of society, and where the larger good of society is the ultimate justification for protecting private property.

While questions about property rights are surrounded by ideology, legal complications, and arguments about the larger good of society, at the core of these questions lie fundamental disputes about the distribution of wealth. Who gets to use a field, the extent of a pharmaceutical company's patent rights, the preservation of a rich man's houses—each of these examples illustrates a conflict over the distribution of wealth as much as it illustrates a complication of how we define and protect property rights. Property rights are the rules of the game by which society's wealth gets divided up, and how we shape those rules is very much connected to how we define the larger good of society.

PATENTS VERSUS LIFE

The relationship between property rights and the larger good of society has come to a head in recent years in the dispute over patent rights and AIDS drugs. It has become increasingly apparent that, when it comes to protecting the property rights of the pharmaceutical companies that hold patents on these life-saving drugs, it-*doesn't*-work-to-do-so.

In low-income countries, multinational pharmaceutical companies have attempted to enforce their patents on life-saving AIDS drugs and prevent the provision of these drugs at affordable prices. The matter has been especially important in several African countries where governments, ignoring the companies' patents, have taken steps to allow local production or importation of low-cost generic forms of the drugs. Large pharmaceutical corporations such as Glaxo, Merck, and Roche have fought back, and their resistance has received extensive support from the U.S. government. In 1998, for example, the South African government of Nelson Mandela passed a law allowing local firms to produce low-cost versions of the AIDS drugs on which U.S. pharmaceutical firms hold patents. The Clinton administration responded on behalf of the firms, accusing the South Africans of "unfair trade practices" and threatening the country with trade sanctions if it implemented the law. The drug companies have since backed off, seeking compromises that would allow access to the drugs in particular cases but that would avoid precedents undermining their property rights in the patents.

The conflict between patent rights and the availability of AIDS drugs, however, has continued and spread. In Thailand, for example, the Government Pharmaceutical Organization (GPO) sought permission from the country's Commerce Department to produce a drug, didanosine, for which Bristol-Myers Squibb holds the patent. In spite of the fact that the locally produced drug would allow treatment of close to a million HIV-positive people in Thailand who would otherwise be unable to afford the didanosine, the permission was rejected because the Thai Commerce Department feared trade retaliation from the United States. Instead, the GPO was only allowed to produce a form of the drug that has greater side effects. Early in 2004, however, Bristol-Myers Squibb ceded the issue. Fearing public outcry and damaging precedents in the courts, the company surrendered in Thailand its exclusive patent rights to manufacture and sell the drug.

These conflicts have not been confined to the particular case of AIDS drugs, but have also been major issues in World Trade Organization (WTO) negotiations on the international extension of patent rights in general. Popular pressure and government actions in several low-income regions of the world have forced compromises from the companies and at the WTO.

But the dispute is far from over, and it is not just about formal issues of property rights and patents. At its core, it is a dispute over whether medical advances will be directed toward the larger good of society or toward greater profits for the pharmaceutical companies and their shareholders. It is a dispute over the distribution of wealth and income.

"FREE THE MOUSE!"

Patents and, similarly, copyrights are a form of property (known as "intellectual property") that is quite clearly a creation of society, and the way society handles patents and copyrights does a great deal to shape the distribution of wealth and income. Acting through the state (the Department of Commerce in the United States), society gives the creator of a new product exclusive rights—in effect, monopoly control—to make, use, or sell the item, based on the general rationale that doing so will encourage the creation of more products (machines, books, music, pharmaceuticals, etc.).

The general rationale for these property rights, however, does not tell us very much about their nature. How long should patents and copyrights last? What can and what cannot be patented? What, exactly, constitutes an infringement of the copyright holder's property rights? And what if the rationale is wrong in the first place? What if patent and copyright protections are not necessary to promote creative activity? The answer to each of these questions is contested terrain, changing time and again as a consequence of larger political and social changes.

Beyond the issue of AIDS drugs, there are several other patent or copyright-related conflicts that illustrate how these rights change through conflict and the exercise of political power. One case is the Napster phenomenon, where people have shared music files over the Internet and generated outcry and lawsuits from music companies. This battle over property rights, inconceivable a generation ago, is now the subject of intense conflict in the courts.

An especially interesting case where rights have been altered by the effective use of political power has been the Mickey Mouse matter. In 1998, Congress passed the Sonny Bono Copyright Term Extension Act, extending copyright protection 20 years beyond what existing regulations provided for. One of the prime beneficiaries of—and one of the strongest lobbyists for—this act was the Disney company; the act assures Disney's control over Mickey Mouse until 2023—and Pluto, Goofy, and Donald Duck until 2025, 2027, and 2029, respectively.

Not surprisingly, the Copyright Extension Act aroused opposition, campaigning under the banner "Free the Mouse!" Along with popular efforts, the act was challenged in the courts. While the challenge had particular legal nuances, it was based on the seemingly reasonable argument that the Copyright Extension Act, which protects creative activity retroactively, could have no impact now on the efforts of authors and composers who created their works in the first half of the 20th century. The Supreme Court, apparently deciding that its view of the law trumped this reasonable argument, upheld the act. Congress and the Court provided a valuable handout to Disney and other firms, but it is hard to see how a 20-year extension of copyright protection will have any significant impact on creative efforts now or in the future.

"COULD YOU PATENT THE SUN?"

Indeed, in a recent paper issued by the Federal Reserve Bank of Minneapolis, economists Michele Boldrin and David K. Levine suggest that the government's granting of protection through patents and copyrights may not be necessary to encourage innovation. When government does grant these protections, it is granting a form of monopoly. Boldrin and Levine argue that when "new ideas are built on old ideas," the monopoly position embodied in patents and copyrights may stifle rather than encourage creativity. Microsoft, a firm that has prospered by building new ideas on old ideas and then protecting itself with patents and copyrights, provides a good example, for it is also a firm that has attempted to control new innovations and limit the options of competitors who might bring further advances. (Microsoft, dependent as it is on microprocessors developed in federal research programs and on the government-sponsored emergence of the Internet, is also a good example of the way property is often brought into being by public, government actions and then appropriated by private interests. But that is another story.)

Boldrin and Levine also point out that historically there have been many periods of thriving innovation in the absence of patents and copyrights. The economic historian David Landes relates how medieval Europe was "one of the most inventive societies that history has known." Landes describes, as examples, the development of the water wheel (by the early 11th century), eyeglasses (by the early 14th century), and the mechanical clock (by the late 13th century). Also, first invented by the Chinese in the ninth century, printing rapidly developed in Europe by the middle of the 15th century with the important addition of movable type. Yet the first patent statute was not enacted until 1474, in Venice, and the system of patents spread widely only with the rise of the Industrial Revolution. (There had been earlier ad hoc patents granted by state authorities, but these had limited force.)

Even in the current era, experience calls into question the necessity of patents and copyrights to spur innovations. The tremendous expansion of creativity on the Internet and the associated advances of open-access software, in spite of Microsoft's best efforts to limit potential competitors, illustrate the point.

The most famous inventor in U.S. history, Benjamin Franklin, declined to obtain patents for his various devices, offering the following principle in his autobiography: "That as we enjoy great Advantages from the Inventions of Others, we should be glad of an Opportunity to serve others by any Invention of ours, and this we should do freely and generously." Probably the most outstanding example of successful research and scientific advance without the motivation of patents and consequent financial rewards is the development of the polio vaccine. Jonas Salk, the principal creator of the polio vaccine, like Franklin, did not seek patents for his invention, one that has saved and improved countless lives around the world. Salk was once asked who would control the new drug. He replied: "Well, the people, I would say. There is no patent. Could you patent the sun?"

*   *   *   *   *

It turns out, then, that there is no simple answer to the question: "Why do we protect private property?" because the meaning of private property rights is not fixed but is a continually changing product of social transformation, social conflict, and political power. The courts are often the venue in which property rights are defined, but, as illustrated by the Pennsylvania and Iowa cases, the definitions provided by the courts change along with society.

The scourge of AIDS combined with the advent of the current wave of globalization have established a new arena for conflict over patent laws governing pharmaceuticals, and an international social movement has arisen to contest property laws in this area. The advances of information technology have likewise generated a new round of legal changes, and the interests, demands, and actions of a vast array of music listeners will be a major factor affecting those changes. With the emergence of the environmental movement and widespread concern for the protection of the natural environment, traditional views of how owners can use their land are coming into question. When society begins to question property rights, it is also questioning the distribution of wealth and income, and it is questioning the distribution of power.

Few realms of property rights can be taken for granted for very long. Whether we are talking about property in the most tangible form as land or property in the intangible form of patents and copyrights, the substance of property rights—who has a right to what and why—is continually changing.

Homeownership has long been one of the cornerstones of the American Dream. Howard Karger points out that buying a home can be a much riskier exercise for low-income versus middle- or upper-income families. Karger questions whether homeownership really benefits lower-income Americans, especially with all the risky financing options that helped create the subprime mortgage crisis.

THE HOMEOWNERSHIP MYTH

BY HOWARD KARGER

A nyone who has given the headlines even a passing glance recently knows the subprime mortgage industry is in deep trouble. Since 2006 more than 20 subprime lenders have quit the business or gone bankrupt. Many more are in serious trouble, including the nation's number two subprime lender, New Century Financial. The subprime crisis is also hitting Wall Street brokerages that invested in these loans, with reverberations from Tokyo to London. And the worst may be yet to come. At least $300 billion in subprime adjustable-rate mortgages will reset this year to higher interest rates. CNN reports that one in five subprime mortgages issued in 2005-2006 will end up in foreclosure. If these dire predictions come true, it will be the equivalent of a nuclear meltdown in the mortgage and housing industries.

What's conspicuously absent from the news reports is the effect of the subprime lending debacle on poor and working-class families who bought into the dream of homeownership, regardless of the price. Sold a false bill of goods, many of these families now face foreclosure and the loss of the small savings they invested in their homes. It's critical to examine the housing crisis not only from the perspective of the banks and the stock market, but also from the perspective of the families whose homes are on the line. It is also critical to uncover the systemic reasons for the recent burst of housing-market insanity that saw thousands upon thousands of families getting signed up for mortgage loans that were highly likely to end in failure and foreclosure.

Like most Americans, I grew up believing that buying a home represents a rite of passage in U.S. society. Americans widely view homeownership as the best choice for everyone, everywhere and at all times. The more people who own their own homes, the common wisdom goes, the more robust the economy, the stronger the community, and the greater the collective and individual benefits. Homeownership is the ticket to the middle class through asset accumulation, stability, and civic participation.

For the most part, this is an accurate picture. Homeowners get a foothold in a housing market with an almost infinite price ceiling. They enjoy important tax benefits. Owning a home is often cheaper than renting. Most important, homeownership builds equity and accrues assets for the next generation, in part by promoting forced savings. These savings are reflected in the data showing that, according to the National Housing Institute's Winton Picoff, the median wealth of low-income homeowners is 12 times higher than that of renters with similar incomes. Plus, owning a home is a status symbol: homeowners are seen as winners compared to renters.

Homeownership may have positive effects on family life. Ohio University's Robert Dietz found that owning a home contributes to household stability, social involvement, environmental awareness, local political participation and activism, good health, low crime, and beneficial community characteristics. Homeowners are better citizens, are healthier both physically and mentally, and have children who achieve more and are better behaved than those of renters.

Johns Hopkins University researchers Joe Harkness and Sandra Newman looked at whether homeownership benefits kids even in distressed neighborhoods. Their study concluded that "[h]omeownership in almost any neighborhood is found to benefit children. ... Children of most low-income renters would be better served by programs that help their families become homeowners in their current neighborhoods instead of helping them move to better neighborhoods while remaining renters." (Harkness and Newman also found, however, that the positive effects of homeownership on children are weaker in unstable low-income neighborhoods. Moreover, the study cannot distinguish whether homeownership leads to positive behaviors or whether owners were already predisposed to these behaviors.)

Faith in the benefits of homeownership—along with low interest rates and a range of governmental incentives—have produced a surge in the number of low-income homeowners. In 1994 Bill Clinton set—and ultimately surpassed—a goal to raise the nation's overall homeownership rate to 67.5% by 2000. There are now 71 million U.S. homeowners, representing close to 68% of all households. By 2003, 48% of black households owned their own homes, up from 34.5% in 1950. Much of this gain has been among low-income families.

Government efforts to increase homeownership for low-income families include both demand-side (e.g., homeowner tax credits, housing cost assistance programs) and supply-side (e.g., developer incentives) strategies. Federal housing programs insure more than a million loans a year to help low-income homebuyers. Fannie Mae and Freddie Mac—the large, federally chartered but privately held corporations that buy mortgages from lenders, guarantee the notes, and then resell them to investors—have increasingly turned their attention to low-income homebuyers as the upper-income housing market becomes more saturated. Banking industry regulations such as the Community Reinvestment Act and the Home Mortgage Disclosure Act encourage homeownership by reducing lending discrimination in underserved markets.

The Housing and Urban Development department (HUD) has adapted some of its programs originally designed to help renters to focus on homeownership. For instance, cities and towns can now use the federal dollars they receive through HOME (the Home Investment Partnerships Act) and Community Development Block Grants to provide housing grants, down payment loans, and closing cost assistance. The American Dream Downpayment Initiative, passed by Congress in 2003, authorized up to $200 million a year for down payment assistance to low-income families. Private foundations have followed suit. The Ford Foundation is currently focusing its housing-related grants on homeownership rather than rental housing; the foundation views homeownership as an important form of asset-building and the best option for low-income people.

While homeownership has undeniable benefits, that doesn't mean it is the best option for everyone. For many low-income families, buying a home imposes burdens that end up outweighing the benefits. It is time to re-assess the policy emphasis on homeownership, which has been driven by an honest belief in the advantages of homeownership, but also by a wide range of business interests who stand to gain when a new cohort of buyers is brought into the housing market.

THE DOWNSIDES OF HOMEOWNERSHIP

Low-income families can run into a range of pitfalls when they buy homes. These pitfalls may stem from the kinds of houses they can afford to buy (often in poor condition, with high maintenance costs); the neighborhoods they can afford to buy in (often economically distressed); the financing they can get (often carrying high interest rates, high fees, and risky gimmicks); and the jobs they work at (often unstable). Taken together, these factors can make buying a home a far riskier proposition for low-income families than it is for middle- and upper-income households.

Most low-income families only have the financial resources to buy rundown houses in distressed neighborhoods marked by few jobs, high crime rates, a dearth of services, and poor schools. Few middle-class homebuyers would hitch themselves to 30-year mortgages in these kinds of communities; poor families, too, have an interest in making the home-buying commitment in safe neighborhoods with good schools.

Homeownership is no automatic hedge against rising housing costs. On the contrary: lower-end affordable housing stock is typically old, in need of repair, and expensive to maintain. Low-income families often end up paying inflated prices for homes that are beset with major structural or mechanical problems masked by cosmetic repairs. A University of North Carolina study sponsored by the national nonprofit organization NeighborWorks found that almost half of low-income home-buyers experienced major unexpected costs due to the age and condition of their homes. If you rent, you can call the landlord; but a homeowner can't take herself to court because the roof leaks, the plumbing is bad, or the furnace or hot water heater quits working.

Besides maintenance and repairs, the expenses of home ownership also include property taxes and homeowners insurance, both of which have skyrocketed in cost in the last decade. Between 1997 and 2002 property tax rates rose nationally by more than 19%. Ten states (including giants Texas and California) saw their prop-erty tax rates rise by 30% or more during that period. In the suburbs of New York City, property tax rates grew two to three times faster than personal income from 2000 to 2004.

Nationally, the average homeowner's annual insurance premiums rose a whopping 62% from 1995 to 2005—twice as fast as inflation. Low-income homeowners in distressed neighborhoods are hit especially hard by high insurance costs. According to a Conning and Co. study, 92% of large insurance companies run credit checks on potential customers. These credit checks translate into insurance scores that are used to determine whether the carrier will insure an applicant at all, and if so, what they will cover and how much they will charge. Those with poor or no credit are denied coverage, while those with limited credit pay high premiums. Needless to say, many low-income homeowners do not have stellar credit scores. Credit scoring may also partly explain why, according to HUD, "Recent studies have shown that, compared to homeowners in predominantly white-occupied neighborhoods, hom-eowners in minority neighborhoods are less likely to have private home insurance, more likely to have policies that provide less coverage in case of a loss, and are likely to pay more for similar policies."

With few cash reserves, low-income families are a heartbeat away from financial disaster if their wages decline, property taxes or insurance rates rise, or expensive re-pairs are needed. With most—or all—of their savings in their homes, these families often have no cushion for emergencies. HUD data show that between 1999 and 2001, the only group whose housing conditions worsened—meaning, by HUD's definition, the only group in which a larger share of households spent over 30% of gross household income on housing in 2001 than in 1999—were low- and mod-erate-income homeowners. The National Housing Conference reports that 51% of working families with critical housing needs (i.e., those spending more than 50% of gross household income on housing) are homeowners.

Most people who buy a home imagine they will live there for a long time, benefiting from a secure and stable housing situation. For many low-income fam-ilies, this is not what happens. Nationwide data from 1976 to 1993 reveal that

36% of low-income homeowners gave up or lost their homes within two years and 53% exited within five years, according to a 2005 study by Carolina Katz Reid of the University of Washington. Reid found that very few low-income families ever bought another house after returning to renting. A 2004 HUD research study by Donald Haurin and Stuart Rosenthal reached similar conclusions. Following a national sample of African Americans from youth (ages 14 to 21) in 1979 to middle age in 2000, the researchers found that 63% of the sample owned a home at some point, but only 34% still did in 2000.

Low-income homeowners, often employed in unstable jobs with stagnant incomes, few health care benefits, limited or no sick days, and little vacation time, may find it almost impossible to keep their homes if they experience a temporary job loss or a change in family circumstances, such as the loss of a wage earner. Homeownership can also limit financial opportunities. A 1999 study by economists Richard Green (University of Wisconsin) and Patric Hendershott (Ohio State University) found that states with the highest homeownership rates also had the highest unemployment rates. Their report concluded that homeownership may constrain labor mobility since the high costs of selling a house make unemployed homeowners reluctant to relocate to find work.

Special tax breaks have been a key selling point of homeownership. If mortgage interest and other qualifying expenses come to less than the standard deduction ($10,300 for joint filers in 2006), however, there is zero tax advantage to owning. That is one reason why only 34% of taxpayers itemize their mortgage interest, local property taxes, and other deductions. Even for families who do itemize, the effective tax saving is usually only 10 to 35 cents for every dollar paid in mortgage interest. In other words, the mortgage deduction benefits primarily those in high income brackets who have a need to shelter their income; it means little to low-income homeowners.

Finally, homeownership promises growing wealth as home prices rise. But the homes of low-income, especially minority, homeowners generally do not appreciate as much as middle-class housing. Low-income households typically purchase homes in distressed neighborhoods where significant appreciation is unlikely. Among other reasons, if financially-stressed property owners on the block can't afford to maintain their homes, nearby property values fall. For instance, Reid's longitudinal study surveyed low-income minority homeowners from 1976 to 1994 and found that they realized a 30% increase in the value of their homes after owning for 10 years, while middle- and upper-income white homeowners enjoyed a 60% jump.

THE NEW WORLD OF HOME LOANS

The new home loan products, marketed widely in recent years but especially to low- and moderate-income families, are generally adjustable-rate mortgages (ARMS) with some kind of twist. Here are a few of these "creative" (read: confusing and risky) mortgage options.

Option ARMs: With this loan, borrowers choose each month which of three or four different—and fluctuating—payments to make:

- full (principal+interest) payment based on a 30-year or 15-year repayment schedule.
- interest-only payment—does not reduce the loan principal or build homeowner equity. Borrowers who pay only interest for a period of time then face a big jump in the size of monthly payments or else are forced to refinance.
- minimum payment—may be lower than one month's interest; if so, the shortfall is added to the loan balance. The result is "negative amortization": over time, the principal goes up, not down. Eventually the borrower may have an "upside down" mortgage where the debt is greater than the market value of the home.

According to the credit rating firm Fitch Ratings, up to 80% of all option ARM borrowers choose the minimum monthly payment option, so it's no surprise that in 2005, 20% of Option ARMS were "upside down." When a negative amortization limit is reached, the minimum payment jumps up to fully amortize the loan for the remaining loan term. In other words, borrowers suddenly have to start paying the real bill.

Even borrowers who pay more than the monthly minimums can face payment shocks. option ARMS often start with a temporary super-low teaser interest rate (and correspondingly low monthly payments) that allows borrowers to qualify for "more house." The catch? Since the low initial monthly payment, based on interest rates as low as 1.25%, is not enough to cover the real interest rate, the borrower eventually faces a sudden increase in monthly payments.

Balloon Loan: This loan is written for a short 5- to 7-year term during which the borrower pays either interest and principal each month or, in a more predatory form, interest only. At the end of the loan term, the borrower must pay off the entire loan in a lump sum—the "balloon payment." At that point, buyers must either refinance or lose their homes. Balloon loans are known to real estate pros as "bullet loans," since if the loan comes due—forcing the owner to refinance—during a period of high interest rates, it's like getting a bullet in the heart. According to the national organizing and advocacy group ACORN, about 10% of all subprime loans are balloons.

Balloon loans are sometimes structured with monthly payments that fail to cover the interest, much less pay down the principal. Although the borrower makes regular payments, her loan balance increases each month: negative amortization. Many borrowers are unaware that they have a negative amortization loan until they have to refinance.

Shared Appreciation Mortgage (SAM): These are fixed-rate loans for up to 30 years that have easier credit qualifications and lower monthly payments than conventional mortgages. In exchange for a lower interest rate, the borrower relinquishes part of the future value of the home to the lender. Interest rate reductions are based on how much appreciation the borrower is willing to give up. SAMs discourage "sweat equity" since the homeowner receives only some fraction of the appreciation resulting from any improvements. Not surprisingly, these loans have been likened to sharecropping.

Stated-Income Loan: Aimed at borrowers who do not draw regular wages from an employer but live on tips, casual jobs that pay under the table, commissions, or investments, this loan does not require W-2 forms or other standard wage documentation. The trade-off: higher interest rates.

No-Ratio Loan: The debt-income ratio (the borrower's monthly payments on debt, including the planned mortgage, divided by her monthly income) is a standard benchmark that lenders use to determine how large a mortgage they will write. In return for a higher interest rate, the no-ratio loan abandons this benchmark; it is aimed at borrowers with complex financial lives or those who are experiencing divorce, the death of a spouse, or a career change.

—Amy Gluckman

"FUNNY MONEY" MORTGAGES AND OTHER TRAVESTIES

Buying a home and taking on a mortgage are scary, and people often leave the closing in a stupor, unsure of what they signed or why. My partner and I bought a house a few years ago; like many buyers, we didn't retain an attorney. The title company had set aside one hour for the closing. During that time more than 125 single-spaced pages (much of it in small print) were put in front of us. More than 60 required our signature or initials. It would have been difficult for us to digest these documents in 24 hours, much less one. When we asked to slow down the process, we were met with impatience. After the closing, Anna asked, "What did we sign?" I was clueless.

Yet buying a home is the largest purchase most families will make in their lifetimes, the largest expenditure in a family budget, and the single largest asset for two-thirds of homeowners. It's also the most fraught with danger.

For low-income families in particular, homeownership can turn out to be more a crushing debt than an asset-building opportunity. The primary reason for this is the growing chasm between ever-higher home prices and the stagnant incomes of millions of working-class Americans. The last decade has seen an unprecedented surge in home prices, which have risen 35% nationally. While the housing bubble is largely confined to specific metropolitan areas in the South, the Southwest, and the two coasts (home prices rose 50% in the Pacific states and 60% in New England), there are also bubbles in midwestern cities like Chicago and Minneapolis. And although the housing bubble is most pronounced in high-end properties, the prices of low-end homes have also spiked in many markets.

Current incomes simply do not support these inflated home prices. For example, only 18% of Californians can afford the median house in the state using traditional loan-affordability calculations. Even the fall in mortgage interest rates in the 1990s and early 2000s was largely neutralized by higher property taxes, higher insurance premiums, and rising utility costs.

This disparity might have put a dent in the mortgage finance business. But no: in 2005, Americans owed $5.7 trillion in mortgages, a 50% increase in just four years. Over the past decade the mortgage finance industry has developed creative schemes designed to squeeze potential homebuyers, albeit often temporarily, into houses they cannot afford. It is a sleight of hand that requires imaginative and risky financing for both buyers and financial institutions.

Most of the "creative" new mortgage products fall into the category of subprime mortgages—those offered to people whose problematic credit drops them into a lower lending category. Subprime mortgages carry interest rates ranging from a few points to ten points or more above the prime or market rate, plus onerous loan terms. The subprime mortgage industry is growing: lenders originated $173 billion in subprime loans in 2005, up from only $25 billion in 1993. By 2006 the subprime market was valued at $600 billion, one-fifth of the $3 trillion U.S. mortgage market.

Subprime lending can be risky. In the 37 years since the Mortgage Bankers Association (MBA) began conducting its annual national mortgage delinquency survey, 2006 saw the highest share of home loans entering foreclosure. In early 2007, according to the MBA, 13.5% of subprime mortgages were delinquent (compared to 4.95% of prime-rate mortgages) and 4.5% were in foreclosure. By all accounts, this is just the tip of the iceberg. However, before the current collapse the rate of return for subprime lenders was spectacular. Forbes claimed that subprime lenders could realize returns up to six times greater than the best-run banks. In the past there were two main kinds of home mortgages: fixed-rate loans and adjustable-rate loans (ARMs). In a fixed-rate mortgage, the interest rate stays the same throughout the 15- to 30-year loan term. In a typical ARM the interest rate varies over the course of the loan, although there is usually a cap. Both kinds of loans traditionally required borrowers to provide thorough documentation of their finances and a down payment of at least 10% of the purchase price, and often 20%.

Adjustable-rate loans can be complicated, and a Federal Reserve study found that fully 25% of homeowners with ARMs were confused about their loan terms. Nonetheless, ARMs are attractive because in the short run they promise a home with an artificially low interest rate and affordable payments.

Even so, traditional ARMs proved inadequate to the tasks of ushering more low-income families into the housing market and generally keeping home sales up in the face of skyrocketing home prices. So in recent years the mortgage industry created a whole range of "affordability" products with names like "no-ratio loans," "option ARMS," and "balloon loans" that it doled out like candy to people who were never fully apprised of the intricacies of these complicated loans. (See sidebar for a glossary of the new mortgage products.) These new mortgage options have opened the door for almost anyone to secure a mortgage, whether or not their circumstances auger well for repayment. They also raise both the costs and risks of buying a home—sometimes steeply—for the low- and moderate-income families to whom they're largely marketed.

Beyond the higher interest rates (at some point in the loan term if not at the start) that characterize the new "affordability" mortgages, low-income homebuyers face other costs as well. For instance, predatory and subprime lenders often require borrowers to carry credit life insurance, which pays off a mortgage if the homeowner dies. This insurance is frequently sold either by the lender's subsidiary or else by a company that pays the lender a commission. Despite low payouts, lenders frequently charge high premiums for this insurance.

As many as 80% of subprime loans include prepayment penalties if the borrower pays off or refinances the loan early, a scam that costs low-income borrowers about $2.3 billion a year and increases the risk of foreclosure by 20%. Prepayment penalties lock borrowers into a loan by making it difficult to sell the home or refinance with a different lender. And while some borrowers face penalties for paying off their loans ahead of schedule, others discover that their mortgages have so-called "call provisions" that permit the lender to accelerate the loan term even if payments are current.

And then there are all of the costs outside of the mortgage itself. Newfangled mortgage products are often sold not by banks directly, but by a rapidly growing crew of mortgage brokers who act as finders or "bird dogs" for lenders. There are approximately 53,000 mortgage brokerage companies in the United States employing an estimated 418,700 people, according to the National Association of Mortgage Brokers; BusinessWeek notes that brokers now originate up to 80% of all new mortgages.

Largely unregulated, mortgage brokers live off loan fees. Their transactions are primed for conflicts of interest or even downright corruption. For example, borrowers pay brokers a fee to help them secure a loan. Brokers may also receive kickbacks from lenders for referring a borrower, and many brokers steer clients to the lenders that pay them the highest kickbacks rather than those offering the lowest interest rates. Closing documents use arcane language ("yield spread premiums," "service release fees") to hide these kickbacks. And some hungry brokers find less-than-kosher ways to make the sale, including fudging paperwork, arranging for inflated appraisals, or helping buyers find co-signers who have no intention of actually guaranteeing the loan.

Whether or not a broker is involved, lenders can inflate closing costs in a variety of ways: charging outrageous document preparation fees; billing for recording fees in excess of the law; "unbundling," whereby closing costs are padded by duplicating charges already included in other categories.

All in all, housing is highly susceptible to the predations of the fringe economy. Unscrupulous brokers and lenders have considerable latitude to ply their trade, especially with vulnerable low-income borrowers.

TIME TO CHANGE COURSE

Despite the hype, homeownership is not a cure-all for low-income families who earn less than a living wage and have poor prospects for future income growth. In fact, for some low-income families homeownership only leads to more debt and financial misery. With mortgage delinquencies and foreclosures at record levels, especially among low-income households, millions of people would be better off today if they had remained renters. Surprisingly, rents are generally more stable than housing prices. From 1995 to 2001 rents rose slightly faster than inflation, but not as rapidly as home prices. Beginning in 2004 rent increases began to slow—even in hot markets like San Francisco and Seattle—and fell below the rate of inflation.

In the mid-1980s, low- and no-downpayment mortgages led to increased foreclosures when the economy tanked. Today, these mortgages are back, along with a concerted effort to drive economically marginal households into homeownership and high levels of unsustainable debt. To achieve this goal, the federal government spends $100 billion a year for homeownership programs (including the $70-plus billion that the mortgage interest deduction costs the Treasury).

Instead of focusing exclusively on homeownership, a more progressive and balanced housing policy would address the diverse needs of communities for both homes and rental units, and would facilitate new forms of ownership such as community land trusts and cooperatives. A balanced policy would certainly aim to expand the stock of affordable rental units. Unfortunately, just the opposite is occurring: rental housing assistance is being starved to feed low-income homeownership programs. From 2004 to 2006, President Bush and the Congress cut federal funding for public housing alone by 11%. Over the same period, more than 150,000 rental housing vouchers were cut.

And, of course, policymakers must act to protect those consumers who do opt to buy homes: for instance, by requiring mortgage lenders to make certain not only that a borrower is eligible for a particular loan product, but that the loan is suitable for the borrower.

The reason the United States lacks a sound housing policy is obvious if we follow the money. Overheated housing markets and rising home prices produce lots of winners. Real estate agents reap bigger commissions. Mortgage brokers, appraisers, real estate attorneys, title companies, lenders, builders, home remodelers, and everyone else with a hand in the housing pie does well. Cities raise more in property taxes, and insurance companies enroll more clients at higher premiums. Although housing accounts for only 5% of GDP, it has been responsible for up to 75% of all U.S. job growth in the last four years, according to the consulting firm Oxford Analytica. Housing has buffered the economy, and herding more low-income families into homes, regardless of the consequences, helps keep the industry ticking in the short run. The only losers? Renters squeezed by higher rents and accelerating conversion of rental units into condos. Young middle-income families trying to buy their first house. And, especially, the thousands of low-income families for whom buying a home turns into a financial nightmare.

Sources: Carolina Katz Reid, Studies in Demography and Ecology: Achieving the American Dream? A Longitudinal Analysis of the Homeownership Experiences of Low-Income Households, Univ. of Washington, CSDE Working Paper No. 04-04; Dean Baker, "The Housing Bubble: A Time Bomb in Low-Income Communities?" Shelterforce Online, Issue #135, May/June 2004, www.nhi.org/online/issues/135/bubble.html; Howard Karger, Shortchanged: Life and Debt in the Fringe Economy (Berrett-Koehler, 2005); National Multi Housing Council (www.nmhc.org).

The quality of public schools in the U.S. consistently reflects the income levels of the families whose children attend them. Citing examples of four statesthat have taken alternative approaches to public education funding, Mchael Engel argues that there is no excuse for low-income children to be stuck in underfunded schools.

SCHOOL FINANCE: INEQUALITY PERSISTS

BY MICHAEL ENGEL

The states vary widely among themselves in terms of support for public education, and there are multiple ways of measuring that variation. Accoring to the federal government's National Center for Education Statistics (NCES), median per pupil expenditure in 2003-2004 ranged from $5,862 in Utah to $14,667 in Alaska; the national median was $7,860. A more significant statistic, calculated by the Census Bureau, is the amount spent by each state per $1,000 of personal income. This measures spending against how much the state's population can potentially afford. In 2003-2004, Florida was at the bottom with $34.36, and Alaska was at the top with $62.92. The figure for the nation as a whole was $43.68.

Perhaps more important is the inequality in spending among school districts *within* each state. The "federal range ratio" for school spending, as reported by the NCES, compares per pupil expenditure in districts spending the least and those spending the most. In Montana, for example, districts at the fifth percentile (those that spend less per pupil than 95% of the districts in the state) spend $5,526 per pupil, versus $19,400 per pupil at the 95th percentile; thus Montana's federal range ratio is 2.51, the highest in the country. (A federal range ratio of zero would denote equal spending across all districts; a federal range ratio of one describes a state where districts at the 95th percentile spend twice as much per pupil as districts at the 5th percentile.) States with relatively low range ratios—for instance, Maryland at 0.32 and Florida at 0.38—are the most "egalitarian."

Putting these three sets of figures together offers a detailed picture of educational inequality in the United States (see Table 1). Interestingly, West Virginia, one of the poorest states in the union, spends more than the median amounts *and* has the lowest federal range ratio in the country. The state's school districts are county-wide, which

TABLE 1

Profile of Public School Spending in Selected States, 2004

		MEDIAN PER PUPIL EXPENDITURE	
		Below the National Median	*Above the National Median*
FEDERAL RANGE RATIO	0.5 or under (Relatively Equal)	Florida Georgia Louisiana	Maryland North Carolina Wisconsin
	0.51 – 0.99 (Moderately Unequal)	Michigan Virginia	Kansas New Jersey New York Pennsylvania Vermont
	1.00 and up (Highly Unequal)	Arizona California Colorado Illinois Oregon Texas Washington	Montana New Mexico

Source: National Center for Education Statistics, "Current Expenditures for Public Elementary and Secondary Education: School Year 2003-04," Table 4, July 2006.

may explain its relatively equitable school funding: wealthier suburban towns cannot fund their own schools well without also supporting the schools in nearby cities.

So far, these data reveal the wide spreads between high- and low-budget school districts. But *which* children are getting the short end of the stick? Here we can look to the Education Trust, whose analysts have calculated the state and local dollars per pupil available to the highest- versus the lowest-poverty school districts and to the districts with the highest versus the lowest minority populations in each state (for 2004). They found that in about half of the states, the one-fourth of school districts with the highest share of poor students had less in state and local dollars to spend per pupil than the one-fourth of districts with the lowest share of poor students.

The variation from one state to another is striking. At the more egalitarian end of the spectrum are states such as New Mexico, Massachusetts, Minnesota, and New Jersey, where the highest-poverty districts have between $1,000 and $2,000 *more* to spend per pupil than the lowest-poverty districts. At the other end are Illinois, New Hampshire, New York, and Pennsylvania, where the highest-poverty districts have between $1,000 and $2,000 *less* to spend per pupil than the lowest-poverty districts.

As the Education Trust analysts note, though, it costs more—not the same—to provide an equal education to poor children. So these figures actually understate the disparity. The report offers the same comparisons cost-adjusted by 40% to account for the higher expense of educating poor children. (See Figure 2.) Using the cost-adjusted figures, the highest-poverty districts have less to spend per pupil than the lowest-poverty district in two-thirds of the states. The adjusted figures show a funding gap in Illinois and New York that exceeds $2,000 per pupil. (Just imagine how an additional $60,000 a year could transform the educational environment for a class of 30 fourth graders!) In terms of discrimination against both the poor and minorities, the worst offenders are Arizona, Illinois, Montana, New Hampshire, New York, Texas, and Wyoming. States that rank high in shortchanging minority districts include Kansas, Nebraska, North Dakota, South Dakota, and Wisconsin.

In states with large urban centers surrounded by wealthy suburbs, the differences in school funding can be especially dramatic. Among the 69 school districts within 15 miles of downtown Chicago, for instance, the city itself ranks 50th in per-pupil spending, according to NCES data. Chicago spends $8,356 per pupil; compare that to $18,055 for Evanston and $15,421 for Oak Park, both wealthy suburbs. In fact, Illinois has a terrible record in every respect, but the state Supreme Court has twice explicitly rejected any judicial responsibility for reform. Among the 41 school districts in New York state within 20 miles of downtown Manhattan, New York City ranks 37th, with spending of $13,131 per pupil, compared with Great Neck at $20,995, Lawrence at $22,499, and Manhasset at $22,199. Even among suburbs, poorer ones with larger minority populations such as Mount Vernon fall far behind whiter and more prosperous communities. In New York, court battles continue while the legislature stalls, ignoring deadlines for reform already set by the courts.

These inequalities extend even to differences in funding within school districts, mostly in the form of teacher salary differentials. A 2005 report by the Education Trust-West *California's Hidden Teacher Spending Gap* concluded that "the concentration of more experienced and more highly credentialed teachers (along with their corresponding high salaries) in whiter and more affluent schools drives huge funding gaps between schools—even between schools within the very same school district."

Financial inequality in U.S. public schools is not an anomaly, nor is it the result of a lack of possible remedies. States have undertaken countless so-called reforms over the past 20 years—to little effect. Only a few states, however, have taken any *serious* steps to guarantee even an adequate, much less an equal, education for all their children.

TABLE 2

Funding Gaps for School Districts with the Highest Poor and Minority Enrollments (with 40% adjustment for low-income students)

	Gap between Spending per Student in the Highest- and Lowest-Poverty Districts	Gap between Spending per Student in the Highest- and Lowest-Minority Districts
United States	−$1,307	−$1,213
States that Shortchange (Gap of $600 or more in per pupil spending favoring the lowest-poverty or lowest-minority districts)	New York (−$2,927) Illinois (−$2,355) Pennsylvania (−$1,511) New Hampshire (−$1,297) Montana (−$1,148) Michigan (−$1,072) Vermont (−$894) Kansas (−$885) Texas (−$757) Wisconsin (−$742) Arizona (−$736) Alabama (−$656)	New York (−$2,636) New Hampshire (−$2,392) Montana (−$1,838) Kansas (−$1,630) Illinois (−$1,524) Nebraska (−$1,374) North Dakota (−$1,290) Wisconsin (−$1,270) Texas (−$1,167) South Dakota (−$1,140) Wyoming (−$1,041) Colorado (−$1,032) Maine (−$874) Idaho (−$849) Pennsylvania (−$709) Arizona (−$680) Rhode Island (−$639) Vermont (−$613) Connecticut (−$602
States that Help (Gap of $600 or more in per pupil spending favoring the highest-poverty or highest-minority districts)	Alaska ($2,054) New Jersey ($1,069) Minnesota ($950) Massachusetts ($694) New Mexico ($679)	Massachusetts ($1,139) Indiana ($1,096) New Jersey ($1,087) Ohio ($942) Missouri ($662) Minnesota ($623)

Note: Dollar amounts have been adjusted to account for regional cost differences and for the additional cost of educating students with disabilities.

Source: Education Trust, *Funding Gaps 2006,* Tables 3 & 4.

COURTROOM REMEDIES

As of 2003, cases challenging the constitutionality of education finance systems had been heard in the courts of 44 states; in 18 of those states, the systems were declared unconstitutional. In 12 states the courts refused to act at all. The court decisions are all over the map in terms of setting standards of adequacy, equity, or equality, requiring legislative action, or prescribing specific remedies. Often it has taken a series of decisions over a number of years to force any change at all. The main overall effect of these rulings has been to push reluctant state legislatures, including those in some states where courts had not yet issued decisions, to modify their educational finance systems.

The outcomes, again, are all over the map, but very few have enacted serious and thorough reforms. For the most part, states have merely tinkered with the existing methods of aiding local schools. The most prevalent method—used in forty-one states—is foundation aid, which sets a statewide minimum per- pupil expenditure and appropriates state funds to make up the difference between that amount and the amounts localities are able (or required) to raise from property taxes. Each state uses a different formula, some so complex as to defy comprehension. Most reforms have involved a change in that formula to benefit poor districts, or a higher foundation level financed by increased state appropriations, or separate and additional grant programs.

A less common and even more complex method is known as "district power equalizing", which essentially guarantees a minimum property tax base to each community. In other words, the state determines the amount of revenue that is to be raised by any given local property tax rate and offers aid to communities whose property tax base is too poor to reach that level. Thus if the state determines a 5% rate should raise $10 million, a community that can only raise $7 million at that tax rate will receive $3 million in state aid. A more radical version, such as the one enacted in Vermont, provides for "recapturing" and redistributing the excess revenues raised by wealthier communities.

Some states combine both methods. In any case, although several states, such as New Jersey and Massachusetts, have managed to improve their formulas to the benefit of poorer communities, none of these adjustments address the basic cause of inequality, namely, reliance on local funding. Overall, in that regard there has been no improvement in twenty years. The state share of public school funding across the nation peaked at 49% in 1985; the federal share peaked at 9% in 1980. Federal aid to elementary and secondary education was $41 billion in 2003, a paltry 2% of the entire federal budget. To the extent that communities continue to have to rely on local property taxes to fund their schools, there is no question that serious inequities will persist.

At least four states, however, have gone beyond the norm. It is instructive to examine their experience with devising school funding systems that ostensibly aim for equality, that is, making sure that no district has a significant financial advantage over any other.

Hawaii is unique in the nation in that the whole state is one school district, and the state government is responsible for appropriating funds to the individual schools. On the surface, this appears to be a perfect example of equal education. Unfortunately, it is not. Until quite recently, funds were appropriated on an enrollment basis, without allowing for the extra costs involved in educating students in high-poverty areas or those with special needs. Moreover, Hawaii ranks 50th in terms of the percent of total state and local government revenues allocated for public education. Per pupil expenditure is just slightly above the national median, and the state ranks 35th in spending per $1,000 of personal income. Thus Hawaii resembles a number of southern states in uniformly underfunding all its public schools.

Kansas adopted a new school finance system in 1992, prompted by a lower court decision invalidating the existing one. The School District Finance and Quality Performance Act set a uniform statewide property tax rate, and established a $3,600 foundation funding level per pupil. The pupil count was weighted to take into account factors such as poverty. State aid was to make up the difference between that foundation level and what each community could raise with the property tax. But an escape hatch was provided by allowing a "local option budget" for communities to raise additional monies, up to 25% over the foundation level. The subsequent failure of the state to fully fund this reform led to widespread use of the local option budget. Richer communities were thus able to raise more money, so pre-existing inequalities continued. According to the Education Trust report, Kansas had one of the largest minority funding gaps in the country in 2003, and the poverty gap increased substantially between 1997 and 2003. The Kansas courts are thus still involved in the issue of educational finance.

Michigan's reforms were not inspired by any court actions. Rather, facing widespread anger over high property taxes, in 1993 Republican governor John Engler bit the bullet by getting the legislature to eliminate the property tax as the basis for school funding. He then forced the issue further by slashing the state education budget, creating a financial crisis for the schools. As a result, voters in 1994 approved a 2% sales tax increase to fund education. Reform legislation set a statewide property tax rate, and localities were not allowed to exceed that rate. State aid would be based on a foundation plan. The result was that the state share of school spending more than doubled. But property taxes still accounted for one-third of school budgets, and with the rate frozen by state mandate, communities with low property values still fell behind. Combined with insufficient state funding (per pupil spending is below the national median), this means that although progress was achieved, Michigan still has a way to go to provide equal and adequate funding to the schools serving its poorest children.

Vermont's Act 60 came closest to bringing schools toward the ideal of educational equality. In 1995, the state's supreme court ruled that the existing finance system violated the state constitution. Two years later the legislature responded with Act 60, the most radical reform in the country. The new law set a statewide property tax rate and foundation spending level. Localities were allowed to levy additional property taxes, but if revenues from a locality exceeded the foundation amount, that excess reverted to the state and was put into a "sharing pool" used to aid poorer communities. This was essentially a district power equalizing program with a socialist twist. Rich communities were hit hard, and their budget process became guesswork since they had no way of knowing in a timely way how much property tax revenue they would be able to keep for the following year. A political uproar ensued; Act 60 was succeeded by Act 68 in 2004, which kept the statewide property tax and increased the state sales tax, but ended the sharing pool. How this will play out is as yet not clear, but as of 2003-2004, Vermont ranked 2nd in per $1000 spending and 8th in per pupil spending with a relatively low poverty gap.

PROSPECTS FOR CHANGE

The complexity and confusion of school finance systems and of all of the efforts to reform them obscure a simple and obvious solution, which no state has chosen: progressive taxation. If public schools were funded entirely by state and local taxes whose effective rates increase with income and wealth, if state aid was weighted sharply in favor of districts with higher educational costs, if federal aid was increased and similarly appropriated, and if strict limits were placed on local supplementation, financial inequality among schools would be history.

To free-market ideologues and neoclassical economists, these alternatives are obviously anathema. But they are rarely mentioned even by liberal or progressive politicians concerned about educational inequality. For they involve confronting two of the most sensitive issues in American politics: taxes and race. All state and local revenue systems in the United States are regressive to one extent or another. And as Jonathan Kozol points out, racial segregation makes it easy for the majority of public officials, and of whites in general, to ignore the disastrous conditions in predominantly-black schools.

It would thus take enormous public pressure to force the government to choose a new course and pursue financial equality. If that were done, we could build a system of public schools that would offer all students genuinely equal opportunity to learn, and the false promise of the Bush administration—"No Child Left Behind"—could actually become a reality.

Sources: Jonathan Kozol, *Savage Inequalities* (Crown, 1991); *The Shame of the Nation* (Crown, 2005); John Yinger, ed., *Helping Children Left Behind* (MIT Press, 2004); Education Trust, *The Funding Gap 2005*, *The Funding Gap 2006*; Education Trust—West, *California's Hidden Teacher Spending Gap* (2005); US Census Bureau, *Survey of Local Government Finances* (www.census.gov/govs/www/estimate.html); U.S. Dept. of Education, National Center for Education Statistics, *Education Finance Statistics Center* (www.nced.ed.gov/edfin); National Conference of State Legislatures, *Education Finance Database* (www.ncsl.org/programs/educ/ed_finance); Hawaii Superintendent of Education, *16th Annual Report* (2005); Teachers College, Columbia University, National Access Network (www.schoolfunding.info/).

From *Dollars & Sense* magazine, spring 2007.

While vacationing on a beach in the tropics may sound like paradise, few tourists are aware of the human and environmental costs that lie behind suchtrips—especially when governments favor tourists over their own people. Vasuki Nesiah explains how Sri Lanka's tsunami reconstruction plans displaced devastated coastal residents to make way for tourism industry expansion.

FISHERFOLK OUT, TOURISTS IN

BY VASUKI NESIAH

Two days after the south Asian tsunami struck last December, as thousands around him were grappling with its devastating impact, former German chancellor Helmut Kohl was airlifted from the roof of his holiday resort in southern Sri Lanka by the country's air force. Kohl is, of course, among the most elite of tourists, and his privileges are not representative of all tourists. Nonetheless, that aerial exit is symptomatic of the tourist industry's alienation from the local community. His easy flight away from the devastation, at a time when official relief supplies were still to reach the majority of victims, was an early indicator of the interplay between tsunami relief and the tourism industry. Kohl was barely airborne, and the waves barely receding, when plans were already afoot to ensure that the beaches of Sri Lanka were cleared of fisherfolk and rendered pristine for a new wave of tourists.

"NATURAL" DISASTERS?

Right from the start, global attention to the tsunami was no doubt heightened by the fact that tourists were among the victims. Reporters conducted their share of riveting tsunami escape interviews in airport departure lounges: first-rate, first-person accounts with first-world tourists. This is not the first time viewers in the rich countries have been plied with images of "natives" being overwhelmed by natural disasters, passively awaiting international humanitarian relief and rescue. Some parts of the globe are just scripted into tragedy and chaos; first-world television screens are accustomed to their loss, their displacement, their overwhelming misery. Against this backdrop, the tales of tourists offered a more newsworthy break from stories that simply echo yesterday's news reports about locals caught up in floods in Bangladesh or mudslides in Haiti.

But while being located in the trajectory of tsunami waves or monsoons is a given, the acute vulnerability of countries like Sri Lanka, Haiti, or Bangladesh to natural disasters only appears spontaneous. It is the socio-political landscape that determines the extent of exposure to adverse impact from such natural disasters. The political economy of exposure to natural disaster is disastrous for those made vulnerable—but not natural. For example, coastal mangrove forests would have contained the fury of the tsunami waves, except that they've been rapidly destroyed in recent years to make way for resorts and industrial shrimp farms. (See "The Tsunami and the Mangroves," page 102.)

Defining that vulnerability as natural is, however, important to the tourism industry, whose job it is to produce exotic destinations through comparison and contrast. The devastation of repeated natural disasters is simply the "native predicament" in places like Sri Lanka, and one of the principle drives behind western tourism to the global South hinges on that predicament. Tourism often is, after all, a quest for a departure from the everyday of western suburbia—but in a neatly packaged module that insulates the visitor from the actual risks of the locale. Trafficking in that balance of otherness and insulation is the task of the tour masters.

The tsunami penetrated that insulation to some degree. However, even through the bloodletting of the last two decades, tourists visiting Sri Lanka have been remarkably insulated from it all: both from the civil war and from the country's impoverished social and economic circumstances. In fact, on the tourism industry's map, Sri Lanka is an adventure zone whose attraction lies at least partly in those circumstances, which make it a cheap vacation spot, a low-cost listing in a travel catalog of exotic but consumer-friendly destinations.

WHAT DOES TOURISM DO?
Does the tourist industry simply feed off a pre-existing socio-economic predicament and perhaps even mitigate it, or does the industry exacerbate that predicament and entrench a country like Sri Lanka in an itinerary of peripheral economies served up for tourist consumption?

The argument is not that tourism per se is bad for Sri Lanka. Clearly the broader tradition of tourism and international travel has had a mixed, complex history. For the many who came, surfed, littered, took photographs, bought sex, batik shirts, or barefoot sarongs and left, there are others who ended up engaged by newly discovered solidarities. Even the interface with colonial exploration was double-edged. As political scientist Kumari Jayewardene and others have shown us, we have always had a line of itinerant travelers who washed onto our shore as tourists of one sort or another, only to develop more fundamental commitments to local communities—

THE TSUNAMI AND THE MANGROVES

Since the 1980s, Asia has been plundered by large industrialized shrimp farms that have brought environmentally unfriendly aquaculture to its shores. Nearly 72% of global shrimp farming takes place in Asia, where the World Bank has been its largest funder. Even before the tsunami struck last December, shrimp cultivation, once termed a "rape-and-run" industry by the U.N. Food and Agricultural Organization, had already caused havoc in the region. Shrimp farms are only productive for two to five years. The ponds are then abandoned, leaving behind toxic waste, destroyed ecosystems, and displaced communities that have lost their traditional livelihoods. The whole cycle is then repeated in another pristine coastal area.

Now the shrimp farms—along with rapid tourism development—are also responsible for a share of the death and destruction the tsunami brought. Shrimp farming was expanded at the cost of tropical mangrove forests, which are among the world's most important ecosystems. Mangrove swamps have long been nature's protection for coastal regions, holding back large waves, weathering the impact of cyclones, and serving as a nursery for the three-fourths of commercial fish species that spend part of their life cycle there.

Ecologists tell us that mangroves provide double protection against storms and tsunamis. The first layer of red mangroves with their flexible branches and tangled roots hanging in the coastal waters absorb the first shock waves. The second layer of tall black mangroves then acts like a wall, withstanding much of the sea's fury.

But shrimp farming has continued its destructive spree, eating away more than half of the world's mangroves. Since the 1960s, for instance, aquaculture and industrial development in Thailand have resulted in a loss of over 65,000 hectares of mangroves. In Indonesia, Java has lost 70% of its mangroves, Sulawesi 49%, and Sumatra 36%. At the time the tsunami struck in all its fury, logging companies were busy axing mangroves in the Aceh province of Indonesia to export to Malaysia and Singapore.

In India, mangrove cover has been reduced by over two-thirds in the past three decades. In Andhra Pradesh, more than 50,000 people have been forcibly removed to make way for shrimp farms; throughout the country, millions have been displaced.

Whatever remained of the mangroves in India was cut down by the hotel industry, aided and abetted by the Ministry of Environment and Forests and the Ministry of Industries. Five-star hotels, golf courses, industries, and mansions sprung up all along the coast, warnings from environmentalists notwithstanding. These two ministries worked overtime to dilute the Coastal Regulation Zone rules, allowing the hotels to take over even the 500-meter buffer zone that was supposed to be maintained along the beach.

The recent tourism boom throughout the Asia-Pacific region coincided with the destructive fallout from industrial shrimp farms. In the past two decades, the entire coastline along the Bay of Bengal, the Arabian Sea, and the Strait of Malacca in the Indian Ocean, as well as all along the South Pacific Ocean, has witnessed massive investment in hotels and tourism facilities. By 2010, the region is projected to surpass the Americas to become the world's number two tourist destination, with 229 million arrivals.

If only the mangroves were intact, the damage from the tsunami would have been greatly minimized. That's what happened in Bangladesh in 1960, when a tsunami wave hit the coast in an area where mangroves were intact. Not a single person died. These mangroves were subsequently cut down and replaced with shrimp farms. In 1991, thousands of people were killed when a tsunami of the same magnitude hit the same region.

In Tamil Nadu, in south India, Pichavaram and Muthupet, with dense mangroves, suffered low human casualties and less economic damage from the recent tsunami than other areas. Likewise, Myanmar and the Maldives suffered much less from the killing spree of the tsunami because the tourism industry had so far not spread its tentacles to the virgin mangroves and coral reefs surrounding their coastlines. The large coral reef surrounding the Maldives islands absorbed much of the tidal fury, limiting the human loss to a little over 100 dead. Like mangrove swamps, coral reefs absorb the sea's fury by breaking the waves.

Let's weigh the costs and benefits of destroying the mangroves. Having grown tenfold in the last 15 years, shrimp farming is now a $9 billion industry. It is estimated that shrimp consumption in North America, Japan, and Western Europe has increased by 300% within the last 10 years. But one massive wave of destruction caused by this tsunami in 11 Asian countries has exacted a cost immeasurably greater than the economic gain that the shrimp industry claims to have created.

World governments have so far pledged $4 billion in aid, and private relief agencies are spending additional billions. The World Bank gave $175 million right away, and then-World Bank president James Wolfensohn said, "We can go up to even $1 billion to $1.5 billion depending on the needs...." But if only successive presidents of the World Bank had refrained from aggressively promoting ecologically unsound but market friendly economic policies, a lot of human lives and dollars could have been saved.

—Devinder Sharma

commitments that then fed into, or even helped catalyze, traditions of dissent and struggles for justice that have had enormous reach in our collective histories.

Such solidarity aside, tourism can be a significant source of revenue, employment, and infrastructure development. It also has a range of indirect effects since tourism generates demand in many sectors; every job created in the tourism industry is said to result in almost 10 jobs in other industries, with enhanced demand in areas like agriculture and small industries, a whole spectrum of service-sector employment, and so on—the kind of thing that excites Central Bank policymakers, not to mention the middlemen who profit from those batik shirts and barefoot sarongs, from the increased demand for sex work and other informal sector labor. At a micro level, the jobs generated by the industry have enabled some financial autonomy for some sections of the working poor. Even when pay and working conditions are exploitative, this is an autonomy that may have particular significance for women and other groups who yield less financial decisionmaking power in the "old" economy.

Yet this baby came with a lot of muddy bath water even before the tsunamis washed in. The growth it has generated has often been of an unbalanced kind that worsened the country's financial vulnerability with little accountability to local communities. As they discovered through the shifting fortunes of the ceasefire, the post-9/11 drop in international travel, and recessions in distant lands, communities that work in the tourism industry have a heightened dependence on a fickle, fluctuating transnational market. The majority of the jobs tourism creates in the formal sector are service-sector jobs that are exploitative, badly paid, seasonal, and insecure; these problems are replicated many times over in the industry's large informal sector, ranging from prostitution to handicrafts. Its untrammeled exploitation of the coast has created unsustainable demands on the local environment that have had particularly bad impacts on coastal ecology. Equally pernicious, it has transformed more and more public land such as beaches into private goods, fencing out local residents.

RECONSTRUCTION FOR WHOM?

The tragedy is that many of tourism's downsides may be exacerbated by the tsunami reconstruction plans. From Thailand to Sri Lanka, the tourist industry saw the tsunami through dollar signs. The governments concerned were on board from the outset, quickly planning massive subsidies for the tourism industry in ways that suggest the most adverse distributive impact. Infrastructure development will be even further skewed to cater to the industry rather than to the needs of local communities. Within weeks of the tsunami, the Alliance for the Protection of National Resources and Human Rights, a Sri Lankan advocacy group, expressed concern that "the developing situation is disastrous, more disastrous than the tsunami itself, if it is possible for anything to be worse than that."

The tsunami arrived at a critical moment in the recent history of Sri Lanka's political economy. Beginning in the late 1970s, Sri Lankan governments of both major parties followed the neoliberal prescriptions to cut tariffs and quotas, privatize, and deregulate more slavishly than many other Asian states. In 2002, the then-ruling center-right UNP issued a major blueprint for continued liberalization, "Regaining Sri Lanka," under the rubric of the "Poverty Reduction Strategy Plans" (PRSPs) that the World Bank and the IMF now require. But public opposition to these policies has intensified over time. In 2004 a center-left coalition won election on an anti-liberalization platform. Once in office, however, the chief party in the coalition appeared unwilling to truly change direction, and the "Regaining Sri Lanka" plan is still very much on the table.

Now, activists are warning that many of the plan's liberalization proposals will be revived and pushed through with little public dialogue and debate, given the emergency powers the government has given itself under cover of tsunami relief and reconstruction. In January, for example, the government revived a plan for water privatization that had earlier been tabled after public opposition. Official reconstruction plans are being prepared by a newly created agency, TAFREN, which a recent statement by a coalition of over 170 civil-society organizations describes as "composed entirely of big business leaders with vested interests in the tourist and construction industries, who are completely unable to represent the interests of the affected communities."

Proposals announced by TAFREN and by various government officials call for the building of multi-lane highways and the wholesale displacement of entire villages from the coast. Coastal lands are to be sliced up into designated buffer zones and tourism zones. The government is preventing those fishing families who wish to do so from rebuilding their homes on the coast, ostensibly because of the risk of future natural disasters; at the same time, it's encouraging the opening of both new and rebuilt beachfront tourist hotels.

The plans are essentially roadmaps for multinational hotel chains, telecom companies, and the like to cater to the tourism industry. Small-scale fishing operations by individual proprietors will become more difficult to sustain as access to the beach becomes increasingly privatized and fishing conglomerates move in. The environmental deregulation proposed in the PRSP will open the door to even more untrammeled exploitation of natural resources. None of the reconstruction planning is being channeled through decision-making processes that are accountable or participatory. Ultimately, it looks like reconstruction will be determined by the deadly combination of a rapacious private sector and government graft: human tragedy becomes a commercial opportunity, tsunami aid a business venture.

Not unpredictably, even the subsidies planned for the tourism industry in the wake of the tsunami are going to the hotel owners and big tour operators, not to the porters and cleaning women who were casual employees in hotels. Many of the local residents who were proprietors or workers in smaller tourism-related businesses, now unemployed, are not classified as tsunami-affected, so they are denied even the meager compensation they should be entitled to. The situation is much worse for the vast informal sector of sex workers, souvenir sellers, and others whose livelihood depended on the tourism industry. If the tsunami highlighted the acute vulnerability that accompanies financial dependence on the industry, the tsunami reconstruction plans look set to exacerbate this vulnerability even further.

A needs assessment study conducted by the World Bank in collaboration with the Asian Development Bank and Japan's official aid agency pegged the loss borne by the tourism industry at $300 million, versus only $90 million for the fishing industry. The ideological assumptions embedded in an assessment methodology that rates a hotel bed bringing in $200 a night as a greater loss than a fisherman bringing in $50 a month have far-reaching consequences. With reconstruction measures predicated on this kind of accounting, we are on a trajectory that empowers the tourism industry to be an even more dominant player than it was in the past, and, concomitantly, one that disempowers and further marginalizes the coastal poor.

TRAVEL AND DISPLACEMENT

Much has been made of the unsightly fishing shanties that will not be rebuilt. Instead, fishing communities are going to be transformed into even more unsightly urban squalor, their residents crowded into "modern" apartment complexes like the sardines they may fish. However, this will be further inland. As they sit on the beach watching the ocean loll onto Lanka's shore, tourists will enjoy the coast in a sanitized, "consumer friendly" environment. Ironically, they may even be sitting in *cadjan* cabanas, a nostalgic nod to the *cadjan* homes of fishing communities of the past—a neatly consumable experience of the exotic without the interference of a more messy everyday.

But perhaps this *is* the new everyday that is proposed: the teeming hordes in designated settlements, a playground for tourists elsewhere. It's a product of the mercantile imagination—the imagination of tourist industry fat cats who will be raking in the tsunami windfall. With the building of planned superhighways, tourists will be able to zoom from airport to beach, shopping mall to spa, while the people who lived in these regions will become less mobile as they are shut out from entire stretches of coastal land. If tourism is about carefully planned displacement from the ordinary for a privileged few, the crossing of boundaries for recreation and adventure, here it is tied to the forced displacement of fishing communities and the instituting of new boundaries that exclude and dispossess.

From *Dollars & Sense* magazine, July/August 2005.

In the last three decades, the rich have gotten richer—relatively quickly—while wages at the bottom of the income scale have stagnated. John Miller critiques The Wall Street Journal for claiming that such inequality comes with the territory in an expanding economy. Miller suggests that the Journal's editors should go back and read Adam Smith, who feared the corrupting effects of large-scale inequality.

MIND-BOGGLING INEQUALITY

BY JOHN MILLER

D o soaring corporate profits (higher as a share of national income than at any time since 1950) and a green Christmas on Wall Street (green as in record-setting multimillion dollar bonuses for investment bankers) have you worried about economic inequality? How about real wages that are lower and poverty rates higher than when the current economic expansion began five years ago? If that is not enough to make you worry, try this. The editors of the *Wall Street Journal* are spilling a whole lot of ink these days to convince their readers that today's inequality is just not a problem. Besides that, there is not much to be done about inequality, say the editors, since taxes are already soaking the rich.

Not even Ben Bernanke, the new head of the Fed, is prepared to swallow the editors' line this time. Inequality in the U.S. economy "is increasing beyond what is healthy," Bernanke told Congress, although like the editors he finds it a "big challenge to think about what to do about it."

There is real reason to worry. By nearly every measure, inequality today is at a level not seen since the Great Depression. And by historical standards, the rich have hardly overpaid in taxes for their decades-long economic banquet.

Once you remove the *Journal* editors' spin, the "actual evidence" from the Congressional Budget Office (CBO) makes clear that the charge of worsening inequality and a declining tax burden on the rich is anything but "trumped up." The CBO's latest numbers document a lopsided economic growth that has done little to improve the lot of most households while it has paid off handsomely for those at the top. From 1979 to 2004, the poorest quintile saw their average real (i.e., inflation-adjusted) income barely budge, increasing just 2.0% over the entire period.

The middle-income quintile enjoyed a larger but still modest real-income gain of 14.6% over the 25-year span, while the best-off fifth enjoyed a 63.0% gain. But the 153.9% jump in the real income of the richest 1% far outdistanced even the gains of the near rich. (See figure.)

The *Journal*'s editors are right about one thing: a widening income gap is a long-term trend that has persisted regardless of the party in power. The well-to-do made out like bandits during the Clinton years as well as the Bush years. In fact, postwar inequality, after peaking in 2000, did retreat somewhat in the first four Bush years as the stock market bubble burst, cutting into the income share of the most well-off, who hold the vast majority of corporate stock. (In 2004, the wealthiest 1% of U.S. households held 36.9% of common stock by value; the wealthiest 10% held 78.7%.)

The increase in the gulf between the haves and the have-nots during the Bush years, however, has hardly been modest. In 2004, as in 1999 and in 2000, the share of pre-tax income going to the richest 1% is greater than the share they received in any year since 1929, according to the ground-breaking historical study of inequality by economists Thomas Piketty and Emmanuel Saez. (See "Slicing Up at the Great Barbeque," p.126, for further discussion of the study.) *Barron's* magazine, the Dow Jones business and financial weekly, put it succinctly in their recent cover story, "Rich America, Poor America": "never in history have the haves had so much."

FEAST AND FAMINE

The editors' banquet scenario is unconvincing, to say the least. First off, before we examine the bill for the banquet, we ought to look at what the 100 guests were served. Not everyone got the same meal; in fact, the economic banquet of the last two and a half decades was a feast for some and a famine for others. Most people got modest portions indeed. The income, or serving size if you will, of the average guest was just one sixteenth of the economic feast lavished on the richest 1%. Surely even *Wall Street Journal* editors wouldn't expect the average taxpayer to subsidize the culinary indulgences of the rich.

Second, the well-to-do picked up much less of the tab for their banquet than the *Journal*'s editorials suggest. True enough, the richest 1% of taxpayers now pay more than one-third of all income taxes. But the federal tax bill is not confined to income taxes alone. It also includes payroll taxes (like FICA, the Social Security tax) and excise taxes (for example, on cars) that fall more heavily on low-income households than the income tax does, making up much of their tax bill. Taking those taxes into account does make a substantial difference in the share of the total federal tax bill shouldered by the rich. In 2004, the richest 1% paid just over one-quarter (25.3%), not one-third, of all federal taxes. (See table.) No working American ate for free.

PERCENT CHANGE IN REAL HOUSEHOLD INCOME 1979-2004 BY INCOME GROUP

[Average household pre-tax cash income*]

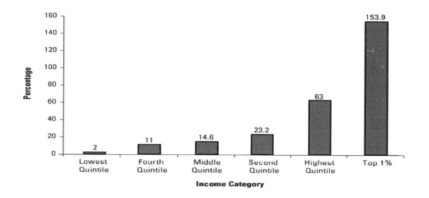

Source: Congressional Budget Office, *Historical Effective Tax Rates: 1979 to 2004*, Appendix Table 1C.

* Pre-tax cash income is the sum of wages, salaries, self-employment income, rents, taxable and non-taxable interest, dividends, realized capital gains, cash transfer payments, and retirement benefits plus employers' share of payroll taxes and employee contributions to 401(k) retirement plans.

Beyond federal tax liabilities, the banquet tab also includes state and local taxes. Those taxes, especially state sales taxes, fall most heavily on those who were served the smallest portions: low-income earners. Once state and local taxes are included, the tax share of the richest 1% falls to just over one-fifth, not much more than their share of national income as calculated by the IRS. According to these estimates, provided by the Washington-based think tank Citizens for Tax Justice, the U.S. tax code taken in its entirety does little to redistribute income. By any definition, our tax system is at best mildly progressive, and surely not "highly progressive" as the *Journal* claims.

On top of all that, when the bill for today's economic banquet came due, the Bush administration somehow decided that the guests as a group had overpaid. The purported excess over the amount of the bill should, at least according to the Bush administration's reasoning, go back to each member of the group in tax cuts, in proportion with what they contributed toward paying the bill. Those who contributed the most should get the most back; those who contributed less should get less back. And those whom the rest are treating to dinner, of course, should get nothing back.

But the Bush tax cuts don't manage to conform to even this version of fairness, at least not when it comes to the share of the cuts going to the super-rich. The richest 1% of taxpayers, with average household income well over $1 million, get a whop-

SHARE OF TOTAL TAX LIABILITIES AND EFFECTIVE TAX RATES PAID BY DIFFERENT INCOME GROUPS, 2004

	Share of Total Tax Liabilities		Effective Tax Rate	
Income Category	Federal	Federal, State, and Local	Federal	Federal, State, and Local
Lowest Quintile	0.9%	2.2%	7.9%	19.7%
Second Quintile	4.5%	5.5%	11.4%	23.3%
Middle Quintile	9.7%	10.5%	15.8%	27.0%
Fourth Quintile	17.6%	19.0%	18.7%	29.8%
Highest Quintile	67.1%	62.6%	21.6%	31.8%
TOP 1%	25.3%	20.8%	24.6%	32.8%

Sources: Congressional Budget Office, *Historical Effective Tax Rates: 1979 to 2004*, Appendix Tables 1b. Citizens for Tax Justice, "Overall Tax Rates Have Flattened Sharply Under Bush," 4/13/04.

ping 35.9% of the benefits of the Bush tax cuts, or an annual tax cut of $48,311 during this decade, well in excess of their one-quarter (or 25.3% to be exact) share of the federal tax burden.

All told, the U.S. tax system does not soak the rich, especially after the Bush tax cuts. In 2004, the effective federal tax rate—that is, the share of total income anyone hands over to the government in federal taxes—for the richest 1% was 24.6%, according to Citizens for Tax Justice, far lower than it was in the 1970s. By historical standards, or by any reasonable definition, taxes on the rich have not reached the saturation point.

On top of that, the effective tax rate for all federal, state, and local taxes combined for the poorest fifth of households is 19.7%—well over half the effective tax rate of 32.8% that the richest 1% pay—and that's *after* taking into account the Earned Income Tax Credit that some low-income households receive. With an average income of $1,259,700, as opposed to $15,400, that rate falls far short of exhausting the ability of the superrich to pay. It hardly represents a contribution to the bill for the economic banquet of the last two and a half decades that is in proportion to the large and lavish meal they've enjoyed.

WHAT WOULD ADAM SMITH SAY?

There is no reason to be flummoxed about how to address worsening inequality, even in the short run. *Wall Street Journal* columnist David Wessel, in a November 2006 article on how Democrats might tackle the wealth gap, had no problem enumerating several measures that would lessen inequality. Those included raising the minimum wage, restraining CEO pay, expanding the earned-income tax credit, and rolling back President Bush's upper-income tax cuts.

Just the thought that Congress might actually pass some of these measures was enough for the Journal's editors to minimize the reality of rising inequality and to extol the supposed tax generosity of the rich.

Too bad. Unlike the *Wall Street Journal*'s editors, even Adam Smith, the patron saint of capitalism, recognized the corrupting effect of inequality in a market economy. As Smith put it in *The Theory of Moral Sentiments*, his often overlooked lectures on ethics, the "disposition to admire, and almost to worship, the rich and the powerful, and to despise, or, at least, to neglect persons of poor and mean condition is the great and most universal cause of the corruption of our moral sentiments."

A fitting description of the attitude the *Wall Street Journal*'s editors seem to have toward the rich and the poor. Business executives and policymakers would do well to skip the *Journal* and go back to Smith.

Resources: Congressional Budget Office, "Historical Effective Federal Tax Rates: 1979 to 2004," 12/04; Citizens for Tax Justice, "Overall Tax Rates Have Flattened Sharply Under Bush," 4/13/04; David Wessel, "Fed Chief Warns of Widening Inequality," *Wall Street Journal*, 2/7/07; David Wessel, "Democrats target wealth gap and hope not to hit economy," *Wall Street Journal*, 11/21/06; Adam Smith, *The Theory of Moral Sentiments*, Sec. III, Chap. III, in The Essential Adam Smith ed. Robert Heilbroner (Norton, 1986), p. 86; "Incomes and Politics," *Wall Street Journal* editorial, 9/2/06; "The Top 1% Pay 35%," *Wall Street Journal editorial*, 12/20/06.

The elite media tell us that countries grow faster when their trade and investment policies favor neoliberal globalization. But their definitions of economic success focus on corporate freedom to dominate nations, rater than economic and political freedom for the citizens of developing countries. John Miller debunks some of the mainstream media myths about free-market globalization.

GLOBALIZATION: GOOD FOR WHAT AILS YOU?

BY JOHN MILLER

OPEN-DOOR POLICY

Now would seem a good time [for politicians tempted by protectionism] to recall how well their countries and others have done by flinging doors open to trade, capital, services and people.

The emergence of China and India as global giants in the making dates directly to their decisions to liberalize. The current U.S. expansion is powered in part by capital from abroad. The Asian Tigers grew off trade. The singular achievement of the European Union was to create the biggest zone on the planet for the free trade of goods, capital and people.

In the past four decades, open economies (mostly from Europe, East Asia, North America) have fared far better than closed ones (Africa, Latin America, parts of Eastern Europe). Economists Jeffrey Sachs and Andrew Warner found that from 1970-1989 average annual growth in open developed economies was 2.3%, compared with 0.7% in the closed. In developing countries, those numbers were 4.5% and 0.7%. That trend hasn't changed much as trade and foreign investment have powered global growth.

As befits the dismal science, not to mention the dismal profession of politics, this evidence hasn't settled the intellectual argument.

—Wall Street Journal *editorial (3/30/06)*

GLOBALIZING GOOD GOVERNMENT

The Federal Reserve Bank of Dallas set out to document the connection between globalization and public policy. We found that the more globalized nations tend to pursue policies that achieve faster economic growth, lower inflation, higher incomes and greater economic freedom. The least globalized countries are prone to policies that interfere with markets and lead to stagnation, inflation and diminished competitiveness.

The gist is clear: as nations become more integrated into the world economy, they tend to maintain fewer barriers to trade and the movement of money. They are less likely to impose punishing corporate taxes and onerous regulations. Their technology policies are more favorable to innovation. Nations more open to the world economy score above the less globalized countries in respect for the rule of law and protection of property rights. More globalized countries also offer greater political stability.

Globalization's critics argue that a more open world economy sets off a race to the bottom by encouraging countries to jettison protections for consumers, workers and the environment. In reality, the opposite is true. If our data demonstrate anything, it is that globalization prompts a race to the top by pushing countries to abandon policies that burden their economies in favor of those that fuel growth and economic opportunity.

—Op-ed by Richard W. Fisher and W. Michael Cox, New York Times *(4/10/06)*

Got a problem with a corrupt, inefficient government? Does economic growth in your country just limp along? Try globalization, neoliberal globalization that is. Rapid growth and good government are sure to follow.

That is not some online advertisement, but comes straight from the opinion pages of the *Wall Street Journal* and the *New York Times*.

In March, the *Journal* editors published their umpteenth editorial praising globalization. And the *Times*, home of Thomas Friedman, elite journalism's best known apologist for globalization, devoted most of an April op-ed page to "Globalizing Good Government," complete with tables and elaborate illustrations, penned by Richard W. Fisher and W. Michael Cox, president and chief economist at the Federal Reserve Bank of Dallas.

There is just one problem with this latest round of pro-globalization hype: it is simply not true. Debunking the hype is particularly easy this time, since the evidence presented in each of the two editorials exposes the distortions in the other.

GLOBALIZATION AND GROWTH

We have been over this ground before. Study after study has failed to link more open trade and investment policy to more rapid economic growth. Most of these studies rely on a sleight of hand: they substitute "trade," a *performance* variable that reflects multiple factors (usually measured as the sum of exports and imports over Gross Domestic Product), for the *policy* variable "trade openness" (typically measured by tariff and non-tariff barriers to trade). There is indeed a tight correlation between trade and economic growth. But that correlation tells us only that countries that trade a lot grow a lot. It says nothing about whether free trade or managed trade policies best promote trade and economic growth.

None of that stopped the *Journal* editors from once again asserting that globalization leads to faster economic growth. But give them credit for this much. In an attempt to avoid those earlier mistakes, the editors reached all the way back to an influential 1995 paper by Harvard economists Jeffrey Sachs and Andrew Warner that does address the right question: how the policy variable "openness to international trade" relates to how fast a country grows. For them, the evidence from Sachs and Warner's paper, "Economic Reform and the Process of Global Integration," settles the intellectual argument that an "open-door policy" is the key to fast economic growth in today's global economy.

The Sachs and Warner paper constructs a complex aggregate measure of openness to international trade out of average tariff rates, non-tariff barriers, state control of exports, and the premium in black-market prices. And, as the editors report, the Sachs and Warner study finds that from 1970 to 1989, "open" developed countries grew more quickly than those closed to international trade according to their composite measure. The same was true for "open" developing economies: they grew more quickly than developing economies closed to international trade by their measure.

A closer look at the Sachs and Warner measure of openness, however, reveals some serious flaws in their study, as mainstream economists Francisco Rodriguez and Dani Rodrik point out in their exhaustive 2000 survey of the major studies of trade policy and economic growth. First, most of the correlation between growth and the measure of openness in their study comes from the premium in black-market prices and the state monopoly of exports and not the more standard measures of trade openness, tariff and non-tariff barriers to trade. (Sachs and Warner argue that a black-market exchange rate for a country's currency that is 20% lower than the official rate suggests that non-market forces are interfering with trade. Similarly, a state monopoly almost by definition indicates that trade is not governed by market forces.) In addition, Sachs and Warner's measure biases the result by leaving out two of the fastest growing economies with state monopolies on exports, Indonesia and Mauritius.

Finally, the robust connection between high black-market premiums and state monopoly of exports on the one hand, and slower economic growth on the other, can be explained by other institutional variables. Countries with a state monopoly of exports (especially after Indonesia and Mauritius are excluded) are concentrated in Sub-Saharan Africa, one of the slowest growing regions of the world economy. But the slow growth in that region might equally well be explained by the fact that it is saddled with massive foreign debt that consumes 40% of its export revenues, and by the fact that it lacks infrastructure, skills, and political stability.

Likewise, large and sustained black market premiums are usually due to serious macroeconomic policy problems, such as a massive current account deficit and large levels of external debt, that are likely to have depressed economic growth (as opposed to a lack of openness to trade).

For all these reasons, Rodriguez and Rodrik are skeptical that the Sachs-Warner measure is "a meaningful indicator of trade policy." Likewise, it pays to be skeptical when the *Journal* editors parrot their claim that trade openness promotes rapid economic growth.

Beyond the technical problems with the study their editorial relies on, the rest of what the editors write casts doubt on their claims. For instance, India and China might be more open to international trade than in the past, but they hardly make good poster children for neoliberal globalization. For instance, China remains a country that does not have a convertible currency, maintains state control of its banking system, and allows little foreign ownership in equity markets.

Nor does the rapid growth of the Asian Tigers make the case for openness. South Korea and Taiwan, whose most formative growth period was during the 1960s and 1970s, faced a world economy with far less capital mobility *and* engaged that world with policies antithetical to free trade—export subsidies, domestic-content requirements, import-export linkages, and restrictions on capital flows, including on foreign direct investment.

Overall, Rodriguez and Rodrik find "little evidence that open trade policies—in the sense of lower tariff and non-tariff barriers to trade—are significantly associated with economic growth."

GLOBALIZATION AND GOOD GOVERNMENT

The *Wall Street Journal* editors have done us a service by focusing our attention on the effects of globalization on economic growth. That alone should inoculate readers against the misleading arguments in "Globalizing Good Government." Despite claiming that "globalization prompts a race to the top … that fuels growth and economic opportunity," authors Fisher and Cox never provide data to show that globalization is associated with faster economic growth. And that is the Achilles' heel of their editorial, and of the Dallas Fed study, "Racing to the Top: How Global Competition Disciplines Public Policy," on which it is based.

"Racing to the Top" divides 60 countries into four groups—least globalized, less globalized, more globalized, and most globalized—using the A.T. Kearney/Foreign Policy Magazine Globalization Index. The index has its problems, for it indiscriminately mixes together performance variables (such as the level of trade or direct foreign investment) with policy variables (such as tariff levels).

The index does, however, suggest the slipshod way the *Wall Street Journal* editors use countries as examples to justify free-market globalization. Ireland, the editors' favorite, is appropriately enough number two, in the top "most globalized" tier, while France and Germany, whose labor policies the editors rail against, only make it into the second tier. But Asian Tigers South Korea and Taiwan, two of the editors' exemplars of openness, are in the second and third tier of the globalization index. And India and China, the other *Journal* examples of successful globalization, are among the least globalized economies in the world.

Back to Fisher and Cox, who use the Kearney index to show that the more globalized economies have many of the characteristics of what they consider good government and sound economic policy. For instance, more globalized economies have more open trade and investment policies (although their measure of openness has all the flaws of the Sachs and Warner measure), lower corporate taxes, lower inflation rates, less regulation of business, more political stability, more rule of law, more strictly enforced property rights, and less corruption (at least as the Dallas Fed and the Frazier Institute, the Canadian free-market think tank, measure these things). That is enough for Fisher and Cox to conclude, "the more globalized nations tend to pursue policies that achieve faster economic growth, lower inflation, higher incomes, and greater economic freedom."

But nowhere in their study or in their op-ed piece do Fisher and Cox show that economic growth rates pick up with globalization. That is because they can't. Journalist David Shipley emphasizes this point nicely in *Extra!*, the publication of the left media group Fairness & Accuracy in Reporting. He finds that in 2003-2004, the most globalized countries according to the Kearney index grew the most slowly and the more globalized countries the next most slowly, while the less globalized grew second most quickly and the least globalized fastest of all—just the opposite of the Fisher and Cox claim that more globalized nations tend to pursue policies that achieve faster economic growth!

That inverse relationship between globalization and economic growth holds up over longer periods as well. For the period from 1988 to 2005, the less and least globalized economies with the poorer measures of government performance in the Dallas Fed study grew on average 4.1% and 4.0% a year respectively, while the most and more globalized economies with the supposedly better government performance grew just 3.1% and 3.2% a year respectively.

Only their pro-globalization predilections could explain why the *Times* editors never asked to see growth statistics to back up Fisher's and Cox's assertion. But blaming their editors lets Fisher and Cox off far too easily. The authors were no doubt aware that the data are inconsistent with the contention that globalization leads to faster growth. Consider how gingerly they treat China, whose rapid growth rates, along with those of India, helped to push up the average growth of the least globalized nations. They make a feeble attempt to finesse the obvious contradiction, claiming that China's growth is the result of its abundant cheap labor and foreign investment, and cannot be sustained if China maintains the vestiges of its state-dominated past and its lack of labor flexibility.

So the evidence is clear: freer trade, greater capital market openness, fewer regulations, and lower corporate taxes, all correspond to slower growth. Each of those measures increases as the Kearney index moves from the least globalized to the most globalized category and growth rates slow. That should be enough to give the *Times* editors, and even the *Journal* editors, pause.

Beyond that contradiction, what Fisher and Cox say constitutes good government and economic freedom needs to be held up to closer scrutiny. For instance, since when did lower taxes become desirable in and of themselves? Aren't lower taxes desirable only if they lead to faster economic growth? It is not clear that they do. Economists Joel Slemrod and Jon Bakija, in their respected primer on tax policy, *Taxing Ourselves*, report that "sophisticated statistical analyses of the relationship between economic growth and the level of taxation, which attempt to hold constant the impact of the other determinants of growth to isolate the tax effect, have come to no consensus."

Neoliberal policies stand in the way of most people gaining control over their economic lives and obtaining genuine economic freedom in today's global economy. True, the Economic Freedom Index put out by the Heritage Foundation and the *Wall Street Journal* correlates nicely with the Kearney globalization index. But it does nothing other than measure corporate and entrepreneurial freedom from accountability, including "burdensome" taxes on corporate profits and "meddlesome" legislation requiring honest corporate accounting or environmental safeguards.

Even if neoliberal globalization did promote economic freedom, political freedom is another matter. Take the city-state Singapore, which tops the Kearney index of the most globalized nations. Singapore is only "partially free" according to Freedom House, which the *Journal* editors have called "the Michelin Guide to democracy's development." In Singapore, freedom of the press and rights to demonstrate are limited, films and TV are censored, preventive detention is legal, and you can do jail time for littering.

Other measures in the Dallas Fed study are just as problematic. For example, Fisher and Cox see globalization as a force for better labor policies. They rightly lament that the international mobility of most workers remains limited, despite countries becoming more globalized. At the same time, they complain that many nations maintain laws that hinder the hiring and firing of workers. They add, "job protection may sound appealing at first, but such policies impede workers' ability to compete." The nations that impose "huge burdens" on employers that lay off workers—including the equivalent of 90 weeks of pay in China—are relatively poor countries. Countries that impose fewer burdens on employers are usually richer. But, hiring labor in China has not been a problem. Fisher and Cox suggest as much when they attribute China's rapid growth to an abundance of cheap labor. The abuse of Chinese factory workers, however, is a problem regularly acknowledged even in the business press, and one that the deregulation of Chinese labor markets would only worsen.

GLOBALIZATION AND THE ELITE MEDIA

Nowadays studies that endorse neoliberal, free-market globalization, no matter how flawed, make good copy in the liberal and conservative elite media. That crowd is prepared to believe that the world is flat—the title of Thomas Friedman's latest paean to globalization—if it fits their worldview.

Sources: From *Dollars & Sense* magazine, July/August2006; "Open-Door Policy," Wall Street Journal, 3/30/06; March 30, 2006; "Globalizing Good Government," by Richard W. Fisher and W. Michael Cox, The New York Times, April 10, 2006; Richard W. Fisher and W. Michael Cox, "Racing To The Top: How Global Competition Disciplines Public Policy," 2005 Annual Report of the Federal Reserve Bank of Dallas; A.T. Kearney, Inc., "Measuring Globalization: The Global Top 20," Foreign Policy, May/June 2005; Joel Slemrod and Jon Bakija, Taxing Ourselves: A Citizen's Guide to the Debate Over Taxes; Francisco Rodriguez and Dani Rodrik, "Trade Policy and Economic Growth: A Skeptic's Guide To The Cross-National Evidence," May 2000; Jeffrey Sachs and Andrew Warner, "Economic Reform and the Process of Global Integration," Brookings Papers on Economic Activity, 1995: 1.

From *Dollars & Sense* magazine, July/August 2006.

Whether economic inequality is rising or falling globally is a matter of intense debate, a key question in the larger dispute over how three decades of intensified economic globalization have affected the world's poor. Bob Sutcliffe is an economist at the University of the Basque Country in Bilbao, Spain, and the author of 100 Ways of Seeing an Unequal World. He has been analyzing both the statistical details and the broader political-economic import of the debate and shared some of his insights in a recent interview with Dollars & Sense.

RICH AND POOR IN THE GLOBAL ECONOMY

A *Dollars & Sense* Interview with Bob Sutcliffe

Dollars & Sense: If someone asked you whether global inequality has grown over the past 25 years, I assume you'd say, "It depends—on how inequality is defined, on what data is used, on how that data is analyzed." Is that fair?

Bob Sutcliffe: Yes, it's fair, but it's not enough. First, the most basic fact about world inequality is that it is monstrously large; that result is inescapable, whatever the method or definition. As to its direction of change in the last 25 years, to some extent there are different answers. But also there are different questions. Inequality is not a simple one-dimensional concept that can be reduced to a single number. Single overall measures of world inequality (where all incomes are taken into account) give a different result from measures of the relation of the extremes (the richest compared with the poorest). Over the last 25 years, you find that the bottom half of world income earners seems to have gained something in relation to the top half (so, in this sense, there is less inequality), but the bottom 10% have lost seriously in comparison with the top 10% (thus, more inequality), and the bottom 1% have lost enormously in relation to the top 1% (much more inequality). None of these measures is a single true measure of inequality; they are all part of a complex structure of inequalities, some of which can lessen as part of the same overall process in which others increase.

We do have to be clear about one data-related question that has caused huge confusion. To look at the distribution of income in the world, you have to reduce incomes of different countries to one standard. Traditionally it has been done by using exchange rates; this makes inequality appear to change when exchange rates change, which is misleading. But now we have data based on "purchasing power parity" (the comparative buying power, or real equivalence, of currencies). Using PPP values achieves for comparisons over space what inflation-adjusted index numbers have achieved for comparisons over time. Although many problems remain with PPP values, they are the only way to make coherent comparisons of incomes between countries. But they produce estimates that are astonishingly different from exchange rate-based calculations. For instance, U.S. income per head is 34 times Chinese income per head using exchange rates, but only 8 times as great using PPP values. (And, incidentally, on PPP estimates the total size of the U.S. economy is now only 1.7 times that of China, and is likely to be overtaken by it by 2011.) So when you make this apparently technical choice between two methods of converting one currency to another, you come up not only with different figures on income distribution but also with two totally different world economic, and thus political, perspectives.

D&S: So even if some consensus were reached on the choices of definition, data, and method, you're urging a complex, nuanced portrait of what is happening to global inequality, rather than a yes or no answer. Could you give a brief outline of what you think that portrait looks like?

BS: Most integral measures—integral meaning including the entire population rather than comparing the extremes—that use PPP figures suggest that overall income distribution at the global level during the last 25 years has shown a slight decline in inequality, though there is some dissent on this. In any event this conclusion is tremendously affected by China, a country with a fifth of world population which has been growing economically at an unprecedented rate. Second, there seems to me little room for debate over the fact that the relative difference between the very rich and the very poor has gotten worse. And the smaller the extreme proportions you compare, the greater the gap. So the immensely rich have done especially well in the last 25 years, while the extremely poor have done very badly. The top one-tenth of U.S. citizens now receive a total income equal to that of the poorest 2.2 billion people in the rest of the world.

There have also been clear trends within some countries. Some of the fastest growing countries have become considerably more unequal. China is an example, along with some other industrializing countries like Thailand. The most economically liberal of the developed countries have also become much more unequal—for instance, the United States, the United Kingdom, and Australia—and so have the post-communist countries. The most extreme figures for inequality are found in a group of poor countries including Namibia and Botswana in southern Africa and Paraguay and Panama in Latin America.

Finally, the overall index of world inequality (measured by the Gini coefficient, a measure of income distribution) is about the same as that for two infamously unequal countries, South Africa and Brazil. And in the last few years it has shown no signs of improvement whatsoever.

D&S: People use the terms "unimodal" and "bimodal" to describe the global distribution of income. Can you explain what these mean? Also, you have referred elsewhere to a possible trimodal distribution—what does that refer to?

BS: The mode of a distribution is its most common value. In many countries there is one level of income around which a large proportion of the population clusters; at higher or lower levels of income there are progressively fewer people, so the distribution curve rises to a peak and then falls off. That is a unimodal distribution. But in South Africa, for example, due to the continued existence of entrenched ethnic division and economic inequality, the curve of distribution has two peaks—a low one, the most common income received by black citizens, and another, higher one, the the most common received by whites. This is a bimodal distribution because there are two values that are relatively more common than those above or below them. Because of its origins you could call it the "Apartheid distribution." The world distribution is in many respects uncannily like that of South Africa. It could be becoming trimodal in the sense that the frequency distribution of income has three peaks—one including those in very poor countries which have not been growing economically (e.g., parts of Africa), one in those developing countries which really have been developing (e.g., in South and East Asia), and one in the high-income industrialized countries. It's a kind of "apartheid plus" form of distribution.

D&S: In 2002, you wrote that many institutions, like the United Nations and the World Bank, were not being exactly honest in this debate—for example, emphasizing results based on data or methods that they elsewhere acknowledged to be poor. Has this changed over the past few years? Has the quality of the debate over trends in global income inequality improved?

BS: The most egregious pieces of statistical opportunism have declined. But I think there is a strong tendency in general for institutions to seize on optimistic conclusions regarding distribution in order to placate critics of the present world order. This increasingly takes the form of putting too much weight on measures of welfare other than income, for instance, life expectancy, for which there has been more international convergence than in the case of income. But there has been very little discussion of the philosophical basis for using life expectancy instead of or combined with income to measure inequality. If poor people live longer but in income terms remain as relatively poor as ever, has the world become less unequal?

The problem of statistical opportunism is not confined to those who are defending the world economic order; it also exists on the left. So, on the question of inequality, there is a tendency to accept whatever numerical estimate shows greatest inequality on the false assumption that this confirms the wickedness of capitalism. But capitalist inequality is so great that the willful exaggeration of it is not needed as the basis of anti-capitalist propaganda. It is more important for the left to look at the best indicators of the changing state of capitalism, including indicators of inequality, in order to intervene more effectively.

Finally, the quality of the debate, regardless of the intentions of the participants, is still greatly restricted by the shortage of available statistics about inequalities. That has improved somewhat in recent years although there are many things about past and present inequalities which we shall probably never know.

D&S: Do you see any contexts in which it's more important to focus on absolute poverty levels and trends in those levels rather than on inequality?

BS: The short answer is no, I do not. Plans for minimum income guarantees or for reducing the number of people lacking basic necessities can be important. But poverty always has a relative as well as an absolute component. It is a major weakness of the Millenium Development Goals, for example, that they talk about halving the number of people in absolute extreme poverty without a single mention of inequality. [The Millenium Development Goals is a U.N. program aimed at eliminating extreme poverty and achieving certain other development goals worldwide by 2015. —*Eds.*] And there is now a very active campaign on the part of anti-egalitarian, pro-capitalist ideologues in favor of the complete separation of the two. That is wrong not only because inequality is what partly defines poverty but more importantly because inequality and poverty reduction are inseparable. To separate them is to say that redistribution should not form part of the solution to poverty. Everyone is prepared in some sense to regard poverty as undesirable. But egalitarians see riches as pathological too. The objective of reducing poverty is integrally linked to the objective of greater equality and social justice.

D&S: Can you explain the paradox that China's economic liberalization since the late 1970s has increased inequality within China and at the same time reduced global inequality? Some researchers and policymakers interpret China's experience over this period as teaching us that it may be necessary for poor countries to sacrifice some equality in order to fight poverty. Do you agree with this—if not, how would you respond?

BS: When you measure *global* inequality, you are not just totalling the levels of inequality in individual countries. In theory all individual countries could become more unequal and yet the world as a whole become more equal, or vice versa. In China, a very poor country in 1980, average incomes have risen much faster than the world average and this has reduced world inequality. But different sections of the population have done much better than others so that inequality within China has grown. If and when China becomes on average a richer country than it is now, further unequal growth there may contribute to increasing rather than decreasing world inequality.

China's growth has been very inegalitarian, but it has been very fast. And the proportion of the population in poverty seems to have been reduced. But it is possible to envisage a more egalitarian growth path which would have been slower in aggregate but which would have reduced the number of poor people at least as much if not more than China's actual record. So I do not think it is right to say that higher inequality is the cause of reduced poverty, though it may for a time be a feature of the rapid growth which in turn creates employment and reduces poverty.

This does not mean that all increases in inequality are necessarily pathological. The famous Kuznets curve sees inequality first rising and then falling during economic growth as an initially poor population moves by stages from low-income, low-productivity work into high-income, high-productivity work, until at the end of the process 100% of the population is in the second group. If you measure inequality during such a process, it does in fact rise and then fall again to its original level—in this example at the start everyone is equally poor, at the end everyone is equally richer. That might be called transitional inequality; many growth processes may include an element of it. In that case equality is not really being "sacrificed" to reduce poverty—poverty is reduced by a process which increases inequality and then eliminates it again. But at the same time inequality may be growing for many other reasons which are not, like the Kuznets effect, self-eliminating, but rather cumulative. When inequality grows, this malign variety tends to be more important than the self-eliminating variety. But many economists are far too ready to see growing inequality as the more benign, self-eliminating variety.

D&S: Where do you think the question of what is happening to global income inequality fits into the broader debate over neoliberalism and globalization?

BS: Many people say that since some measures of inequality started to improve in about 1980 and that is also when neoliberalism and globalization accelerated, it is those processes which have produced greater equality. There are many problems with this argument, among them the fact that at least on some measures global inequality has grown since 1980. In any case, measures which show global inequality falling in this period are, as we have seen, very strongly influenced by China. China's extraordinary growth has, of course, in part been expressed in and permitted by greater globalization (its internationalization has grown faster than its production), and it is also clear that liberalization of economic policy has played a role, though China hardly has a neoliberal economy. But to permit is not to cause. The real cause is surely to be found not so much in economic policy as in a profound social movement in which a new and highly dynamic capitalist class (combined with a supportive authoritarian state) has once again become an agent of massive capitalist accumulation, as seen before in Japan, the United States, and Western Europe. So, an important part of what we are observing in figures which show declining world inequality is not any growth of egalitarianism, but the dynamic ascent of Chinese and other Asian capitalisms.

This interview also appears on the website of the Political Economy Research Institute at the University of Massachusetts-Amherst, along with Bob Sutcliffe's working paper "A More or Less Unequal World? World Income Distribution in the 20th Century." See <www.umass.edu/peri>.

From *Dollars & Sense* magazine, March/April 2005.

The Consequences of Inequality

> *When income inequality increases, the rest of the economy suffers too. Since the 1970s, pro-corporate and anti-union economic policies have helped accelerate inequality in the United States. James M. Cypher explains some of the causes and effects of the growing concentration of income and wealth.*

SLICING UP AT THE GREAT BARBEQUE:

Who Gorges, Who Serves, and Who Gets Roasted?

BY JAMES CYPHER

conomic inequality has been on the rise in the United States for 30-odd years. Not since the Gilded Age of the late 19th century—during what Mark Twain referred to as "the Great Barbeque"—has the country witnessed such a rapid shift in the distribution of economic resources.

Still, most mainstream economists do not pay too much attention to the distribution of income and wealth—that is, how the value of current production (income) and past accumulated assets (wealth) is divided up among U.S. households. Some economists focus their attention on theory for theory's sake and do not work much with empirical data of any kind. Others who *are* interested in these on-the-ground data simply assume that each individual or group gets what it deserves from a capitalist economy. In their view, if the share of income going to wage earners goes up, that must mean that wage earners are more productive and thus deserve a larger slice of the nation's total income—and vice versa if that share goes down.

Heterodox economists, however, frequently look upon the distribution of income and wealth as among the most important shorthand guides to the overall state of a society and its economy. Some are interested in economic justice; others may or may not be, but nonetheless are convinced that changes in income distribution signal underlying societal trends and perhaps important points of political tension. And the general public appears to be paying increasing attention to income and wealth inequality. Consider the strong support voters have given to recent ballot questions raising state minimum wages and the extensive coverage of economic inequality that has suddenly begun to appear in mainstream news outlets like the *New York Times*, the *Los Angeles Times*, and the *Wall Street Journal*, all of which published lengthy article series on the topic in the past few years. Just last month, news outlets around the country spotlighted the extravagant bonuses paid out by investment firm Goldman Sachs, including a $53.4 million bonus to the firm's CEO.

By now, economists and others who do pay attention to the issue are aware that income and wealth inequality in the United States rose steadily during the last three decades of the 20th century. But now that we are several years into the 21st, what do we know about income and wealth distribution today? Has the trend toward inequality continued, or are there signs of a reversal? And what can an understanding of the entire post-World War II era tell us about how to move again toward greater economic equality?

The short answers are: (1) Income distribution is even more unequal that we thought; (2) The newest data suggest the trend toward greater inequality continues, with no signs of a reversal; (3) We all do better when we all do better. During the 30 or so years after World War II the economy boomed and every stratum of society did better—pretty much at the same rate. When the era of shared growth ended, so too did much of the growth: the U.S. economy slowed down and recessions were deeper, more frequent, and harder to overcome. Growth spurts that did occur left most people out: the bottom 60% of U.S. households earned only 95 cents in 2004 for every dollar they made in 1979. A quarter century of falling incomes for the vast majority, even though average household income rose by 27% in real terms. Whew!

THE CLASSLESS SOCIETY?

Throughout the 1950s, 1960s, and 1970s, sociologists preached that the United States was an essentially "classless" society in which everyone belonged to the middle class. A new "mass market" society with an essentially affluent, economically homogeneous population, they claimed, had emerged. Exaggerated as these claims were in the 1950s, there was some reason for their popular acceptance. Union membership reached its peak share of the private-sector labor force in the early 1950s; unions were able to force corporations of the day to share the benefits of strong economic growth. The union wage created a target for non-union workers as well, pulling up all but the lowest of wages as workers sought to match the union wage and employers often granted it as a tactic for keeping unions out. Under these circumstances, millions of families entered the lower middle class and saw their standard of living rise markedly. All of this made the distribution of income more equal for decades until the late 1970s. Of course there were outliers—some millions of poor, disproportionately blacks, and the rich family here and there.

Something serious must have happened in the 1970s as the trend toward greater economic equality rapidly reversed. Here are the numbers. The share of income received by the bottom 90% of the population was a modest 67% in 1970, but by 2000 this had shrunk to a mere 52%, according to a detailed study of U.S. income distribution conducted by Thomas Piketty and Emmanuel Saez, published by the prestigious National Bureau of Economic Research in 2002. Put another way, the top 10% increased their overall share of the nation's total income by 15 percentage points from 1970 to 2000. This is a rather astonishing jump—the *gain* of the top 10% in these years was equivalent to more than the *total income received annually* by the bottom 40% of households.

To get on the bottom rung of the top 10% of households in 2000, it would have been necessary to have an adjusted gross income of $104,000 a year. The real money, though, starts on the 99th rung of the income ladder—the top 1% received an unbelievable 21.7% of all income in 2000. To get a handhold on the very bottom of this top rung took more than $384,000.

The Piketty-Saez study (and subsequent updates), which included in its measure of annual household income some data, such as income from capital gains, that generally are not factored in, verified a rising *trend* in income inequality which had been widely noted by others, and a *degree* of inequality which was far beyond most current estimates.

The Internal Revenue Service has essentially duplicated the Piketty-Saez study. They find that in 2003, the share of total income going to the "bottom" four-fifths of households (that's 80% of the population!) was only slightly above 40%. (See Figure 1.) Both of these studies show much higher levels of inequality than were previously thought to exist based on widely referenced Census Bureau studies. The Census studies still attribute 50% of total income to the top fifth for 2003, but this number appears to understate what the top fifth now receives—nearly 60%, according to the IRS.

A BRAVE NEW (GLOBALIZED) WORLD FOR WORKERS

Why the big change from 1970 to 2000? That is too long a story to tell here in full. But briefly, we can say that beginning in the early 1970s, U.S. corporations and the wealthy individuals who largely own them had the means, the motive, and the opportunity to garner a larger share of the nation's income—and they did so.

Let's start with the motive. The 1970s saw a significant slowdown in U.S. economic growth, which made corporations and stockholders anxious to stop sharing the benefits of growth to the degree they had in the immediate postwar era.

Opportunity appeared in the form of an accelerating globalization of economic activity. Beginning in the 1970s, more and more U.S.-based corporations began to set up production operations overseas. The trend has only accelerated since, in part because international communication and transportation costs have fallen dramatically. Until the 1970s, it was very difficult—essentially unprofitable—for giants like General Electric or General Motors to operate plants offshore and then import their foreign-made products into the United States. So from the 1940s to the 1970s, U.S.

FIGURE 1

Income Share by Quintile: Selected Years 1979-2003

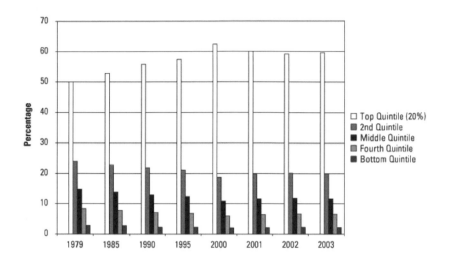

Source: "Further Analysis Of The Distribution Of Income And Taxes, 1979-2002," Michael Strudler and Tom Petska, Statistics of Income Division, Internal Revenue Service, and Ryan Petska, Quantitative Economics and Statistics, Ernst and Young LLP. Accompanying Excel files include data to 2003. Available at www.irs.gov/taxstats/article/0,,id=131260,00.html.

workers had a geographic lever, one they have now almost entirely lost. This erosion in workers' bargaining power has undermined the middle class and decimated the unions that once managed to assure the working class a generally comfortable economic existence. And today, of course, the tendency to send jobs offshore is affecting many highly trained professionals such as engineers. So this process of gutting the middle class has not run its course.

Given the opportunity presented by globalization, companies took a two-pronged approach to strengthening their hand vis-à-vis workers: (1) a frontal assault on unions, with decertification elections and get-tough tactics during unionization attempts, and (2) a debilitating war of nerves whereby corporations threatened to move offshore unless workers scaled back their demands or agreed to givebacks of prior gains in wage and benefit levels or working conditions.

A succession of U.S. governments that pursued conservative—or pro-corporate—economic policies provided the means. Since the 1970s, both Republican and Democratic administrations have tailored their economic policies to benefit corporations and shareholders over workers. The laundry list of such policies includes

- new trade agreements, such as NAFTA, that allow companies to cement favorable deals to move offshore to host nations such as Mexico;
- tax cuts for corporations and for the wealthiest households, along with hikes in the payroll taxes that represent the largest share of the tax burden on the working and middle classes;
- lax enforcement of labor laws that are supposed to protect the right to organize unions and bargain collectively.

EXPLODING MILLIONAIRISM

Given these shifts in the political economy of the United States, it is not surprising that economic inequality in 2000 was higher than in 1970. But at this point, careful readers may well ask whether it is misleading to use data for the year 2000, as the studies reported above do, to demonstrate rising inequality. After all, wasn't 2000 the year the NASDAQ peaked, the year the dot-com bubble reached its maximum volume? So if the wealthiest households received an especially large slice of the nation's total income that year, doesn't that just reflect a bubble about to burst rather than an underlying trend?

To begin to answer this question, we need to look at the trends in income and wealth distribution *since* 2000. And it turns out that after a slight pause in 2000-2001, inequality has continued to rise. Look at household income, for example. According to the standard indicators, the U.S. economy saw a brief recession in 2000-2001 and has been in a recovery ever since. But the median household income has failed to recover.* In 2000 the median household had an annual income of $49,133; by 2005, after adjusting for inflation, the figure stood at $46,242. This 6% drop in median household income occurred while the inflation-adjusted Gross Domestic Product *expanded* by 14.4%.

When the Census Bureau released these data, it noted that median household income had gone up slightly between 2004 and 2005. This point was seized upon by Bush administration officials to bolster their claim that times are good for American workers. A closer look at the data, however, revealed a rather astounding fact: Only 23 million households moved ahead in 2005, most headed by someone aged 65 or above. In other words, subtracting out the cost-of-living increase in Social Security benefits and increases in investment income (such as profits, dividends, interest, capital gains, and rents) to the over-65 group, workers again suffered a *decline* in income in 2005.

Another bit of evidence is the number of millionaire households—those with net worth of $1 million or more excluding the value of a primary residence and any IRAs. In 1999, just before the bubbles burst, there were 7.1 million millionaire households in the United States. In 2005, there were 8.9 million, a record number. Ordinary

FIGURE 2

Real Wages and Productivity of U.S. Production Workers, 1972-2005

— Hourly Output per Nonagricultural Worker
— Average Real Hourly Wage of Production Workers

Source: *Economic Report of the President 2006*, Tables B-47 and B-49.

workers may not have recovered from the 2000-2001 rough patch yet, but evidently the wealthiest households have!

Many economists pay scant attention to income distribution patterns on the assumption that those shifts merely reflect trends in the productivity of labor or the return to risk-taking. But worker productivity *rose* in the 2000-2005 period, by 27.1% (see Figure 2). At the same time, from 2003 to 2005 average hourly pay *fell* by 1.2%. (Total compensation, including all forms of benefits, rose by 7.2% between 2000 and 2005. Most of the higher compensation spending merely reflects rapid increases in the health insurance premiums that employers have to pay just to maintain the same levels of coverage. But even if benefits are counted as part of workers' pay—a common and questionable practice—productivity growth outpaced this elastic definition of "pay" by 50% between 1972 and 2005.)

And at the macro level, recent data released by the Commerce Department demonstrate that the share of the country's GDP going to wages and salaries sank to its lowest postwar level, 45.4%, in the third quarter of 2006 (see Figure 3). And this figure actually overstates how well ordinary workers are doing. The "Wage & Salary" share includes *all* income of this type, not just production workers' pay. Corporate

FIGURE 3

Wages/Salaries vs. Corporate Profits as Shares of U.S. Income, 1972-2006

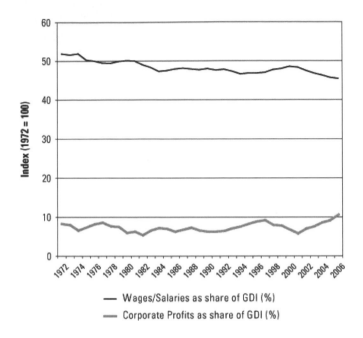

— Wages/Salaries as share of GDI (%)
— Corporate Profits as share of GDI (%)

Source: U.S. Dept. of Commerce, Bureau of Economic Analysis, *National Income and Product Accounts 2006*, Table 1.10.

executives' increasingly munificent salaries are included as well. Workers got rough-ly 65% of total wage and salary income in 2005, according to survey data from the U.S. Department of Labor; the other 35% went to salaried professionals—medical doctors and technicians, managers, and lawyers—who comprised only 15.6% of the sample.

Moreover, the "Wage & Salary" share shown in the National Income and Prod-uct Accounts includes bonuses, overtime, and other forms of payment not included in the Labor Department survey. If this income were factored in, the share going to nonprofessional, nonmanagerial workers would be even smaller. Bonuses and other forms of income to top employees can be many times base pay in important areas such as law and banking. Goldman Sachs's notorious 2006 bonuses are a case in point; the typical managing director on Wall Street garnered a bonus ranging be-tween $1 and $3 million.

So, labor's share of the nation's income is falling, as Figure 3 shows, but it is actually falling much faster than these data suggest. Profits, meanwhile, are at their highest level as a share of GDP since the booming 1960s.

These numbers should come as no surprise to anyone who reads the paper: story after story illustrates how corporations are continuing to squeeze workers. For instance, workers at the giant auto parts manufacturer Delphi have been told to prepare for a drop in wages from $27.50 an hour in 2006 to $16.50 an hour in 2007. In order to keep some of Caterpillar's manufacturing work in the United States, the union was cornered into accepting a contract in 2006 that limits new workers to a maximum salary of $27,000 a year—no matter how long they work there—compared to the $38,000 or more that long-time Caterpillar workers make today. More generally, for young women with a high school diploma, average entry-level pay fell to only $9.08 an hour in 2005, down by 4.9% just since 2001. For male college graduates, starter-job pay fell by 7.3% over the same period.

AIDING AND ABETTING

And the federal government is continuing to play its part, facilitating the transfer of an ever-larger share of the nation's income to its wealthiest households. George W. Bush once joked that his constituency was "the haves and the have-mores"—this may have been one of the few instances in which he was actually leveling with his audience. Consider aspects of the four tax cuts for individuals that Bush has implemented since taking office. The first two cut the top *nominal* tax rate from 39.6% to 35%. Then, in 2003, the third cut benefited solely those who hold wealth, reducing taxes on dividends from 39.6% to 15% and on capital gains from 20% to 15%. (Bush's fourth tax cut—in 2006—is expected to drop taxes by 4.8% percent for the top one tenth of one percent of all households, while the median household will luxuriate with an extra nickel per day.)

So, if you make your money by the sweat of your brow and you earned $200,000 in 2003, you paid an *effective* tax rate of 21%. If you earned a bit more, say another $60,500, you paid an effective tax rate of 35% on the additional income. But if, with a flick of the wrist on your laptop, you flipped some stock you had held for six months and cleared $60,500 on the transaction, you paid the IRS an effective tax rate of only 15%. What difference does it make? Well, in 2003 the 6,126 households with incomes over $10 million saw their taxes go down by an average of $521,905 from this one tax cut alone.

These tax cuts represent only one of the many Bush administration policies that have abetted the ongoing shift of income away from most households and toward the wealthiest ones. And what do these top-tier households do with all this new-found money? For one thing, they save. This is in sharp contrast to most households. While the top fifth of households by income has a savings rate of 23%, the bottom 80% as a group dissave—in other words, they go into debt, spending more than they earn. Households headed by a person under 35 currently show a negative savings rate of 16% of income. Today *overall* savings—the savings of the top fifth minus the dis-savings of the bottom four-fifths—are slightly negative, for the first time since the Great Depression.

Here we find the crucial link between income and wealth accumulation. Able to save nearly a quarter of their income, the rich search out financial assets (and sometimes real assets such as houses and businesses) to pour their vast funds into. In many instances, sometimes with inside information, they are able to generate considerable future income from their invested savings. Like a snowball rolling downhill, savings for the rich can have a turbo effect—more savings generates more income, which then accumulates as wealth.

LIFESTYLES OF THE RICH

Make the rich even richer and the creative forces of market capitalism will be unleashed, resulting in more savings and consequently more capital investment, raising productivity and creating abundance for all. At any rate, that's the supply-side/neoliberal theory. However—and reminiscent of the false boom that defined the Japanese economy in the late 1980s—the big money has not gone into productive investments in the United States. Stripping out the money pumped into the residential real estate bubble, inflation-adjusted investment in machinery, equipment, technology, and structures increased only 1.4% from 1999 through 2005—an average of 0.23% per year. Essentially, productive investment has stagnated since the close of the dot-com boom.

Instead, the money has poured into high-risk hedge funds. These are vast pools of unregulated funds that are now generating 40% to 50% of the trades in the New York Stock Exchange and account for very large portions of trading in many U.S. and foreign credit and debt markets.

And where is the income from these investments going? Last fall media mogul David Geffen sold two paintings at record prices, a Jasper Johns ($80 million) and a Willem de Kooning ($63.5 million), to two of "today's crop of hedge-fund billionaires" whose cash is making the art market "red-hot," according to the *New York Times*.

Other forms of conspicuous consumption have their allure as well. Boeing and Lufthansa are expecting brisk business for the newly introduced 787 airplane. The commercial version of the new Boeing jet will seat 330, but the VIP version offered by Lufthansa Technik (for a mere $240 million) will have seating for 35 or fewer, leaving room for master bedrooms, a bar, and the transport of racehorses or Rolls Royces. And if you lose your auto assembly job? It should be easy to find work as a dog walker: High-end pet care services are booming, with sales more than doubling between 2000 and 2004. Opened in 2001, Just Dogs Gourmet expects to have 45 franchises in place by the end of 2006 selling hand-decorated doggie treats. And then there is Camp Bow Wow, which offers piped-in classical music for the dogs (oops, "guests") and a live Camper Cam for their owners. Started only three years ago, the company already has 140 franchises up and running.

According to David Butler, the manager of a premiere auto dealership outside of Detroit, sales of Bentleys, at $180,000 a pop, are brisk. But not many $300,000 Rolls Royces are selling. "It's not that they can't afford it," Butler told the *New York Times*, "it's because of the image it would give." Just what is the image problem in Detroit? Well, maybe it has something to do with those Delphi workers facing a 40% pay cut. Michigan's economy is one of the hardest-hit in the nation. GM, long a symbol of U.S. manufacturing prowess, is staggering, with rumors of possible bankruptcy rife. The best union in terms of delivering the goods for the U.S. working class, the United Auto Workers, is facing an implosion. Thousands of Michigan workers at Delphi, GM, and Ford will be out on the streets very soon. (The top three domestic car makers are determined to permanently lay off three-quarters of their U.S. assembly-line workers—nearly 200,000 hourly employees. If they do, then the number of autoworkers employed by the Big Three—Ford, Chrysler, and GM—will have shrunk by a staggering 900,000 since 1978.) So, this might not be the time to buy a Rolls. But a mere $180,000 Bentley—why not?

HAD ENOUGH OF THE "HAVES"?

In the era Twain decried as the "great barbeque," the outrageous concentration of income and wealth eventually sparked a reaction and a vast reform movement. But it was not until the onset of the Great Depression, decades later, that massive labor/social unrest and economic collapse forced the country's political elite to check the growing concentration of income and wealth.

Today, it does not appear that there are, as yet, any viable forces at work to put the brakes on the current runaway process of rising inequality. Nor does it appear that this era's power elite is ready to accept any new social compact. In a recent report on the "new king of Wall Street" (a co-founder of the hedge fund/private-equity buyout corporation Blackstone Group) that seemed to typify elite perspectives on today's inequality, the New York Times gushed that "a crashing wave of capital is minting new billionaires each year." Naturally, the Times was too discreet to mention is that those same "crashing waves" have flattened the middle class. And their backwash has turned the working class every-which-way while pulling it down, down, down.

But perhaps those who decry the trend can find at least symbolic hope in the new boom in yet another luxury good. Private mausoleums, in vogue during that earlier Gilded Age, are back. For $650,000, one was recently constructed at Daytona Memorial Park in Florida—with matching $4,000 Medjool date palms for shade. Another, complete with granite patio, meditation room, and doors of hand cast bronze, went up in the same cemetery. Business is booming, apparently, with 2,000 private mausoleums sold in 2005, up from a single-year peak of 65 in the 1980s. Some cost "well into the millions," according to one the nation's largest makers of cemetery monuments. Who knows: maybe the mausoleum boom portends the ultimate (dead) end for the neo-Gilded Age.

Resources: Jenny Anderson, "As Lenders, Hedge Funds Draw Insider Scrutiny," *NY Times* 10/16/06; Steven Greenhouse, "Many Entry-Level Workers Feel Pinch of Rough Market," *NY Times* 9/4/06; Greenhouse and David Leonhardt, "Real Wages Fail to Match a Rise in Productivity," *NY Times* 8/28/06; Paul Krugman, "Feeling No Pain," *NY Times* 3/6/06; Krugman, "Graduates vs. Oligarchs," *NY Times* 2/27/06; David Cay Johnston, *Perfectly Legal* (Penguin Books, 2003); Johnston, "Big Gain for Rich Seen in Tax Cuts for Investments," *NY Times* 4/5/06; Johnston, "New Rise in Number of Millionaire Families," *NY Times* 3/28/06; Johnston, "'04 Income in US was Below 2000 Level," *NY Times* 11/28/06*; Leonhardt, "The Economics of Henry Ford May Be Passé," *NY Times* 4/5/06; Rick Lyman, "Census Reports Slight Increase in '05 Incomes," *NY Times* 8/30/06; Micheline Maynard and Nick Bunkley, "Ford is Offering 75,000 Employees Buyout Packages," *NY Times* 9/15/06; Jeremy W. Peters, "Delphi Is Said to Offer Union a One-Time Sweetener," *NY Times* 3/28/06; Joe Sharky, "For the Super-Rich, It's Time to Upgrade the Old Jumbo Jet," *NY Times* 10/17/06; Guy Trebay, "For a Price, Final Resting Place that Tut Would Find Pleasant" *NY Times* 4/17/06.

From *Dollars & Sense* magazine, January/February 2007.

Progressives who decry economic inequality just don't know how the economy works—or so say conservative pundits. According to those on the right, inequality fuels economic growth. But as Chris Tilly explains, exactly the opposite is true. In fact, equality boosts economic growth, while inequality puts on the brakes.

GEESE, GOLDEN EGGS, AND TRAPS

Why Inequality Is Bad for the Economy

BY CHRIS TILLY

Whenever progressives propose ways to redistribute wealth from the rich to those with low and moderate incomes, conservative politicians and economists accuse them of trying to kill the goose that lays the golden egg. The advocates of unfettered capitalism proclaim that inequality is good for the economy because it promotes economic growth. Unequal incomes, they say, provide the incentives necessary to guide productive economic decisions by businesses and individuals. Try to reduce inequality, and you'll sap growth. Furthermore, the conservatives argue, growth actually promotes equality by boosting the have-nots more than the haves. So instead of fiddling with who gets how much, the best way to help those at the bottom is to pump up growth.

But these conservative prescriptions are absolutely, dangerously wrong. Instead of the goose-killer, equality turns out to be the goose. Inequality stifles growth; equality gooses it up. Moreover, economic expansion does *not* necessarily promote equality—instead, it is the types of jobs and the rules of the economic game that matter most.

INEQUALITY: GOOSE OR GOOSE-KILLER?

The conservative argument may be wrong, but it's straightforward. Inequality is good for the economy, conservatives say, because it provides the right incentives for innovation and economic growth. First of all, people will only have the motivation to work hard, innovate, and invest wisely if the economic system rewards them for good economic choices and penalizes bad ones. Robin Hood-style policies that collect from the wealthy and help those who are worse off violate this principle. They reduce the payoff to smart decisions and lessen the sting of dumb ones. The result: people and companies are bound to make less efficient decisions. "We must allow [individuals] to fail, as well as succeed, and we must replace the nanny state with a regime of self-reliance and self-respect," writes conservative lawyer Stephen Kinsella in *The Freeman: Ideas on Liberty* (not clear how the free woman fits in). To prove their point, conservatives point to the former state socialist countries, whose economies had become stagnant and inefficient by the time they fell at the end of the 1980s.

If you don't buy this incentive story, there's always the well-worn trickle-down theory. To grow, the economy needs productive investments: new offices, factories, computers, and machines. To finance such investments takes a pool of savings. The rich save a larger fraction of their incomes than those less well-off. So to spur growth, give more to the well-heeled (or at least take less away from them in the form of taxes), and give less to the down-and-out. The rich will save their money and then invest it, promoting growth that's good for everyone.

Unfortunately for trickle-down, the brilliant economist John Maynard Keynes debunked the theory in his *General Theory of Employment, Interest, and Money* in 1936. Keynes, whose precepts guided liberal U.S. economic policy from the 1940s through the 1970s, agreed that investments must be financed out of savings. But he showed that most often it's changes in investment that drive savings, rather than the other way around. When businesses are optimistic about the future and invest in building and retooling, the economy booms, all of us make more money, and we put some of it in banks, 401(k)s, stocks, and so on. That is, saving grows to match investment. When companies are glum, the process runs in reverse, and savings shrink to equal investment. This leads to the "paradox of thrift": if people try to save too much, businesses will see less consumer spending, will invest less, and total savings will end up diminishing rather than growing as the economy spirals downward. A number of Keynes's followers added the next logical step: shifting money from the high-saving rich to the high-spending rest of us, and not the other way around, will spur investment and growth.

Of the two conservative arguments in favor of inequality, the incentive argument is a little weightier. Keynes himself agreed that people needed financial consequences to steer their actions, but questioned whether the differences in payoffs needed to be so huge. Certainly state socialist countries' attempts to replace material incentives with moral exhortation have often fallen short. In 1970, the Cuban government launched the *Gran Zafra* (Great Harvest), an attempt to reap 10 million tons of sugar cane with (strongly encouraged) volunteer labor. Originally inspired by Che Guevara's ideal of the New Socialist Man (not clear how the New Socialist Woman fit in), the effort ended with Fidel Castro tearfully apologizing to the Cuban people in a nationally broadcast speech for letting wishful thinking guide economic policy.

But before conceding this point to the conservatives, let's look at the evidence about the connection between equality and growth. Economists William Easterly of New York University and Gary Fields of Cornell University have recently summarized this evidence:

- Countries, and regions within countries, with more equal incomes grow faster. (These growth figures do not include environmental destruction or improvement. If they knocked off points for environmental destruction and added points for environmental improvement, the correlation between equality and growth would be even stronger, since desperation drives poor people to adopt environmentally destructive practices such as rapid deforestation.)
- Countries with more equally distributed land grow faster.
- Somewhat disturbingly, more ethnically homogeneous countries and regions grow faster—presumably because there are fewer ethnically based inequalities.

In addition, more worker rights are associated with higher rates of economic growth, according to Josh Bivens and Christian Weller, economists at two Washington think tanks, the Economic Policy Institute and the Center for American Progress.

These patterns recommend a second look at the incentive question. In fact, more equality can actually *strengthen* incentives and opportunities to produce.

EQUALITY AS THE GOOSE

Equality can boost growth in several ways. Perhaps the simplest is that study after study has shown that farmland is more productive when cultivated in small plots. So organizations promoting more equal distribution of land, like Brazil's Landless Workers' Movement, are not just helping the landless poor—they're contributing to agricultural productivity!

Another reason for the link between equality and growth is what Easterly calls "match effects," which have been highlighted in research by Stanford's Paul Roemer and others in recent years. One example of a match effect is the fact that well-educated people are most productive when working with others who have lots of schooling. Likewise, people working with computers are more productive when many others have computers (so that, for example, e-mail communication is widespread, and know-how about computer repair and software is easy to come by). In very unequal societies, highly educated, computer-using elites are surrounded by majorities with little education and no computer access, dragging down their productivity. This decreases young people's incentive to get more education and businesses' incentive to invest in computers, since the payoff will be smaller.

Match effects can even matter at the level of a metropolitan area. Urban economist Larry Ledebur looked at income and employment growth in 85 U.S. cities and their neighboring suburbs. He found that where the income gap between those in the suburbs and those in the city was largest, income and job growth was slower for everyone.

"Pressure effects" also help explain why equality sparks growth. Policies that close off the low-road strategy of exploiting poor and working people create pressure effects, driving economic elites to search for investment opportunities that pay off by boosting productivity rather than squeezing the have-nots harder. For example, where workers have more rights, they will place greater demands on businesses. Business owners will respond by trying to increase productivity, both to remain profitable even after paying higher wages, and to find ways to produce with fewer workers. The CIO union drives in U.S. mass production industries in the 1930s and 1940s provide much of the explanation for the superb productivity growth of the 1950s and 1960s. (The absence of pressure effects may help explain why many past and present state socialist countries have seen slow growth, since they tend to offer numerous protections for workers but no right to organize independent unions.) Similarly, if a government buys out large land-holdings in order to break them up, wealthy families who simply kept their fortunes tied up in land for generations will look for new, productive investments. Industrialization in Asian "tigers" South Korea and Taiwan took off in the 1950s on the wings of funds freed up in exactly this way.

INEQUALITY, CONFLICT, AND GROWTH

Inequality hinders growth in another important way: it fuels social conflict. Stark inequality in countries such as Bolivia and Haiti has led to chronic conflict that hobbles economic growth. Moreover, inequality ties up resources in unproductive uses such as paying for large numbers of police and security guards—attempts to prevent individuals from redistributing resources through theft.

Ethnic variety is connected to slower growth because, on the average, more ethnically diverse countries are also more likely to be ethnically divided. In other words, the problem isn't ethnic variety itself, but racism and ethnic conflict that can exist among diverse populations. In nations like Guatemala, Congo, and Nigeria, ethnic strife has crippled growth—a problem alien to ethnically uniform Japan and South Korea. The reasons are similar to some of the reasons that large class divides hurt growth. Where ethnic divisions (which can take tribal, language, religious, racial, or regional forms) loom large, dominant ethnic groups seek to use government power to better themselves at the expense of other groups, rather than making broad-based investments in education and infrastructure. This can involve keeping down the underdogs—slower growth in the U.S. South for much of the country's history was linked to the Southern system of white supremacy. Or it can involve seizing the surplus of ethnic groups perceived as better off—in the extreme, Nazi Germany's expropriation and genocide of the Jews, who often held professional and commercial jobs.

Of course, the solution to such divisions is not "ethnic cleansing" so that each country has only one ethnic group—in addition to being morally abhorrent, this is simply impossible in a world with 191 countries and 5,000 ethnic groups. Rather, the solution is to diminish ethnic inequalities. Once the 1964 Civil Rights Act forced the South to drop racist laws, the New South's economic growth spurt began. Easterly reports that in countries with strong rule of law, professional bureaucracies, protection of contracts, and freedom from expropriation—all rules that make it harder for one ethnic group to economically oppress another—ethnic diversity has *no* negative impact on growth.

If more equality leads to faster growth so everybody benefits, why do the rich typically resist redistribution? Looking at the ways that equity seeds growth helps us understand why. The importance of pressure effects tells us that the wealthy often don't think about more productive ways to invest or reorganize their businesses until they are forced to. But also, if a country becomes very unequal, it can get stuck in an "inequality trap." Any redistribution involves a tradeoff for the rich. They lose by giving up part of their wealth, but they gain a share in increased economic growth. The bigger the disparity between the rich and the rest, the more the rich have to lose, and the less likely that the equal share of boosted growth they'll get will make up for their loss. Once the gap goes beyond a certain point, the wealthy have a strong incentive to restrict democracy, and to block spending on education which might lead the poor to challenge economic injustice—making reform that much harder.

DOES ECONOMIC GROWTH REDUCE INEQUALITY?

If inequality isn't actually good for the economy, what about the second part of the conservatives' argument—that growth itself promotes equality? According to the conservatives, those who care about equality should simply pursue growth and wait for equality to follow.

"A rising tide lifts all boats," President John F. Kennedy famously declared. But he said nothing about which boats will rise fastest when the economic tide comes in. Growth does typically reduce poverty, according to studies reviewed by economist Gary Fields, though some "boats"—especially families with strong barriers to participating in the labor force—stay "stuck in the mud." But inequality can increase at the same time that poverty falls, if the rich gain even faster than the poor do. True, sustained periods of low unemployment, like that in the late 1990s United States, do tend to raise wages at the bottom even faster than salaries at the top. But growth after the recessions of 1991 and 2001 began with years of "jobless recoveries"—growth with inequality.

For decades the prevailing view about growth and inequality within countries was that expressed by Simon Kuznets in his 1955 presidential address to the American Economic Association. Kuznets argued that as countries grew, inequality would first increase, then decrease. The reason is that people will gradually move from the low-income agricultural sector to higher-income industrial jobs—with inequality peaking when the workforce is equally divided between low- and high-income sectors. For mature industrial economies, Kuznets's proposition counsels focusing on growth, assuming that it will bring equity. In developing countries, it calls for enduring current inequality for the sake of future equity and prosperity.

But economic growth doesn't automatically fuel equality. In 1998, economists Klaus Deininger and Lyn Squire traced inequality and growth over time in 48 countries. Five followed the Kuznets pattern, four followed the reverse pattern (decreasing inequality followed by an increase), and the rest showed no systematic pattern. In the United States, for example:

- incomes became more equal during the 1930s through 1940s New Deal period (a time that included economic decline followed by growth)
- from the 1950s through the 1970s, income gaps lessened during booms and expanded during slumps
- from the late 1970s forward, income inequality worsened fairly consistently, whether the economy was stagnating or growing.

The reasons are not hard to guess. The New Deal introduced widespread unionization, a minimum wage, social security, unemployment insurance, and welfare. Since the late 1970s, unions have declined, the inflation-adjusted value of the minimum wage has fallen, and the social safety net has been shredded. In the United States, as elsewhere, growth only promotes equality if policies and institutions to support equity are in place.

TRAPPED?

Let's revisit the idea of an inequality trap. The notion is that as the gap between the rich and everybody else grows wider, the wealthy become more willing to give up overall growth in return for the larger share they're getting for themselves. The "haves" back policies to control the "have-nots," instead of devoting social resources to educating the poor so they'll be more productive.

Sound familiar? It should. After two decades of widening inequality, the last few years have brought us massive tax cuts that primarily benefit the wealthiest, at the expense of investment in infrastructure and the education, child care, and income supports that would help raise less well-off kids to be productive adults. Federal and state governments have cranked up expenditures on prisons, police, and "homeland security," and Republican campaign organizations have devoted major resources to keeping blacks and the poor away from the polls. If the economic patterns of the past are any indication, we're going to pay for these policies in slower growth and stagnation unless we can find our way out of this inequality trap.

From *Dollars & Sense* magazine, July/August 2004.

The 1990s saw concentrated wealth encroach into politics to an unprecedented degree—resulting in policy changes that produced crises in the accounting, telecom, and banking industries, and led to the Wall Street decline of 2001. Kevin Phillips puts today's plutocracy into historical perspective.

HOW WEALTH DEFINES POWER

The Politics of the New Gilded Age

BY KEVIN PHILLIPS

O f all the great deceptions that come to surround a gathering stock-market boom—from blather about the obsolescence of the business cycle to editorial claptrap about the United States turning into a republic of shareholders—one of the most pernicious has been the failure to recognize the character of the money culture it creates.

The pages of American history tell different stories about enormous wealth. Sometimes it has coexisted reasonably well with democracy, as in the days of Andrew Jackson or during the two decades after World War II. But the reverse has been true of the record concentrations of wealth that have grown up around the three most important financial boom periods: the post-Civil War Gilded Age, the Roaring Twenties, and the just-concluded bull market of the 1980s and '90s.

In a nutshell, these unusual wealth surges have bred unusual corruption. The moral degradation, in fact, has been multiple—financial corruption, political corruption, and philosophic or ideological corruption. Each has reinforced the others. When money is king, politicians get bought on a truly grand scale and philosophy bows to avarice. The genesis is much the same each time. All three booms have involved at least one decade—sometimes several—of hot new technology, surging stock markets, innovative finance, and the sense that the United States has transcended old limitations and rules. Money has fed on itself, creating a cult of railroad barons, automobile kings, hotshot CEOs, and financial masters of the universe. As the boom swells, so does the culture's preoccupation with money—and the competitive urge to ever more willingly cut corners. Human nature just can't resist. The ethical low usually becomes clear after the bull-market peak.

To get a fix on the corruption, it's necessary to begin with a portrait of the unusual wealth-creation dynamics involved. Each of these three periods saw a particularly lucrative convergence of economic forces. First, powerful new technology—railroads, steel, and oil in the Gilded Age; automobiles, radio, motion pictures, aviation, and household appliances in the 1920s; and personal computers, telecommunications, biotechnology, networking, and the Internet in the 1980s and '90s—energized the economy and captured the national imagination.

The second factor was financial innovation—new dimensions of banking, ballooning stock-market volume, innovations from ticker tapes, and investment trusts to computer programs and derivatives. There was also a cockiness each time about the United States having achieved a new level of sophisticated financial regulation—represented in the 1990s by the magic of Alan Greenspan—that would ensure against any calamity.

In all three periods, elements of the technology mania combined with new financial and speculative opportunities to create speculative excesses in bonds, stocks, or both. And each time a speculative bubble burst—in 1893, 1929, and 2000—the weakness in stocks and bonds spread into the real economy. But the wealth created was still notable, even after some or much of it was lost in the downturn.

The Gilded Age after the Civil War—it was 1873 when Mark Twain coined the term—lifted the American economy to not only new heights of success and industrialization, but also of economic polarization, and it introduced the nation to new lows of corruption. When the Civil War broke out in 1861, the largest fortune in the country was in the $15 million range, but by 1876, Commodore Vanderbilt had $100 million, and by the turn of the century both John D. Rockefeller (oil) and Andrew Carnegie (steel) were worth $300 million to $400 million. There had been maybe 300 U.S. millionaires in 1860, but by 1900 there were 4,000 to 5,000. And because there was little change in the value of a dollar between 1860 and 1900, the gains were real and not the product of inflation.

The financial corruption was lethal. Stocks and bonds were manipulated and watered down to such an extent that, after the Panic of 1893, thousands of banks and companies controlling one-third of the nation's railroad system were among the tens of thousands that failed. As for the political corruption of the Gilded Age, the U.S. Senate, then chosen by state legislatures rather than elected by the people, is even more emblematic than the Tweed Ring, Whiskey Ring, or Indian Ring. Millionaires frequently bought themselves Senate seats, and when one honest but naive member proposed legislation to unseat senators who had done so, Sen. Weldon B. Heyburn (R-Idaho) replied, in all seriousness, "We might lose a quorum here, waiting for the courts to act." Meanwhile, the philosophic corruption of the era produced a cult of markets and laissez faire, social Darwinism and survival of the fittest.

The 1920s made their greatest mark in financial corruption: Ponzi and his scheme, banks that peddled junk bonds and stocks, Samuel Insull and his pyramided utility holding companies, and New York Stock Exchange President Richard Whitney, who finally went to jail in 1938. The political side was highlighted by the Teapot Dome scandal and corrupt big-city machines owned by bootleggers and gangsters. The Dow Jones industrial average climbed 500% between 1921 and 1929, and the number of millionaires roughly quintupled to between 30,000 and 35,000 before collapsing in 1929 along with stock prices and the Indian summer of laissez faire.

Which brings us to the 1980s and 1990s and the corruption during those boom-crazed, wealth-fetishizing decades—behavior that was not just a matter of a few bad apples. As financial historians and economists such as Charles Kindleberger have pointed out, financial and political corruption seem to be an inevitable consequence of the psychologics and politics unleashed as a long bull market feeds a culture of money and greed.

The wealth and feeding pattern of the 1980s and '90s can be described in one word: unprecedented. The percentage increase in the Dow Jones industrial average between 1982 and 1999 was greater than the increase between 1921 and 1929, and the buildup in the largest American fortunes can be seen in the annual list of the *Forbes* 400 richest Americans. In 1982, looking at the richest 30 individuals and families, No. 30 had $500 million and No. 1, the du Pont family, had $8.6 billion; by 1999, after a 1,200% rise in the Dow, No. 30 had a fortune of $7 billion and No. 1, Bill Gates of Microsoft, had $85 billion.

Another set of numbers make clear just how rapacious America's top corporate echelon was. At its most intense, this was the mentality that gave us Enron, World-Com and the like. In 1981 the 10 highest-compensated executives in the United States had an average annual compensation of $3.45 million; in 1988 the average compensation for this group had climbed to $19.3 million; in 2000 it had soared to $154 million.

Very little of this incredible gain at the top of the U.S. wealth-and-income structure trickled down. The top 1% of Americans did not do nearly as well as the top one-tenth of 1%, but their fortunes soared in comparison with the middle class. In the autumn of 2001, when the Senate was Democratic and the House Republican, the Congressional Budget Office published data showing changes in household af-ter-tax income adjusted for inflation.

From the 1980s on, the enormous economic opportunities and benefits being concentrated at the top (and spreading down into the upper quintile) through tax cuts; bank, currency, and savings-and-loan bailouts; deregulation; mergers; leveraged buyouts; and a bull market in stocks had the predictable effects. Financial corruption ballooned, exemplified by the looting of savings-and-loan associations, the prolifera-tion of insider-trading scandals, and the criminal machinations of junk-bond king

Michael Milken. On the philosophic front, conservative think tanks promoted laissez faire and theorized about markets replacing politics. With so much at stake in policy-making and regulation, the rich stepped up their political involvement, and more and more money poured into congressional elections.

After a pause at the beginning of the 1990s, the boom, the technology mania, and the stock-market bubble continued to expand until they burst in 2000. After

INCOME IN AFTER-TAX 1997 DOLLARS

	1979	1987	1997
Average Household in Lowest Quintile	$9,300	$8,800	$8,700
Average Household in Middle Quintile	$31,700	$32,000	$33,200
Average Household in Top 1%	$256,400	$421,500	$644,300

Source: Congressional Budget Office.

the crash, a mass of financial corruption and dirty laundry spilled out of the closet, tainting Enron, Citicorp, Merrill Lynch, Bell South, and dozens of others. The warping of ideas and thinking had in many ways resurrected the Gilded Age taste for survival of the fittest (this time globally), glorification of the rich, and deification of markets.

But my purpose here is to emphasize how the concentration and momentum of wealth spilled over, just as they had before, from economic self-interest and buccaneering into the corruption of politics. Money flowed into elections and into the many pockets of well-tailored politicians. If the corruption was not as obvious as in the buying of the U.S. Senate circa 1900, it was even greater in overall scale. Consider these highlights (or lowlights):

- **The presidential "money primary."** In the 1999–2000 election cycle, big donors in both parties were able for the first time to flood the system with enough money to anoint chosen candidates—Republican George W. Bush, Democrat Al Gore—scare off most rivals, and avoid a drawn-out primary contest on either side.

- **The buying of the national parties.** Soft-dollar contributions rose from very little in the early 1980s to some $495 million in the 1999–2000 cycle, more or less enabling wealthy individuals, corporations, and interests to rent the loyalties of both parties.

- **The rising cost of open seats.** Since the 1979–1980 election cycle, the cost of running for open House and Senate seats has roughly quintupled, ensuring that a candidate must either have money of his or her own or accept the conditions and fealty that come with large-scale fundraising.

- **The selling of representatives and senators.** Over the years, politicians have tailored more and more pockets into which money can be stuffed, including campaign war chests, leadership political action committees, personal foundations, allied think tanks and high-paying jobs for spouses, to say nothing of future job opportunities for themselves.

- **The ascendancy of the top 1%.** Not surprisingly, the dominance of money in politics has cemented the dominance of those who have it to give. In the 1999–2000 cycle, the 15,000 top campaign donors (of $10,000 and more) gave more than 40% of the total contributions greater than $1,000. Similarly, about 40% of the donors giving at least $200 were in the top 1% of Americans by income. This goes a long way toward explaining why Congress has voted for top-bracket income-tax cuts and for eliminating the federal inheritance or estate tax, which applies only to the top 1.6% of estates.

- **The purchase of key economic policies.** Since the mid-1990s, the ability of rich individuals and free-spending industries to buy victory on critical issues has been particularly evident in three congressional decisions: the 1995 legislation to shield accounting firms from liability for inaccurate corporate reporting (and the subsequent defeat of efforts to curb accounting industry conflicts of interest); the 1996 Telecommunications Act; and the 1999 legislation repealing the Glass-Steagall Act, a law that for 65 years had prohibited banks from being in the insurance or securities business. Money won each time. The accounting industry flooded Congress with money and marshaled allies to threaten the Securities and Exchange Commission's budget. Sen. John McCain (R-Ariz.), chairman of the Senate Committee on Commerce, called the Telecommunications Act, in which broadcasters got $70 billion worth of free spectrum, "one of the greatest rip-offs since Teapot Dome." In 1999 the finance, insurance and real-estate sector was able to repeal Glass-Steagall in part because it was spending more on lobbying (more than $200 million in 1998) than any other economic sector. It had also become the biggest campaign giver in national politics, up from $109 million in 1991–1992 to a walloping $297 million in 1999–2000.

Alas, the changes won by the accounting, telecommunications, and banking industries—all of them promoting either something for nothing, lowered standards of responsibility, or corner-cutting—only exacerbated the collapse of ethics and responsible behavior. Not surprisingly, each of these industries would be front and center in the excesses and abuses that came to light in 2002 and 2003.

The bottom line, to use that phrase beloved by businessmen, is simply this: As the top 1% of Americans made so much money with the help of the political favoritisms of the 1980s and 1990s, they plowed even more money back into politics to secure and extend that favoritism—and they are still reaping the benefits. Meanwhile, of course, corrupted thinking is pushing the argument that giving a check to a candidate amounts to protected political speech under the First Amendment of the U.S. Constitution. It is amazing—literally amazing—how few opponents of these developments understand their larger historical context and symbolism.

For most Americans, a home is their single largest asset. For others, homeownership seems increasingly out of reach, and, of course, thousands have no place to lay their heads at all. A place to live is one of the most fundamental human needs, but in a society characterized by vast and growing pools of private wealth, it's also a lucrative investment; speculation in real estate markets is pushing many families out of decent housing. Activist Betsy Leondar-Wright recounts her direct experience of the issue.

HOUSING BLUES

BY BETSY LEONDAR-WRIGHT

In 1996, the Seaborn family bought a four-bedroom condo down the street from me in an up-and-coming Boston neighborhood. They paid $150,000. The Seaborns' daughters were best friends with a girl across the street whose family, the Cranes, rented a two-bedroom apartment. The Cranes were beloved members of the community—hosts of picnics and tag sales—and wanted to stay in the neighborhood. They began looking for a house or condo; if they could find something under $250,000, they could swing it. But the neighborhood was gentrifying rapidly, and the Cranes faced getting priced out of the area.

Then, in 2002, Mr. Seaborn got a job in another state with far lower housing costs. Several neighbors suggested that the Seaborns sell their condo to the Cranes. At $250,000, they would have made $100,000 profit in just six years. Instead, they put their condo on the market and sold it for $350,000. They've since moved, to a home on four acres with a pool. In the meantime, the Cranes had another baby, so they now live four people to a two-bedroom apartment. Their rent went up again; soon, they may not be able to stay in the neighborhood even as renters.

Usually we don't see the faces of both the people who make a windfall selling their homes in an overheated housing market and the people who are squeezed out of decent housing, but in this case both the Seaborns and the Cranes (whose names have been changed) were my friends. Watching these two families negotiate their housing choices, I became acutely aware of a "housing divide" that is widening in tandem with the United States' growing wealth gap.

DOWN THE HOUSING LADDER

Over the past 25 years, corporate actions and government policies have put trillions of additional dollars into the hands of the wealthiest Americans. When the rich get an additional surge of wealth, from a stock-market bubble—or a tax break—the new wealth moves in part into speculative investments. Prices for certain commodities—art, gold, and race horses, for example—start to rise.

Most Americans don't care whether race horses become more expensive. But when those dollars flow into real estate, investors' profits trickle down as housing hardship for everyone else. Investors and real estate developers buy and sell residential properties in rapid succession, for a higher price each time; soon they are out of reach for moderate-income homebuyers. As prices rise on rental properties, new owners have to jack up the rents just to cover the mortgage.

In those housing markets that see a steep run-up in prices, a process unfolds along these lines: Newly minted millionaires buy the biggest suburban houses, sometimes tearing down an existing house (or two!) to build a mansion. Professional two-career families who would have lived in those houses can afford only medium-sized suburban houses instead. Young professionals who would have moved to the suburbs instead stay in their urban starter homes for longer, or can't find a starter home and stay in the nicest rental housing. The working families who would have bought starter homes or rented nice apartments instead live in small, dingy rental housing. The working poor families who would have lived in small, dingy apartments instead live in substandard, dilapidated apartments or public housing. And the very poor people who would have lived in substandard or public housing become homeless.

Little or no research has been done to assess or quantify the effect of growing concentrations of wealth on housing markets, according to economists Lance Freeman and Bill Rohe. But this process is readily visible in cities around the country. I saw it firsthand in Boston in the mid-1980s, and again in the late 1990s. I was a community organizer in Jamaica Plain in 1986 when *Forbes Magazine* featured the neighborhood as having the fastest-rising property values in the nation. Flush with the Reagan tax cut, many investors made millions rapidly trading in Boston property. The average length of time new buyers held a Boston residential property was less than a year, according to the neighborhood group City Life/Vida Urbana. Rents and purchase prices soared. Single-room occupancy units and tenements were turned into condominiums, until no very low-rent units remained. Suddenly there were homeless people on the streets who weren't mentally ill or addicted, just poor. The long-time residents, a mix in which working-class Latino families and low-budget white bohemians predominated, lost their homes in droves, and the neighborhood became whiter and much more affluent.

Only the tireless efforts of community groups kept a few affordable apartments in place. City Life/Vida Urbana developed affordable units itself as well as organizing a militant Eviction Free Zone campaign. A coalition put together a "Campaign of Conscience for Housing Justice": Landlords signed a pledge to keep rents reasonable, for example, promising to base rent increases on their actual costs, not overall market trends. Through tenant organizing, mediation, and negotiation, these groups prevented thousands of evictions and other displacements. Still, countless families found themselves sliding down the housing ladder.

What happened to housing in Boston and elsewhere highlights the difference between speculative and productive investments. If supply and demand worked the way the economics textbooks claim, the heightened demand for reasonably priced homes in Boston should have sparked a building boom, with every vacant lot filled in with modest condos, and new Levittowns springing up in the outer suburbs. In fact, developers built almost no new housing except for high-end luxury homes, and that increased supply did not trickle down into lower (or even stable) prices for non-luxury housing. The smart money avoided the risks of new construction and went instead into what seemed like a sure thing: buying and selling existing properties at ever higher prices.

REAL ESTATE ETHICS?

The Seaborns are good people. They were not speculating in real estate, merely selling their primary residence at the price the market offered them. Like most people, they saw no ethical problem in their choice, even if it contributed to making housing unaffordable for someone else. That's the norm for property owners in our society.

Most people bristle at the idea of incorporating any values into their property decisions. With pensions becoming less common, selling a home at an appreciated price has become the most reliable way to retire. But when property values rise rapidly, homeowners profit from the "social appreciation," that is, the price increase in excess of inflation plus the value of any property improvements.

Individual property owners can take steps to keep housing affordable. The Massachusetts-based Equity Trust, an advocacy organization that promotes alternative forms of ownership and investment, ran a program in which homeowners pledged to put some or all of the social appreciation from selling their homes into a pool invested in permanently affordable housing. My partner and I have made such a pledge. Our down payment and equity payments, plus the overall inflation rate, plus any improvements we make on our condo: that's a fair price. Any more and we're hurting someone else's chance to live in decent housing. If our home was affordable for a pair of 40-year-olds with masters degrees when we bought it, it should be affordable for a pair of 40-year-olds with masters degrees when we sell it—not only to people with trust funds. We will take some social appreciation profit only if not doing so would jeopardize our ability to meet our basic needs for food, shelter, and health care. But if, like millions of Americans, we aren't forced to relocate to a more expensive area, but can retire to a less expensive home, then we'll donate the social appreciation to an affordable housing group.

Working toward a fairer economy means taking into consideration all the people affected by personal financial decisions, even real estate decisions. Unless such individual practices are adopted by a significant cross-section of the population, though, they cannot fix a housing market distorted by the speculative investments that concentrated wealth makes possible. Only significant public investment in affordable housing can do that.

The racial wealth gap in America is persistent and large. It's like a fossil, the enduring imprint of policies and practices that closed off myriad avenues of asset-building to African Americans and other people of color throughout U.S. history. But it's also the consequence of an economic system that continues to discriminate today. For all of the attention to white-collar and high-tech jobs going overseas, the more typical laid-off U.S. worker today is a black manufacturing worker. Without steady employment, black workers cannot hope to buy a home, save for retirement, or otherwise build assets; without assets, periods of unemployment pose a severe burden—a vicious circle.

BLACK JOB LOSS DÉJÀ VU

BY BETSY LEONDAR-WRIGHT

I n July 2003, Mary Clark saw a notice posted by the time-clock at the Pillowtex plant where she worked: the plant was closing down at the end of the month. The company would be laying off 4,000 workers. "They acted like we was nobody," she said; Pillowtex even canceled the workers' accrued vacation days. Clark had worked at the textile plant in Eden, North Carolina, for 11 years, inspecting, tagging, and bagging comforters. By 2003, she was earning more than $10 an hour.

Clark's unemployment benefits don't cover her bills. Because Pillowtex had sent her and her coworkers home frequently for lack of work in the final year, her unemployment checks are low, based on that last year's reduced earnings. She lost her health coverage, and now she needs dental work that she cannot afford.

It's happening again.

In the 1970s, a wave of plant closings hit African Americans hard. Two generations after the "Great Migration," when millions of black people had left the South to take factory jobs in Northern and Midwestern cities, the U.S. economy began to deindustrialize and many of those jobs disappeared—in some cases shifting to the low-wage, nonunion South.

The recession of 2001—and the historically inadequate "recovery" since—has again brought about a catastrophic loss of jobs, especially in manufacturing, and once again African Americans have lost out disproportionately. Jobs that moved to the South during the earlier era of deindustrialization are now leaving the country entirely or simply disappearing in the wake of technological change and rising productivity.

Media coverage of today's unemployment crisis often showcases white men who have lost high-paying industrial or information-technology jobs. But Mary Clark is actually a more typical victim. Recent job losses have hit black workers harder than white workers: black unemployment rose twice as fast as white unemployment in this last recession. Once again, African Americans are getting harder hit. Once again, they face a downturn with fewer of the resources and assets that tide families over during hard times. And once again, bearing a disproportionate share of job losses will make it more difficult for them to build wealth and economic security.

LAST HIRED, FIRST FIRED

The tight labor market of the late 1990s was very beneficial for African Americans. The black unemployment rate fell from 18% in the 1981–82 recession, to around 13% in the early 1990s, to below 7% in 1999 and 2000, the lowest black unemployment rate on record. But the 2001 recession (and the job-loss recovery since then) has robbed African Americans of much of those gains.

"The last recession has had a severe and disproportionate impact on African Americans and minority communities," according to Marc H. Morial, president of the National Urban League. In its January 2004 report on black unemployment, the Urban League found that the double-digit unemployment rates in the 14 months from late 2002 through 2003 were the worst labor market for African Americans in 20 years.

The 2001 recession was hard on African American workers both in relation to earlier recessions and in relation to white workers. Unemployment for adult black workers rose by 2.9 percentage points in the recession of the early 1980s, but by 3.5 in the 2001 recession. White unemployment, in contrast, rose by only 1.4 percentage points in the early-1980s recession and by 1.7 in the recent downturn. The median income of black families fell 3% from 2001 to 2003, while white families lost just 1.7%. Today, black unemployment has remained above 10% for over three years.

Official unemployment figures, of course, greatly understate the actual number of adults without jobs. The definition doesn't include discouraged people who have stopped looking for work, underemployed part-timers, students, or those in prison or other institutions. In New York City, scarcely half of African-American men between 16 and 65 had jobs in 2003, according to the Bureau of Labor Statistics' employment-to-population ratios for the city. The BLS ratios, which include discouraged workers and others the official unemployment statistics leave out, were 51.8% for black men, 57.1% for black women, 75.7% for white men, and 65.7% for Latino men. The figure for black men was the lowest on record (since 1979).

ELLEN SHUB

Local 7 ironworker Stephen Henry protests at a fundraiser for George W. Bush at Boston's Park Plaza Hotel, 2004.

Manufacturing job losses in particular have hit black workers harder than white workers. In 2000, there were 2 million African Americans working in factory jobs. Blacks comprised 10.1% of all manufacturing workers, about the same as the black share of the overall workforce. Then 300,000 of those jobs, or 15%, disappeared. White workers lost 1.7 million factory jobs, but that was just 10% of the number they held before the recession. By the end of 2003, the share of all factory jobs held by African Americans had fallen to 9.6%. "Half a percentage point may not sound like much, but to lose that much in such an important sector over a relatively short period, that is going to be hard to recover," Jared Bernstein of the Economic Policy Institute, a progressive economics think tank, told the *New York Times*. Latino workers increased their share of manufacturing jobs in 2002 and 2003 slightly, though their unemployment rate overall rose.

WHERE IS THE NORTH OF TODAY?

Ellen Williams was 16 years old when she left Butler County, Georgia, one of the innumerable backwoods Georgia counties with Jim Crow and "Negroes Need Not Apply," no indoor plumbing, and one-room schoolhouses. When she arrived in Boston in 1946, she thought she'd died and gone to heaven. Though she'd left her family behind, her dream of accessing just a bit of the pie seemed realizable at last.

Momma never quite achieved her dream, but she did have a job for 41 years, a job that helped stabilize our lives. When she retired in the early 1990s, that job provided her a pension she lives on today, back in her beloved Georgia. My mother worked for Raytheon and was a member of the International Brotherhood of Electrical Workers. She never had a car until the early '70s, but she said she never thought of herself as poor, because she had a good job, which gave her a sense of hope.

I understood as a girl that the job was the key to my family's security. Momma could pay our rent, buy groceries, pay the insurance man, and take my sister and me to the doctor. Raytheon was a cornerstone in my family's life.

Momma made sure that her family members in the South did okay, regularly sending money home to help out. Our three-bedroom apartment was a temporary home to at least three other extended family members who fled the economically depressed South in the 1960s. Two of them also managed to get jobs at Raytheon.

It was a struggle for women working in the plants. Promotions weren't as forthcoming, especially if you were Black. Momma said the combined issue of race and gender was a problem even in the union. But she was a card-carrying member of IBEW, and she supported the union for the job security and cushion of wealth—

Some of the largest layoffs have occurred in areas with large African American populations—in April 2004, for example, 1,000 jobs were cut at a Ford plant in St. Louis and 300 at a Boeing plant in San Antonio. Textile plants with mostly black employees have closed in Roanoke Rapids, N.C., Columbus, Ga., and Martinsville, Va. The states with the greatest number of layoffs of 50 workers or more are black strongholds New York and Georgia.

When Autoliv closed its seat belt plant in Indianapolis in 2003, more than 75% of the laid-off workers were African Americans. Many of these workers are young adults who got their jobs during the labor shortage of the late 1990s even without a high school diploma; now they have few options. "They were taken from the street into decent-paying jobs; they were making $12 to $13 an hour. These young men started families, dug in, took apartments, purchased vehicles. It was an up-from-the-street experience for them, and now they are being returned to their old envi-

---

however modest—it gave her. She said, "The union was my key. We had health care, vacation, pension, and the union protected my rights." With the union's support, she took community college courses and broke ground to become one of Raytheon's first women inspectors.

None of my daughters and nieces have worked in manufacturing jobs, and none of them have been union members. They've worked at hotels and in stores. One niece went to community college in a certified nursing assistant program and got a job at a unionized hospital—but it was a temporary contract job for six months, not a permanent union job. Now she works in a nursing home.

Many younger members of my family have moved south again because that's where the jobs are. But companies have a "let me hold my nose, I think I smell a union" attitude. Some of these young people have gone to college and found better-paying jobs—but not everyone can go to college, and the jobs for those without college now have no benefits and no union. Unlike their parents, they can't have a car or purchase a home. No matter what they do, a stable life seems to always be just beyond.

Today as I watch young people of color enter the workforce, it's almost as if we've come full circle, back to that same place my mother started out. She left a state with no opportunity for her and moved to a state with abundant good jobs. The young Black adults coming up today all live in states with a shrinking base of options for those without college educations—but there is now nowhere to move to find abundant good jobs. Where's their boost up the ladder?

— *Attieno Davis*

ronment," Michael Barnes, director of an Indiana AFL-CIO training program for laid-off workers, told the *New York Times.*

The Autoliv workers and the many other laid-off black workers are facing an immediate drop in income. Just as important, their lower income weakens their long-term prospects for accumulating assets. This may seem obvious: lower income, lower wealth. But confronted with the fact of the racial wealth gap, many analysts jump to other explanations: African Americans don't save what they do earn; African Americans have dysfunctional family structures. In fact, income *is* the most significant predictor of wealth and of the wealth gap, according to a careful analysis by sociologist Thomas Shapiro. So layoffs represent a double whammy: an immediate loss of income *and* a long-run loss of wealth.

U.S. Chamber of Commerce executive vice president Bruce Josten isn't too worried about layoffs. "We're talking about transformational evolution—successful companies remaking their own operations so they're able to better focus on what their core mission is. It's not a deal where everyone gains instantly. At a micro level, there's always going to be a community that's hurt," Josten told Knight Ridder. The communities that are hurt come in all colors, but several factors make the micro level pain more severe in communities of color.

HARD TIMES HIT BLACKS HARDER

Prolonged unemployment is scary for most families, but it puts the typical African-American family in deeper peril, and faster. The median white family has more than $106,000 in net worth (assets minus debts; the figures exclude vehicles). The median black family has less than $11,000, a far smaller cushion in tough times.

Laid-off workers often turn to family members for help, but with almost a quarter of black families under the poverty line, and one in nine black workers unemployed, it's less likely that unemployed African Americans have family members with anything to spare. Black per capita income was only 57 cents for every white dollar in 2001.

Thanks to continuing segregation and discrimination in housing, it's more difficult for black families to relocate to find work. New jobs are concentrated in mostly white suburbs with little public transportation.

When homeowners face prolonged unemployment, they can take out a home equity loan or second mortgage to tide them over. But while three-quarters of white families are homeowners, less than half of black families own their own homes. And even those black families who do own a home have, on average, less equity to borrow against. In 2001, black homeowners' median home equity was just $29,100, compared to $75,000 for white homeowners, according to an analysis of data from the Panel Study of Income Dynamics by Elena Gouskova and Frank Stafford.

When African Americans *have* been able to build savings, they have made a strong commitment to homeownership. In 2001, according to the Federal Reserve, 43% of the value of black-owned assets were in primary residences. Another 9% were in vehicles. Only 32% were in financial assets such as savings accounts, stocks, and retirement funds. In a term coined by economist Michael Stone, black homeowners are disproportionately "shelter poor"—they have insufficient money left after paying housing costs to afford other necessities. Thus one of the main risks of black job loss is foreclosure and the loss of hard-won wealth in home equity.

HISTORY REPEATS ITSELF

The term "deindustrialization" came into everyday use in the 1970s, when a wave of plant closings changed the employment landscape. From 1966 to 1973, corporations moved over a million American jobs to other countries. Even more jobs moved from the Northeast and Midwest to the South, where unions were scarce and wages lower. New York City alone lost 600,000 manufacturing jobs in the 1960s.

As today, the workers laid off in the 1960s and 1970s were disproportionately African-American. The U.S. Commission on Civil Rights found that during the recession of 1973 to 1974, 60% to 70% of laid-off workers were African-American in areas where they were only 10% to 12% of the workforce. In five cities in the Great Lakes region, the majority of black men employed in manufacturing lost their jobs between 1979 and 1984. A major reason was seniority: white workers had been in their jobs longer, and so were more likely to keep them during cutbacks.

Another reason was geography. The northern cities that lost the most jobs were some of those with the largest populations of people of color, and those inner-city areas sank deep into poverty and chronically high unemployment as few heavily white areas did.

The race and class politics of deindustrialization are also part of the story. The pro-business loyalties of the federal government dictated policies that encouraged plant closings and did very little to mitigate their effects. Tax credits for foreign investment and for foreign tax payments encouraged companies to move plants overseas. While Northern cities were suffering from deindustrialization, the federal government spent more in the Southern states than in the affected areas: Northeast and Midwest states averaged 81 cents in federal spending for each tax dollar they sent to Washington in the 1970s, while southern states averaged $1.25. Laid-off black factory workers had no clout, so politicians faced little pressure to address their needs.

As dramatic as the movement of jobs from the North to the South and overseas was the shift from city to suburb. The majority of new manufacturing jobs in the 1970s were located in suburban areas, while manufacturing employment fell almost 10% in center cities. In the Los Angeles area, for example, older plants were closing in the city while new ones opened in the San Fernando Valley and Orange County.

THE RACIAL WEALTH GAP HURTS

African-American families own just 15 cents for every dollar of wealth held by white families. The lack of family assets, along with racial discrimination, has a dramatic impact on the education and health outcomes of black Americans. People with assets are able to buy their way into neighborhoods with good schools, and they are able to pay for preventive and emergency health care. While the causal relationships between wealth and life outcomes in areas such as education and health are complex and intertwined with other factors, there's no doubt that the racial wealth gap has fundamental life consequences for black families.

When depressing statistics about black-white gaps—in school achievement, for example—are reported, commentators are quick to attribute them to cultural factors: the higher prevalence of female-headed families in the African-American community, or an "oppositional culture" among African-American teens that equates academic success with selling out. There is no question that African Americans lag behind whites in most measures of educational attainment and academic achievement. Even when family income is accounted for, African-American students demonstrate lower levels of achievement, as measured by standardized tests.

But what about when family wealth is factored in? The ostensibly race-based differences largely vanish, according to sociologist Dalton Conley. Conley analyzed data on high-school and college graduation rates as well as on retention (getting held back a grade), suspension, and expulsion of school-age children. He found that differences in family net worth are a significant explanatory variable for each of these—so much so, for example, that African Americans actually have a higher high-school graduation rate than whites at the same level of family wealth.

"Two families with the same household income [but differing levels of net worth] might have vastly different resources at their disposal to provide advantages to their children. These advantages can be as tangible as extracurricular and private education, financial support during college, or in-kind aid such as supplying educational materials," Conley explains. He also points to research showing that parents' financial contribution to their children's education expenses—whether a computer or a college fund—not only contributes directly to children's academic

The new suburban jobs were usually inaccessible for African Americans and other people of color because of housing costs, job and housing discrimination, lack of public transportation, and lack of informal social networks with suburban employers. In a study of Illinois firms that moved to the suburbs from the central cit-

achievement, it also affects children's educational expectations and, in turn, their own motivation to learn.

— *Amy Gluckman and Adria Scharf*

THE RACIAL WEALTH DIVIDE, EDUCATION, AND HEALTH

Indicator	Year	White	Black	Black as a % of White
Median Household Net Worth	2001	$121,000	$19,000	15.7%
High School Dropout Rate	2001	4.6%	5.7%	123.9%
Completed High School	2002	88.7%	79.2%	89.3%
Completed Four or More Years of College	2002	29.4%	17.2%	58.5%
Infant Mortality Rate (per 1,000)	2001	5.7	14.0	245.6%
Life Expectancy at Birth	2000	77.4	71.7	92.6%

Sources: Arthur B. Kennickell, "A Rolling Tide: Changes in the Distribution of Wealth in the U.S., 1989–2001," Levy Economics Institute, Nov. 2003; National Center for Health Statistics, National Vital Statistics Reports, Dec. 19, 2002, Table 11; National Vital Statistics Reports, Sept. 18, 2003, Table 31; U.S. Census Bureau, Current Population Survey, Educational Attainment Historical Tables, Table A-2; Educational Attainment Historical Tables, Table A-5; U.S. Census Bureau, Current Population Survey, School Enrollment Historical Tables, Table A-4. Table excerpted from "The State of the Dream 2004: Enduring Disparities in Black and White," United for a Fair Economy, January 2004.

ies between 1975 and 1978, black employment in the affected areas fell 24%, while white employment fell less than 10%. In another study, some employers admitted to locating facilities in part so as to avoid black workers. One study of the causes of black unemployment in 45 urban areas found that 25% to 50% resulted from jobs shifting to the suburbs. Even the federal government shifted jobs to the suburbs: although the number of federal civilian jobs grew by 26,558 from 1966 to 1973, federal jobs in central cities fell by 41,419. Over time, suburban white people gained a greater and greater geographic edge in job hunting.

LOOKING FORWARD

Mary Clark has been looking for work for nine months now without success. Stores get applications from hundreds of other laid-off workers; there aren't enough jobs for even a fraction of the unemployed. "It used to be that if one plant shut down, there'd be another one hiring. Now they're all laying off or closing," she says.

For years Clark had helped her grown daughter support her two small children. "Now the roles are reversed, and they help me." She has turned to charities to make ends meet, but some only give aid once a year, and others won't help a single woman without children at home. "It breaks your self-esteem to have to ask for help," Clark says.

Some of her former coworkers are in more desperate straits than she is. Some have lost their homes or gone into bankruptcy. Some people have found jobs far from home and commute for hours a day. Clark sees crime, divorce, and family violence all rising in the area.

What job growth there's been has been concentrated in the low-wage service sector, which pays less than the shrinking manufacturing sector. There's no law of nature that says service jobs are inevitably low paid and without benefits. Or that manufacturing can't revive in the United States. The recent wave of union organizing victories in heavily black industries such as health care represent one source of hope for creating more decent jobs for African Americans.

Dr. Martin Luther King, Jr. said in 1968, "When there is massive unemployment in the black community, it is called a social problem. But when there is massive unemployment in the white community, it is called a depression." The New Deal response to the Great Depression included public works jobs and a strengthened safety net, most of which excluded people of color. Mary Clark clearly recognizes what happens when there is no New Deal for unemployed African Americans: "North Carolina has people who want to work, but we don't have anyone pushing work our way. We need the mills back. We're people used to working, and when you take the work away, what do you have left?

From *Dollars & Sense* magazine, May/June 2004.

Why should middle-class people care about wealth inequality? Sam Pizzigati argues that wealth inequality hurts everyone. The concentration of wealth in the United States has promoted excessive consumption among the very rich, raising consumption standards throughout the society. As Pizzigati explains, these rising standards take a financial and psychological toll on middle-class households which must choose between "keeping up with the Joneses" and losing social status.

THE HAZARDS OF LIFE ON—AND OFF— THE LUXURY LANE

BY SAM PIZZIGATI

How wealthy have the wealthiest Americans become?

This wealthy: A half-century ago, our nation's most affluent loved to fly off to Florida for the winter. Today's wealthy don't just fly their families south. They fly their trees. One deep-pocketed Long Island couple, the *New York Times* reported in 2000, simply could not bear the thought of everyday life without palms eternally swaying. The couple had palm trees installed on its Hamptons estate, then flown, every winter, to Florida.

How wealthy are the wealthy today? This wealthy: A half-century ago, America's wealthiest spent fortunes on country club memberships. Today's fortunate start country clubs just for themselves. Billionaire H. Wayne Huizenga, the *Wall Street Journal* informed us in 1999, founded a private club with only himself and his wife as members. The club features a golf course and 68 boat slips for invited dignitaries.

Wildly excessive consumption, some analysts believe, ought to be a source of entertainment for America's non-rich majority—and nothing more. Rich people, economist Michael Weinstein has quipped, are "fun to watch, fun to ridicule, perhaps even fun to envy." But they aren't, continues Weinstein, "much to worry about."

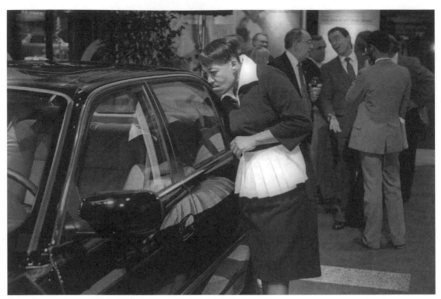

A worker at the North American International Auto Show in Detroit examines one of the luxury automobiles on display.

In fact, rich people—and their consumption patterns—are worth worrying about. What Cornell economist Robert Frank calls "luxury fever" has raised the price of the good life for everyone. In the 1980s and 1990s, as wealth became increasingly concentrated in the United States, luxuries, not basic comforts, came to define the good life. Fancy watches. Expensive cars. Vacation homes. The inevitable result: a general ratcheting up of the sense of what it takes to live a decent life—and more pressure on average Americans. More pressure on middle-income Americans to work the extra hours to make the extra income that affording a decent life demands. More pressure on low-income Americans, already straining just to put food on the table.

Apologists for America's unequal status quo have no sympathy for these pressures. "It's not the high cost of living that gets us, it's the cost of living high," argues W. Michael Cox, chief economist of the Federal Reserve Bank of Dallas. Want a less stressed existence? Just do it. The choice, conservatives assert, is up to every individual.

Some people, to be sure, have been able to jump off the treadmill that has so many Americans getting nowhere fast. But their example has touched off no mass exodus. How could it? Few low-income people can afford to work any fewer hours than they do, not when the cost of renting a decent apartment, in most parts of the United States, now demands a job that pays.

three times the minimum wage. And all working families, low- and middle-income alike, wherever they live, are still reminded daily, by the media, about the acquisitions that define the life that any self-respecting American ought to desire. Average households may be free, in theory, to ignore these luxury-driven consumption standards, but, in real life, they ignore these standards at their peril.

Take a trivial example. Studies have demonstrated that motorists who delay at a green light "are less likely to be honked" from behind if they're driving a luxury automobile, notes Boston College sociologist Juliet Schor. Most people can tolerate intemperate honking. But few can tolerate the full psychological cost of jumping off the treadmill. Once off the treadmill, people risk losing something important, their status in the groups that matter most to them. And our most valued group identity, in any society split into economic classes, usually involves where we stand, or seek to stand, in the class structure. Consumption is an important marker of that standing.

In a relatively equal nation, a society where minor differences in income and wealth separate the classes, people will be less likely to obsess over meeting consumption standards. If nearly everyone can afford much the same things, things overall tend to lose their significance. People are more likely to judge others by who they are, not what they own, in a society where incomes and wealth are distributed fairly equally.

In an unequal society, people can, of course, decline to play by the consumption rules. But most don't. After all, what right do parents have to expose their children to the "loser" label? What right do people have to force their friends to choose between them and the stigma of hanging out with a failure? So most people keep treading. And this treading will never stop—not as long as wealth remains so concentrated.

Uganda has been widely recognized for its successes in stemming the AIDS crisis, but its policies have failed to address the inequalities that make women vulnerable to the disease. Lacking basic legal rights and economic security, Ugandan women have higher infection rates than men. Jessica Weisberg looks at the relationship between women's economic empowerment and the prevention of AIDS.

ABC'S OF AIDS PREVENTION

BY JESSICA WEISBERG

U ganda is one of a handful of countries to have dramatically reduced its overall HIV infection rate in the past 10 years. It's widely viewed as a global leader in AIDS policy and is seen as a model for other countries in Africa and the global South. Its approach, known as "ABC," stands for "Abstinence, Be faithful, and Condoms"—but critics refer to it as "A-B-and sometimes-C" because of policymakers' emphasis on the first two over the third.

Despite Uganda's notable successes in stemming the AIDS epidemic, ABC has serious limitations. The policy primarily targets male behavior and fails to protect a particularly vulnerable population: married women. It offers little to girls forced by poverty to exchange one of their only assets—their bodies—for basic necessities or school fees. And by focusing on prevention, the policy fails to expand affordable and available treatments to those who've already contracted the disease—or address the core economic and social inequalities that make women susceptible to infection.

Nevertheless, President Bush has routinely cited Uganda's emphasis on abstinence and fidelity in defending its own abstinence-oriented global initiatives. In fact, the United States has adopted the ABC model as the centerpiece of its international AIDS policy.

In his 2004 State of the Union address, Bush declared optimistically, "AIDS can be prevented." Prevented? AIDS can be *treated*; with anti-retroviral therapies, widely available since early 1996, the otherwise fatal illness takes on a chronic character. By prevention, the president was referring not to a vaccine but to abstinence. He's been known to say it "works every time."

A few months after the address, in May 2004, Congress passed the President's Emergency Plan for AIDS Relief (PEPFAR). It allocated $15 billion dollars for AIDS programs worldwide over five years, with a focus on 15 "target countries" which are home to more than 50% of all people with HIV: Botswana, Côte d'Ivoire, Ethiopia, Kenya, Mozambique, Namibia, Nigeria, Rwanda, South Africa, Tanzania, Uganda, Zambia, Vietnam, Guyana, and Haiti.

Twenty percent of PEPFAR funding will go to prevention programs. (The balance goes to support services and treatment.) By law, at least one-third of those prevention funds must be used to promote abstinence. The first allocation of $100 million in PEPFAR grants for abstinence programs was announced in October. Nine of the 11 organizations that won the grants were faith-based organizations. Under PEPFAR, such groups are allowed to exclude information about contraception from their educational programs. Ambassador Randall Tobias, head of the State Department's Office of Global AIDS, has cited Uganda's accomplishments when PEPFAR's abstinence program has faced questions.

UGANDA'S WAY

Since Ugandan President Yoweri Museveni initiated the ABC program in the mid-1990s, the country has undergone enormous reductions in HIV prevalence (the percentage of individuals living with HIV/AIDS). The percent of infected individuals in Uganda has declined from around 30% in the early 1990s to 6% in 2004, according to the United Nations and the Ugandan government. Although some scientists question the validity of those specific figures, arguing that survey methodology is flawed and that the reduction in prevalence rates may in part reflect the deaths of those who had HIV in the 1990s, most agree that Uganda has secured the most dramatic turnaround in AIDS of any country to date. Museveni brought this about by aggressively raising AIDS awareness, by using radio and other modes of mass communication, involving churches and nongovernmental organizations, and by crafting messages that resonated with Ugandan culture; for example, he introduced the slogan "zero grazing" to encourage monogamy in the cattle-oriented society.

The effectiveness of Uganda's AIDS prevention and treatment policies has varied, though, with respect to gender. Far more women than men have become infected with HIV since ABC was implemented. According to the Uganda AIDS Commission, there were 99,031 new HIV cases in the country in 2001. Of these, females were three to six times more likely to become infected by HIV than males in the 15 to 19 age bracket, according to the Uganda Women's Network. In the 20 to 24 age bracket, the HIV infection rate among women remains twice as high as that of men.

There are several reasons for this disparity. Most importantly, research indicates that marriage actually increases the chance of HIV infection. In fact, the most dramatic increase in prevalence rates in recent years has occurred among monogamous married women; even as the overall percentage of people with HIV has fallen, the percentage of married women with HIV has increased. One study found that in rural Uganda, 88% of HIV-infected women age 15 to 19 are married.

For the majority of married couples in Uganda, the woman is at least six years younger than her husband. Paul Zeitz of the advocacy group Global AIDS Alliance points out that abstinence programs could "in effect be encouraging women to marry earlier," placing them at risk of infection by older husbands. "What use is abstinence, what use is fidelity if he is already infected and brings it into the marriage?" Stephen Lewis asked the *Agence France Presse*. Zeitz goes so far as to argue: "Abstinence [promotion] could be leading to a public health crisis."

Take Suzan, a 17-year-old mother from Ndeeba, a Kampala suburb, whose 62-year-old husband recently died of AIDS. She was infected by her late husband, and is unable to afford treatment.

With such large age differences between wives and husbands, Ugandan women like Suzan often outlive their husbands. When a man dies, his family typically repossesses his assets, robbing the woman of all her property and making her remaining years all the more difficult. In Suzan's case, her husband's family has taken away both their land and her child.

Another Ugandan woman, Juliet, is a 27-year-old widow with four children. Her in-laws also took away her home and land upon her husband's death. She is now hospitalized with an advanced case of AIDS, and her children are struggling to support themselves.

Women like Suzan and Juliet are overlooked by the ABC program's emphasis on abstinence and fidelity. Both women were abstinent before marriage and then faithful, but neither their own behavior nor the ABC program did anything to protect them from contracting the disease or to treat them once they were infected.

Condoms too are of little use to married women in a culture where extramarital polygamy is common but wives are unaware of their husbands' affairs. Even if women have suspicions, many adhere to patriarchal mores against vocally questioning their husbands' behavior. Those same mores also deter women from telling their husbands to wear condoms.

Harriet Abwoli, interviewed in 2003 for the Human Rights Watch report "Just Die Quietly," described her experience: "He used to force me to have sex with him. He would beat me and slap me when I refused. I never used a condom with him. ... When I got pregnant I went for a medical check-up. When I gave birth, and the child had passed away, they told me I was HIV-positive. I cried. The doctor told me, 'Wipe your tears, the whole world is sick.'"

"Women do not have negotiation power," says researcher Sarah Kalloch, who has done considerable fieldwork in Uganda. "Women do not have control over their own bodies." Kalloch describes instances of wife-swapping, wife inheritance, and widespread marital rape. Rape and domestic violence are "virtually impossible to prosecute" due to legal discrimination. "ABC is not enough for women in Uganda. They need legal rights that give them control over their bodies, their relationships, and who they marry," Kalloch says.

They also need basic economic security. Uganda's abstinence program has attempted to reach "high risk" populations such as soldiers and truck drivers, but has sent mixed messages by disparaging female HIV victims for indulgent or "promiscuous" behavior. So long as extreme economic deprivation continues to force young girls to barter for food and basic economic needs with sex, this sort of message will do little to save those who lack access to income and resources.

In the poverty-stricken northern region of Uganda, it's common for parents to force their teen and pre-teen daughters into sex work. "The mother will simply say to her daughters, 'come back with food,'" said Paul Zeitz of Global AIDS Alliance. Zeitz refers to this practice as "survival sex," since selling sex is not a profession for most of these girls, but a measure driven by dire economic necessity. Most customers are truck drivers and traveling soldiers, who prefer young girls, believing that they are free of HIV. Truck drivers synchronize their routes with school tuition deadlines (which vary by region), when girls are most likely to be waiting at truck stops for customers, according to a study conducted by the group.

When asked if abstinence programs fail women, Randall Tobias said, "One of the best ways to protect vulnerable women from HIV is to instill the 'ABC' message in men...." To Tobias, "the ABC model is a simple conceptualization of the major tenets of what happened in Uganda and can be implemented elsewhere with some local adaptation."

But as Lynn Amowitz, a Harvard medical school professor who has researched women's health and human rights in Afghanistan, observes: "The forms discrimination and stigma take differ from country to country. In some places, it's widow inheritance, in others it's that women are considered minors." Extending abstinence programs to these countries, with their distinct social dynamics, is unlikely to slow the feminization of HIV and AIDS. Without specific prevention programs that take such practices into account, the burden of HIV/AIDS will continue to disproportionately affect women.

Already, 58% of the 25 million people living with AIDS in sub-Saharan Africa are women. Adult women are up to 1.3 times more likely to be infected with HIV than their male counterparts, and women and girls now make up three-quarters of the 6.2 million young people (age 15 to 24) with AIDS. Because women serve as the primary caregivers for their own children and work in disproportionate numbers in schools, as nurses, and in social services, the feminization of AIDS ravages the socioeconomic fabric of their communities. Furthermore, the epidemic will be passed on to future generations, as the likelihood of mother-to-child transmission is estimated at 30%.

TREATMENT POSSIBILITIES

The situation is not hopeless. Life-extending drugs such as nevaripine and anti-retroviral therapies do exist. The World Health Organization (WHO) has engineered generic anti-retrovirals that will reduce the cost of therapy to $148 dollars a year, compared to an average $548 a year for name-brand drugs.

But the Bush administration has put the breaks on treatment. Under PEPFAR, all drugs sold abroad must be approved by the FDA. Even generic drugs that have already undergone the WHO's meticulous prequalification standards must be reexamined by the FDA before they are distributed abroad through the program. This rule will indefinitely delay the availability of affordable medication.

What's more, PEPFAR allocates no funds for distributing nevaripine, which at a cost of $4 per person can reduce the likelihood of mother-to-child transmission by almost 90%. Likewise, it does not fund the development of microbicides, topical products that women could use, undetected, to prevent sexual transmission of HIV. Protesters at the International AIDS Conference in Bangkok last July condemned Ambassador Tobias and President Bush for prioritizing pharmaceutical patent rights over public health needs and ideology over efficacy.

Women's economic marginalization is a global problem, and severe in the 15 countries that PEPFAR will target. President Bush's vague declaration that "AIDS can be prevented" is, in fact, correct. Prevention programs can provide a cost-effective means of gradually reducing HIV prevalence, but only if such programs address specific economic inequities that underlie patterns of transmission, dismantle barriers to economic independence for women, empower married women, and deliver messages in a culturally accessible manner. Just as important, they cannot ignore the necessity of investing in treatment for women and their daughters, who are already infected. Otherwise, women's social and economic powerlessness will continue to render them disproportionately vulnerable to the HIV epidemic. For women, the solution to the AIDS crisis is a lot more complicated than A-B-C.

Resources: "The ABC Debate Heats Up," *Africa News*, July 13, 2004; Garbus, Lisa and Elliot Marseille, *Country AIDS Analysis Project: HIV/AIDS in Uganda*, San Francisco: AIDS Policy Research Center, University of California San Francisco, 2003; "Health: Women Demand Stepped-Up AIDS Treatment, Prevention," Inter Press Service, 2002; Ingham, Richard, "U.N. Envoy Blasts U.S. for "Ideological Agenda" on Abstinence to Combat AIDS," Agence France Presse, Bangkok, July 15, 2004; "Just Die Quietly," Human Rights Watch, 2003; Klein, Alonso Luiza, "Women's Social Representation of Sex, Sexuality, and AIDS in Brazil," *Women's Experiences with HIV/AIDS: An International Perspective*. New York: Columbia University Press, 1996; Ntabade, Catherine, "Abolish Polygamy," The Uganda Women's Network; Otterman, Sharon, "AIDS: The U.S. Anti-AIDS Program," Council of Foreign Relations," November 28, 2003; <www.siecus.org/policy/PUpdates/ pdate0073.html>; "Uganda Puts Morality Before Condoms," Global News Wire, July 15, 2004.

From *Dollars & Sense* magazine, January/February 2005.

D&S co-editor Amy Gluckman and intern Allisa Thuotte spoke with Harvard epidemiologist Ichiro Kawachi in November of 2007 about the impact that rising income inequality can have on our health.

INEQUALITY: BAD FOR YOUR HEALTH

AN INTERVIEW WITH ICHIRO KAWACHI

How do you stay healthy? That's a no brainer, right? Eat the right foods, exercise, quit smoking, get regular medical checkups. Epidemiologist Ichiro Kawachi wants to add a new item to the list: live in a relatively egalitarian society. Kawachi, a professor of social epidemiology at the Harvard School of Public Health, has carried out a wide range of research studies on the social and economic factors that account for average health outcomes in different societies. Among the most novel conclusions of this body of research is that people in societies with high levels of economic inequality are less healthy than those living in more equal societies regardless of their absolute levels of income.

Health policy is at least on the table in this election year. The conversation, however, is almost entirely limited to whether and how to ensure universal health insurance coverage. The work of Kawachi and his colleagues suggests that the public debate about health really needs to be much broader, encompassing a wide range of public policies—in many cases economic policies—that do not explicitly address health but that nonetheless condition how long and how robust our lives will be. Their work traces the multidimensional connection between an individual's health and the qualities of her social world, many of which can shift dramatically when the gap between rich and poor widens.

Dollars & Sense: Your research looks at the relationship between economic factors and health, especially whether living in a more unequal society, in itself, has a negative effect on health outcomes—and you have found evidence that it does. But I want to start by being really clear about what this hypothesis means. There seems to be such a complicated web of possible relationships between income and health.

Ichiro Kawachi: Let's start with how your own income affects your health. Most obviously, income enables people to purchase the goods and services that promote health: purchasing good, healthy food, being able to use the income to live in a safe and healthy neighborhood, being able to purchase sports equipment. Income enables people to carry out the advice of public health experts about how to behave in ways that promote longevity.

But in addition to that, having a secure income has an important psychosocial effect. It provides people with a sense of control and mastery over their lives. And lots of psychologists now say that sense of control, along with the ability to plan for the future, is in itself a very important source of psychological health. Knowing that your future is secure, that you're not going to be too financially stressed, also provides incentives for people to invest in their health Put another way, if my mind is taken up with having to try to make ends meet, I don't have sufficient time to listen to my doctor's advice and invest in my health in various ways.

So there are some obvious ways in which having adequate income is important for health. This is what we call the absolute income effect—that is, the effect of your own income on your own health. If only absolute income matters, then your health is determined by your income alone, and it doesn't matter what anybody else makes. But our hypothesis has been that relative income might also matter: namely, where your income stands in relation to others'. That's where the distribution of income comes in. We have looked at the idea that when the distance between your income and the incomes of the rest of society grows very large, this may pose an additional health hazard.

How could people's relative income have an impact on health, even if their incomes are adequate in absolute terms? There are a couple of possible pathways. One is this ancient theory of relative deprivation: the idea that given a particular level of income, the greater the distance between your income and the incomes of the rest of society, the more miserable you feel. People *are* sensitive to their relative position in society vis-à-vis income. You may have a standard of living above the poverty level; nonetheless, if you live in a community or a society in which everyone else is making so much more, you might feel frustrated or miserable as a result, and this might have deleterious psychological and perhaps behavioral consequences. So that's one idea.

Another hypothesis about why income distribution matters is that when the income or wealth gap between the top and bottom grows, certain things begin to happen within the realm of politics. For example, when the wealthiest segment of society pulls away from the rest of us, they literally begin to segregate themselves in terms of where they live, and they begin to purchase services like health care and education through private means. This translates into a dynamic where wealthy people see that their tax dollars are not being spent for their own benefit, which in turn leads to a reduced basis for cooperation and spending on public goods. So I think there is an entirely separate political mechanism that's distinct from the psychological mechanism involved in notions of relative deprivation.

These are some of the key ways in which income inequality is corrosive for the public's health.

D&S: When you talk about relative deprivation, are you talking primarily about poor people, or does the evidence suggest that inequality affects health outcomes up and down the income ladder? For instance, what about the middle class? I think for the public to understand the inequality effect as something different from just the absolute-income effect, they would have to see that it isn't only poor people who can be hurt by inequality.

IK: Exactly, that's my argument. If you subscribe to the theory that it's only your own income that matters for health, then obviously middle-class people would not have much to worry about—they're able to put food on the table, they have adequate clothing and shelter, they're beyond poverty. What the relative-income theory suggests is that even middle-class people might be less healthy than they would be if they lived in a more egalitarian society.

D&S: That's what I was wondering about. Say we compared a person at the median income level in the United States versus Germany, both of whom certainly have enough income to cover all of the basic building blocks of good health. Would this hypothesis lead you to expect that, other things being equal, the middle-income person in the United States will likely have worse health because economic inequality is greater here?

IK: Yes, that's exactly right. And that's borne out. Americans are much less healthy than Europeans, for example, in spite of having higher average wealth.

D&S: But, unlike most other rich countries, the United States does not have universal health care. Couldn't that explain the poorer health outcomes here?

IK: Not entirely. There was a very interesting paper that came out last year comparing the health of Americans to the health of people in England, using very comparable, nationally representative surveys. They looked at the prevalence of major conditions such as heart attack, obesity, diabetes, hypertension. On virtually every indicator, the *top* third of Americans by income—virtually all of whom had health insurance—were still sicker than the *bottom* third of people in England. The comparison was confined to white Americans and white Britons, so they even abstracted out the contribution of racial disparities.

Health insurance certainly matters—I'm not downgrading its importance—but part of the reason Americans are so sick is because we live in a really unequal society, and it begins to tell on the physiology.

D&S: Has anyone tried to compare countries that have universal health care but have differing levels of inequality?

IK: There have been comparisons across Western European countries, all of which pretty much have universal coverage. If you compare the Scandinavian countries against the U.K. and other European countries, you generally see that the Scandinavians do have a better level of health. The more egalitarian the country, the healthier its citizens tend to be. But that's about as much as we can say. I'm not aware of really careful comparative studies; I'm making a generalization based on broad patterns.

D&S: It sounds like there is still plenty of research to do.

IK: Yes.

D&S: You have already mentioned a couple of possible mechanisms by which an unequal distribution of income could affect health. Are there any other mechanisms that you would point to?

IK: I think those are the two big ones: the political mechanism, which happens at the level of society when the income distribution widens, and then the individual mechanism, which is the relative deprivation that people feel. But I should add that relative deprivation itself can affect health through a variety of mechanisms. For instance, there is evidence that a sense of relative deprivation leads people into a spending race to try to keep up with the Joneses—a pattern of conspicuous, wasteful consumption, working in order to spend, to try to keep up with the lifestyle of the people at the top. This leads to many behaviors with deleterious health consequences, among them overwork, stress, not spending enough time with loved ones, and so forth.

Very interestingly, a couple of economists recently analyzed a study of relative deprivation, which used an index based upon the gap between your income and the incomes of everybody above you within your social comparison group, namely, people with the same occupation, or people in the same age group or living in the same state. What they found was that the greater the gap between a person's own income and the average income of their comparison group, the shorter their lives, the lower their life expectancy, as well as the higher their smoking rates, the higher their utilization of mental health services, and so on. This is suggestive evidence that deprivation relative to average income may actually matter for people's health.

D&S: It's interesting—this part of your analysis almost starts to dovetail with Juliet Schor's work.

IK: Absolutely, that's right. What Juliet Schor writes about in *The Overspent American* is consumerism. It seems to me that in a society with greater income inequality, there's so much more consumerism, that the kind of pathological behavior she describes is so much more acute in unequal societies, driven by people trying to emulate the behavior of those who are pulling away from them.

D&S: Your research no doubt reflects your background as a social epidemiologist. However, it seems as though many mainstream economists view these issues completely differently: many do not accept the existence of *any* causal effect running from income to health, except possibly to the degree that your income affects how much health care you can purchase.

IK: Yes, there is a lot of pushback from economists who, as you say, are even skeptical that absolute income matters for health. What I would say to them is, try to be a little bit open-minded about the empirical evidence. It seems to me that much of the dismissal from economists is not based upon looking at the empirical data. When they do, there is a shift: some economists are now beginning to publish studies that actually agree with what we are saying. For example, the study on relative deprivation and health I mentioned was done by a couple of economists. Another example: some studies by an erstwhile critic of mine, Jeffrey Milyo, and Jennifer Mellor, who in the past have criticized our studies on income distribution and health in the United States as not being robust to different kinds of model specifications—a very technical debate. Anyway, most recently they published an interesting study based on an experiment in which they had participants play a prisoners' dilemma kind of game to see how much they cooperate as opposed to act selfishly. One of the things Mellor and Milyo found was that as they varied the distribution of the honoraria they paid to the participants, the more unequal the distribution of this "income," the more selfishly the players acted. They concluded that their results support what we have been contending, which is that income inequality leads to psychosocial effects where people become less trusting, less cohesive, and less likely to contribute to public spending.

D&S: That's fascinating.

IK: Yes, it's very interesting. So watch this space, because some of the recent evidence from economists themselves has begun to support what we're saying.

D&S: In other parts of the world, and especially in Africa, there are examples of societies whose economies are failing or stagnating *because of* widespread public health issues, for example HIV/AIDS. So it seems as if not only can low income cause poor health, but also that poor health can cause low income. I wonder if your research has anything to say about the complicated web between income and health that those countries are dealing with.

IK: There's no doubt that in sub-Saharan Africa, poor health is the major impediment to economic growth. You have good econometric studies suggesting that the toll of HIV, TB, and malaria alone probably slows economic growth by a measurable amount, maybe 1½% per year. So there's no question that what those countries need is investment to improve people's health in order for them to even begin thinking about escaping the poverty trap.

The same is true in the United States, by the way. Although I've told the story in which the direction of causation runs from income to health, of course poor health is also a major cause of loss of income. When people become ill, for example, they can lose their jobs and hence their income.

What I'll say about the developing world is that in many ways, the continuing lack of improvement in health in, for example, the African subcontinent is itself an expression of the maldistribution of income in the world. As you know, the rich countries are persistently failing to meet the modest amount of funding that's being asked by the World Health Organization to solve many of these problems, like providing malaria tablets and bed nets and HIV pills for everyone in sub-Saharan Africa. If you look at inequality on a global scale, the world itself could benefit from some more redistribution. Today the top 1% of the world's population owns about a third of the world's wealth. So, although certainly the origins of the HIV epidemic are not directly related to income inequality, I think the solution lies in redistributing wealth and income through overseas development aid, from the 5% of the world who live in the rich countries to everyone else.

D&S: Leaving aside some of the countries with the most devastating public health problems, poor countries in general are often focused just on economic growth, on getting their per capita GDP up, but this often means that inequality increases as well—for example, in China. Do you view the inequality effect as significant enough that a developing country concerned about its health outcomes should aim to limit the growth of inequality even if that meant sacrificing some economic growth?

IK: It depends on the country's objectives. But I'd ask the question: what is the purpose of economic growth if not to assure people's level of well-being, which includes their health? Why do people care about economic growth? In order to lead a satisfying and long life, many people would say. If that's the case, then many people living in developing countries may feel exactly as you suggest: they would prefer policies that attend to egalitarian distribution over policies that are aimed purely at growth.

Amartya Sen has written about this; he has pointed to many countries that are poor but nonetheless enjoy a very good level of health. He cites examples like Costa Rica and the Kerala region in India, which are much, much poorer than the United States but enjoy a high level of health. It really depends on the objectives of the country's politicians. In Kerala and Costa Rica, their health record is very much a reflection of how their governments have invested their income in areas that promote health, like education and basic health services—even if doing so means causing a bit of a drag on economic growth.

China also had this record until perhaps ten years ago. Now they're in this era of maximizing growth, and we're seeing a very steep rise in inequality. Although we don't have good health statistics from China, my guess is that this is probably going to tell on its national health status. Actually, we already know that improvement in their child mortality rates for children under five has begun to slow down in the last 20 years, since the introduction of their economic reforms. In the 1950s and 1960s, the records seemed to suggest quite rapid improvements in health in China. But that's begun to slow down.

D&S: Certainly your research on the health effects of inequality could represent a real challenge in the United States in terms of health care policy. In many ways we have a very advanced health care system, but many people are not well served by it. What effect do you think your work could or should have on U.S. health policy?

IK: Regardless of whether you believe what I'm saying about income inequality, the most basic interpretation of this research is that there are many things that determine people's health besides simply access to good health services. We spend a lot of time discussing how to improve health insurance coverage in this country. In the current presidential debates, when they talk about health policy, they're mostly talking about health insurance. But it's myopic to confine discussions of health policy to what's going to be done about health insurance. There are many social determinants of health and thus many other policy options for improving Americans' health. Investing in education, reducing the disparities in income, attacking problems of poverty, improving housing for poor people, investing in neighborhood services and amenities—these are all actually health policies. The most fundamental point about this whole area of research is that there are many determinants of health besides what the politicians call health policy.

D&S: Besides doctors and medical care.

IK: Yes, that's right. I used to be a physician, and physicians do a lot of good, but much of health is also shaped by what goes on outside the health care system. That's probably the most important thing. The second thing is the implication that income certainly matters for health. So policies that affect peoples' incomes, both absolute and relative income, may have health consequences. For instance, I think the kinds of tax policies we have had in recent years—where most of the benefits have accrued to the top 1% and the resulting budget deficits have led to cutbacks of services to the rest of us, especially those in the bottom half of the income distribution—have been a net negative for public health, through the kind of political mechanism I have described.

D&S: It's almost as though there should be a line for health care in the cost-benefit analysis of any change in tax policies or other economic policies.

IK: Absolutely. There's an idea in public health called the health impact assessment. It's a technique modeled after environmental impact assessments, a set of tools that people are advocating should be used at the Cabinet level. The idea is that when, say, the treasury secretary suggests some new economic measure, then we can formally put the proposal through a modeling exercise to forecast its likely effects on health. Health certainly is very sensitive to decisions that are made elsewhere in the Cabinet besides what goes on in Health and Human Services.

D&S: What about global health policy? Are groups like the World Health Organization paying attention to the kind of research that you do?

IK: Yes, they are. Maybe seven or eight years ago, the WHO had a commission on macroeconomics and health, headed by Jeffrey Sachs. The idea was, by increasing funding to tackle big health problems in the developing world, we can also improve their economic performance and end poverty. That commission posed the direction of causality from health to income. In the last three years, the WHO has had a new commission on the social determinants of health, headed by a social epidemiologist from England, Michael Marmot. That group is looking at the other direction of causality—namely, from poverty to ill health—and considering the ways in which government policies in different areas can improve people's social environment in order to improve their health. I think they are due to report next year with some recommendations as well as case examples from different countries, mostly developing countries whose governments have tried to tackle the economic side of things in order to improve health outcomes.

D&S: Right now the United States is continuing on this path of becoming more and more economically stratified. Your work suggests that that doesn't bode well for us in terms of health. I wonder—this is very speculative—but if we stay on this path of worsening inequality, what do you predict our health as a country is likely to look like in 20 or 30 years?

IK: We're already in the bottom third of the 23 OECD countries, the rich countries, in terms of our average health status. Most people are dimly aware that we spend over half of the medical dollars expended on this planet, so they assume that we should therefore be able to purchase the highest level of health. I teach a course on social determinants of health at Harvard, and many of my students are astonished to discover that America is not number one in life expectancy.

I predict that if we continue on this course of growing income inequality, we will continue to slip further. That gains in life expectancy will continue to slow down. Life expectancy is increasing every year, probably because of medical advances, but I suspect that eventually there will be a limit to how much can be delivered through high-tech care and that our health will slip both in relative terms, compared to the rest of the OECD countries, and maybe even in absolute terms, losing some of the gains we have had over the last half century. For example, some demographers are already forecasting that life expectancy will drop in the coming century because of the obesity academic. Add that to the possible effects of income inequality, and I could easily imagine a scenario in which life expectancy might decline in absolute terms as well as in relative terms. We have not yet seen the full impact of the recent rise in inequality on health status, because it takes a while for the full health effects to become apparent in the population.

From *Dollars & Sense* magazine, January/February 2008.

Strategies for Change

According to right-wing pundits, taxing wealth is so crazy an idea that no respectable economist could support it. But economist John Miller shows that some of the most influential political economists of the 19th and 20th centuries did just that. So, too, did Andrew Carnegie, the 19th-century robber baron. Today's supporters of the estate tax and other forms of wealth taxation have plenty of intellectual and historical backing.

TAX WEALTH

Great Political Economists and Andrew Carnegie Agree

BY JOHN MILLER

ART BY NICK THORKELSON

A few years ago, I appeared regularly on talk radio as part of a campaign to block the repeal of the estate tax. As an economist, my job was to correct the distortions and outright hucksterism that the Heritage Foundation and other right-wing think tanks used to demonize the estate tax. In their hands, this modest tax on the inheritance of the richest 2% of U.S. taxpayers became a "death tax" that double-taxed assets in family estates, destroyed family farms and small businesses, and put a brake on economic growth.

Once that was done, assuming anyone was still listening, I was supposed to make the affirmative case for taxing wealth. But before I got very far, whichever conservative expert I was debating would inevitably interrupt and ask, "Isn't what you advocate straight out of Marx's **Communist Manifesto**?" After my first stammering reply, I got pretty good at saying, "Perhaps, but calls for taxing wealth are also straight out of **The Gospel of Wealth** by Andrew Carnegie. Do you think he was anti-capitalist?" Then it was the conservative's turn to stammer.

In fact, Marx, the philosopher of socialism, and Carnegie, the predatory capitalist turned philanthropist, weren't the only ones to call for heavy taxation of estates. Over the 19th and 20th centuries, they were joined by great political economists who, unlike Marx, were more concerned with saving capitalism from its excesses than replacing it. Let's take a look at what all these writers had to say.

KARL MARX

Sure enough, the manifesto of the Communist League, penned by Karl Marx and Fredrick Engels in 1848, called for the heavy taxation and even confiscation of inherited wealth. In the **Communist Manifesto**, Marx and Engels developed a transitional program intended to lead Europe away from the horrors of industrial capitalism—a system guided by "naked self interest"—and toward a socialist society. The ten-step program that Marx and Engels laid out for the most advanced countries began with these demands:

1. Abolition of property in land and aplication of all rents of land to public purposes.
2. A heavy or progressive graduated income tax.
3. Abolition of all rights of inheritance.

These clauses need to be understood in context of the socialist debate of the day and Marx's other writings. The first clause did not target the capitalist who directed production on the farm or in the mine, but the landowner or rentier who collected a return merely by owning the land or mine. It was their rents, not the capitalist's profits, that Marx and Engels argued should go to the state to be used for public purposes.

A heavy or progressive graduated income tax, the second clause, hardly seems radical. The U.S. federal income tax had a top tax bracket of 90% in the early post-World War II period (prior to 1962), although effective income tax rates were far lower than that.

Abolishing rights of inheritance, on the other hand, would be a radical change. The third clause targeted large estates; despite its wording, it was not intended to apply to small holders of property. "The distinguishing feature of Communism," as Marx and Engels made clear, "is not the abolition of property generally, but the abolition of bourgeois property." Marx and Engels were concerned with the social relation of capital based on the private ownership of the means of production. They saw this as the root of capitalist class power and the basis of class antagonisms that involved "the exploitation of the many by the few." The abolition of capitalist private property was surely the backbone of the **Communist Manifesto**, the most influential economic pamphlet ever written.

JOHN STUART MILL

Writing in the middle of the 19th century as well, the far more respectable John Stuart Mill also called for limitations on inheritance. Mill was a radical, but also a member of the English parliament and the author of the **Principles of Political Economy**, the undisputed bible of economists of his day. Mill regarded the laws of distribution of capitalism (who got paid what) to be a matter of social custom and quite malleable, unlike the inalterable market laws that governed production (how commodities were made). Indeed, he devoted long sections of the later editions of **Principles** to then-novel experiments with workers' cooperatives and utopian communities which he thought could distribute resources more equitably.

Mill openly attacked the institution of inheritance and entered a plea for progressive death duties. Observing the gaping inequalities that the industrial system had produced in England, he wrote that there existed "an immense majority" who were condemned from their birth to a life of "never-ending toil" eking out a "precarious subsistence." At the same time, "a small minority" were born with "all the external advantages of life without earning them by any merit or acquiring them by an any exertion of their own."

To curtail this "unearned advantage," Mill called for the "limitation of the sum which any one person may acquire by gift or inheritance to the amount sufficient to constitute a moderate independence." He argued for a "system of legislation that favors equality of fortunes" to allow individuals to realize "the just claim of the individual to the fruits, whether great or small, of his or her own industry." Otherwise,

as he famously observed, all the mechanical inventions of the industrial revolution would only enable "a greater population to live the same life of drudgery and imprisonment and an increased number of manufacturers and others to make fortunes."

HENRY GEORGE

Henry George, a journalist who taught himself economics, burst onto the American scene in 1879 with the publication of **Progress and Poverty**. This instant bestseller launched a crusade for a "single tax" on land that would put an end to the speculation that George saw as the root cause of the country's unjust distribution of wealth. Although rejected by the economics profession, **Progress and Poverty** sold more copies than all the economic texts previously published in the United States. It is easy to see why. In epic prose, George laid out the problem plaguing U.S. society at the close of the 19th century:

"The association of poverty with progress is the greatest enigma of our times. It is the central fact from which spring industrial, social, and political difficulties that perplex the world… It is the riddle which the Sphinx of Fate puts to our civilization and which not to answer is to be destroyed. So long as all the increased wealth which modern progress brings goes but to build up great fortunes, to increase luxury, and make sharper the contrast between the House of Have and the House of Want, progress is not real and cannot be permanent."

George traced the maldistribution of wealth to the institution of private property in land. To end the association of poverty with progress, he argued that "we must make land common property." But, he argued, "it is not necessary to confiscate land; it is only necessary to confiscate rent." Taxation was his means for appropriating rent, and George proposed "to abolish all taxation save that upon land values."

Henry George's single tax on land (excluding improvements) was meant to lift the burden of taxation from labor and all productive effort and place it on the rising of value of land. That rising value, he wrote, was the product of social advancement, and should be socialized. It was unjust for such gains to remain in the hands of an individual land owner—"someone whose grandfather owned a pasture on which two generations later, society saw fit to erect a skyscraper," as Robert Heilbroner, the historian of economic ideas, put it.

Progress and Poverty spawned an impressive grass-roots movement dedicated to undoing the wealth gap. Georgist Land and Labor clubs sprang up across the nation, and despite a concerted counter-attack by the economics profession, Georgists exerted considerable influence on U.S. tax policy. Most recently, Alaska adopted a George-like proposition. The state created the Alaska Permanent Fund and in its constitution vested the ownership of the state's oil and natural resources in the people as a whole. The Permanent Fund distributes substantial oil revenues as citizen dividends to state residents.

JOHN MAYNARD KEYNES

During the Great Depression of the 1930s, John Maynard Keynes, the pre-eminent economist of the 20th century, warned that a worsening maldistribution of wealth threatened to bring capitalism to its knees. Keynes was no radical. Instead, he was concerned with rescuing capitalism from its own excesses. Keynes's analysis of the instabilities of capitalist economies, and his prescriptions for taming them, guided U.S. economic policy from the 1940s through the 1970s and are still tremendously influential today.

"The outstanding faults of the economic society in which we live," he wrote in **The General Theory of Employment, Interest, and Money** in 1936, "are its failure to provide for full employment and its arbitrary and inequitable distribution of wealth and incomes." Keynes argued that income inequality and financial instability made for unstable demand among consumers. Without stable demand for goods and services, corporations invested less and cut jobs. Indeed, during the worst years of the Great Depression, this chain of economic events cost more than one-quarter of U.S. workers their jobs.

By 1936, Keynes wrote, British death duties, along with other forms of direct taxation, had made "significant progress toward the removal of very great disparities of wealth and income" of the 19th century. Still, he thought that much more was needed. In the last chapter of the **General Theory**, Keynes went so far as to propose what he called the "euthanasia of the rentier." By this he meant the gradual elimi-

nation of "the functionless investor," who made money not by working but by investing accumulated wealth. Keynes imagined a capitalist economy in which public policy kept interest rates so low that they eroded the income of the functionless investor and at the same time lowered the cost of capital (or borrowing funds) so that it was abundant enough to provide jobs for everyone. This was Keynes's plan to support continuous full employment.

Neither the United States nor Britain ever instituted such a policy, but Keynes provided the theoretical bulwark for the "mixed economy" in which public and private investment complemented one another. He showed how government spending could compensate for the instability of private investment, with government investment rising when private investment fell. The mixed economy, which moderated capitalist instability during the post-war period, remains, in the words of economist Dani Rodrik, "the most valuable heritage the 20th century bequeaths to the 21st century in the realm of economic policy."

Today, just a few years into the 21st century, a conservative movement is trying to rob us of that bequest. The repeal of the estate tax, all but accomplished in 2001, is the sharp end of the axe its adherents are using to cut government down to size. That move is sure to fuel the very excesses that Keynes worried were likely to undo capitalism during the 1930s. It will starve the public sector of revenue, compromising its ability to stabilize the private economy. By showering tax cuts on the richest of our society, it will also exacerbate inequality at a time when the richest 1% already receive their largest share of the nation's income (before taxes) since 1936, the very year that Keynes published the **General Theory**. Finally, repealing the estate tax is unlikely to improve the management of our economic affairs: as Keynes caustically wrote, "the hereditary principle in the transmission of wealth and the control of business is the reason why the leadership of the capitalist cause is weak and stupid."

ANDREW CARNEGIE

It is not easy for me to invoke Andrew Carnegie's defense of the estate tax. For over a decade, I lived in Pittsburgh, where Andrew Carnegie is remembered as the ruthless capitalist who built his public libraries up and down the Monongahela River valley with the money he sweated out of his immigrant workforce, and only after he had busted the union in the local steel mill. Carnegie actually applauded the maldistribution of wealth that Marx, Mill, George, and even Keynes railed against. As he argued, concentrated wealth "is not to be deplored, but welcomed as highly beneficial. Much better this great irregularity than universal squalor."

But despite these apologetics, Carnegie was deeply troubled by large inheritances. "Why should men leave great fortunes to their children?" he asked in his 1889 book, **The Gospel of Wealth**. "If this is done from affection, is it not misguided affection? Observation teaches that, generally speaking, it is not well for the children that they should be so burdened."

Carnegie was also an unabashed supporter of the estate tax. "The growing disposition to tax more and more heavily large estates left at death," Carnegie declared, "is a cheering indication of the growth of a salutary change in public opinion." He added that "of all forms of taxation, this seems the wisest. … By taxing estates heavily at death, the state marks its condemnation of the selfish millionaire's unworthy life." Finally, Carnegie warned that "the more society is organized around the preservation of wealth for those who already have it, rather than building new wealth, the more impoverished we will all be."

FROM HERE TO THERE

Today, whether one is out to save capitalism from its excesses or to bring capitalist exploitation to a halt, taxing accumulated wealth and especially large estates is essential. On that point, Marx, Mill, George, Keynes, and even Carnegie all agreed. But to subject wealth to fair taxation, we will need to do more than resurrect the ideas of these thinkers. We will need a spate of grassroots organizing—from workers' organizations to organizations of the socially-conscious well-to-do—dedicated to the demand that those who have benefited most from our collective efforts give back the most.

This can be done. A hundred years ago, populists concerned about the concentration of wealth forced Congress to enact the original estate tax. They also pushed through a constitutional amendment allowing a progressive income tax that raised revenue for public services. These kinds of advances can happen again.

It will be no easy task. Politics at the beginning of the 21st century are far less progressive than they were at the beginning of the 20th century. But with the greatest of political economists and even a predatory capitalist on our side, perhaps we have a chance.

Chuck Collins and Dedrick Muhammad propose tying the estate tax to a bold set of asset-building initiatives in order to mobilize support for wealth taxation.

TAX WEALTH TO BROADEN WEALTH

BY CHUCK COLLINS AND DEDRICK MUHAMMAD

For the past decade, a coalition of business lobbyists and wealthy families has waged a crusade to abolish the nation's only tax on inherited wealth. They've misled the public into believing that the estate tax falls on everyone (when it applies to fewer than the wealthiest 1.5%) and that it destroys small businesses and family farms (it doesn't). In 2001, their multimillion-dollar lobbying effort paid off. Congress voted to phase out the estate tax by gradually raising the exemption level from $1 million in 2002 to $3.5 million in 2009. The tax will disappear in 2010—millionaires and billionaires who die that year will pass on their fortunes tax-free. Its fate after 2010 has yet to be determined. The tax will return to its 2002 levels in 2011 unless Congress revisits the issue.

In a time of state budget crises, a skyrocketing national deficit, and continued cuts to the social safety net, this gift to the richest 1.5% comes at too high a price. Last year, the estate tax added $28 billion to the U.S. Treasury and stimulated an estimated $10 billion in charitable giving. Its abolition is expected to cost the nation $1 trillion over 20 years, and will only deepen the growing wealth divide.

Progressives need to respond to this polarizing economic agenda with a bold economic agenda of their own. One proposal that has real potential to galvanize public support for preserving the tax is a plan to link it to wealth-broadening policies that would directly augment people's personal and household assets. If estate tax revenues were dedicated to a "wealth opportunity fund"—a public trust fund—and used to underwrite wealth-expanding programs, the benefits of taxing inherited fortunes would be made clear: the wealth tax would directly reduce asset disparities, including longstanding racial inequities. In the process, the proposal would reassert a positive role for redistributive government spending.

DIVERGING FORTUNES

The concentration and polarization of wealth have reached levels that would have been unfathomable just 30 years ago. Between 1971 and 1998, the share of wealth held by the richest 1% of households grew from 19.9% to 38.1%. Within this top 1%, the largest wealth gains accrued to people with household net worth over $50 million. As New York University economist Edward N. Wolff has observed: "The 1990s also saw an explosion in the number of millionaires and multimillionaires. The number of households worth $1,000,000 or more grew by almost 60%; the number worth $10,000,000 or more almost quadrupled."

Meanwhile, almost one in five households reported zero or negative net worth (excluding the value of their automobiles) throughout the 1990s "boom" years—and racial wealth disparities continued to widen. According to the most recent Survey of Consumer Finances, median net worth for whites rose 16.9% to $120,900 between 1998 and 2001. But median nonwhite and Hispanic household net worth actually fell 4.5%, to $17,100, during the same period.

British commentator Will Hutton observes that "U.S. society is polarizing and its social arteries hardening. The sumptuousness and bleakness of the respective lifestyles of rich and poor represent a scale of difference in opportunity and wealth that is almost medieval."

SHRINK, SHIFT, AND SHAFT

The drive to abolish the estate tax is just one part of a much broader attack on the progressive tax system. Neo-conservatives are pushing their "shrink, shift, and shaft" fiscal agenda: Shrink the regulatory and welfare states (while enlarging the "warfare" and the "watchtower" states); shift the tax burden from progressive taxes (like the estate tax) to regressive payroll and sales taxes; and shaft the overwhelming majority of the population that depends on government programs and services like public schools, libraries, and roads.

In contrast to the period after World War II, when the federal government carried out massive public investment in wealth-broadening initiatives like the GI Bill, the last three years have seen the Bush administration and Congress institute historic federal tax cuts that disproportionately benefit the very wealthy. In five decades, we've gone from a system of progressive taxation that funded America's biggest middle-class expansion to an increasingly regressive tax system inadequate to fund the most basic of social services.

Democrats have been loath to support anything that looks like a tax hike. Many actually voted for the estate tax phase-out. But taxing wealth is good policy, and in the context of a major wealth-building program, it would make good politics.

Consider how such a program would work: By simply freezing the estate tax at its 2009 level (taxing inherited fortunes in excess of $3.5 million at a rate of 45%), the tax could initially generate $20 to $25 billion a year for a wealth opportunity fund. But in the coming decades, an enormous intergenerational transfer of wealth will occur and estate tax revenue will grow to between $157 billion and $750 billion a year, depending on which estimated annual growth rate one uses. (The lower projection assumes 2% real growth in wealth. The higher figure assumes a 4% growth rate. See <www.bc.edu/research/swri> for more information about these assumptions.) If the estate tax were made more progressive, with a top rate returning to 70% on fortunes over $100 million, it would generate enough revenue for a wealth-broadening program of GI Bill-scale.

ASSET BUILDING SOLUTIONS

How should these revenues be spent? Good proposals and pilot projects already exist to broaden assets and reduce wealth disparities. Taken together, these ideas form the modest beginning of a policy agenda for greater wealth equality.

One example is a new wealth-broadening initiative in England, sponsored by Tony Blair's Labor Party. In 2003, the British Parliament established what have become known as "baby bonds"—small government-financed trust funds for each newborn in the country. Small sums will be deposited and invested for each newborn infant, and available for withdrawal at age 18.

In 1998, then-U.S. Senator Robert Kerrey introduced similar legislation to create what he called "KidSave" accounts. The KidSave initiative would guarantee every child $1,000 at birth, plus $500 a year for children ages one to five, to be invested until retirement. Through compound returns over time, the accounts would grow substantially, provide a significant supplement to Social Security and other retirement funds, and enable many more Americans to leave inheritances to their children.

Another important program is the national Individual Development Account (IDA) demonstration project. This project gives low-income people matching funds for their savings. While the number of households that benefit from IDAs has been small to date, and the amounts that low-income people have managed to save have been modest, the idea is to ramp up this concept, through expanded public funding, to assist many more households.

Nationwide, many community-based organizations are working to expand homeownership opportunities using a patchwork of development subsidies, low-interest mortgages, and down-payment assistant programs.

A challenge for all of these wealth-broadening programs, including the British baby bonds, is that they don't have an adequate or dedicated source of revenue to bring the efforts to a meaningful scale. Here is where some interesting theoretical proposals are emerging as to how to pay for asset programs.

Yale professors Bruce Ackerman and Anne Alstott put forward an "equality of opportunity" proposal in their 2001 book, **The Stakeholder Society**. They advocate imposing an annual 2% tax on wealth, to be paid by the wealthiest 41% of the country. The wealth tax would fund an $80,000 "stake" given to every American at age 21, conditioned on graduating from high school. This notion of "stakeholding," or providing people a piece of the nation's wealth as they come of age, has a long history. In 1797, Tom Paine argued that all new democratic republics, including France and the United States, should guarantee every 21-year old citizen a wealth stake. And in the United States, land grants and subsidized housing loans have been among the ways that the government has helped individuals build personal property.

Sources other than a wealth tax could provide an additional stream of revenue for wealth building—one interesting example is a proposed "sky trust," which addresses both the need for asset building and the problem of environmental degradation. Recognizing that the environmental "commons" is being destroyed, Peter Barnes, in **Who Owns the Sky**, proposes a trust capitalized by pollution credits. Polluting companies would purchase carbon and sulfur permits and the permit revenue would be paid into the trust. Barnes compares the idea to the Alaska Permanent Fund, which pays annual dividends to Alaska residents from the state's oil wealth.

By directly contradicting the thrust of the Bush fiscal agenda, which aims to reduce taxation on the wealthiest and dismantle the ladder of economic opportunity for the rest, a wealth-broadening initiative could move progressive constituencies and candidates off of the defense ("We want just half of Bush's tax cut") and behind a positive agenda.

Such an initiative would recapture the possibility of affirmative, activist government, reconnecting the people with the potential for positive government spending—as the GI Bill and homeownership expansion programs did for the post-war generation—and dramatize the limitations of Bush's "want another tax cut?" social policy.

At the same time, this emerging movement must defend existing safety nets and investments in opportunity as a foundation for moving forward. Broadening individual wealth alone has its limitations and is not a substitute for a robust social safety net and adequately funded Social Security program.

THE WEALTH-BROADENING MOVEMENT

From a constituency mobilization perspective, the proposal solves a problem: From the outset, there has been a fundamental imbalance in the estate tax debate. The wealthy individuals and business interests that pay the tax are highly motivated to abolish it. On the other side, the constituencies that would benefit from retaining it are immobilized.

Eliminating the estate tax will lead to budget cuts and a shifting of the tax burden onto those less able to pay—but this has been hard for the public to see. Because the revenues go into the general treasury, its benefits appear remote.

LAST CENTURY'S WEALTH BROADENING PROGRAM

In the two decades after World War II, federal education and housing programs moved millions of families onto the multigenerational wealth-building train. Between 1945 and 1968, the percentage of American families living in owner-occupied dwellings rose from 44% to 63%, thanks in large part to a massive public commitment to subsidized and insured mortgages from the Federal Housing Authority (FHA), the Veteran's Administration (VA), and the Farmers Home Administration (FmHA).

Prior to the 1940s, mortgages averaged only 58% of property value, excluding all but those with substantial savings from owning homes. FHA and other mortgage subsidies enabled lenders to lengthen the terms of mortgages and dramatically lower down payments to less than 10%. Government guarantees alone enabled interest rates to fall two or three points.

Between World War II and 1972, 11 million families bought homes and another 22 million improved their properties, according to Kenneth T. Jackson's history of the FHA, Crabgrass Frontier. The FHA also insured 1.8 million dwellings in multi-family projects. The biggest beneficiary was white suburbia, where half of all housing could claim FHA or VA financing in the 1950s and 1960s. All these housing-subsidy programs helped finance private wealth in the form of homeownership for 35 million

Linking estate tax revenue to a public "trust fund" would help secure support from the vast majority of Americans who are on the wrong side of today's wealth divide by addressing fundamental aspirations of the middle class and the poor alike: the desire for a degree of economic security, a foothold of opportunity, and the means to pass along assets to the next generation.

On the ground, a nascent "wealth broadening movement" already exists, made up of community-development corporations and agencies that promote affordable housing and homeownership, credit unions, and IDAs, as well as savings and investment clubs within religious congregations. These groups aspire to broaden their programs through state and federal legislation, but are hampered by the absence of sizable funding streams. They could provide organizational infrastructure and resources for the effort.

The cumulative impact of a program to broaden wealth by taxing wealth would be to dramatically reduce, over a generation, the disparities of wealth in the United States. This agenda is particularly important for people of color who were themselves excluded, or whose parents or ancestors were excluded, from previous government-led wealth- building opportunities. (See "Last Century's Wealth Broadening Program.")

families between 1933 and 1978. The home mortgage interest deduction also benefited suburban homeowners, and interstate highway construction served as an indirect subsidy, as it opened up inexpensive land for suburban commuters.

Unfortunately, for a host of reasons—including racial discrimination in mortgage lending practices, housing settlement patterns, income inequality, and unequal educational opportunities—many nonwhite and Latino families were left standing at the wealth-building train station.

Today, racial wealth disparities persist, and are far more extreme even than disparities in income. Homeownership rates for blacks and Latinos are currently stalled at the level where whites were at the end of World War II. And while over 70% of non-Latino whites own their own homes today, homeownership rates for blacks and Latinos combined average just 48%.

The post-World War II investment in middle-class wealth expansion was paid for by a system of progressive taxation. The top income-tax rate coming out of the war was 91% (it's 38.6% today)—and the estate tax included a provision that taxed fortunes over $50 million at a 70% rate. In turn, many of the widely shared benefits of post-war spending meant that the progressivity of the tax system enjoyed widespread political support.

Wealth is a great equalizing force. Cutting across racial lines, families with equal wealth have similar educational results, economic practices, and health conditions. Asset assistance will be all the more meaningful to those who possess few or no assets, who are disproportionately people of color. Over 11% of African Americans have no assets, compared to 5.6% of white non-Latino households.

In a sense, this agenda would fulfill the next phase of the American civil rights movement. The movement was able to push through legislation that outlawed gross white supremacist practices, but the reforms never adequately addressed the economic dimension of white supremacy. Efforts such as Dr. Martin Luther King's Poor People's Campaign and the War on Poverty were never fully institutionalized. The implementation of asset-building policies that are racially and ethnically inclusive will strengthen the social fabric for future generations.

Obviously, questions about how to design a program to tax wealth in order to broaden wealth remain. Should wealth-broadening go beyond these notions of individual wealth ownership to include community wealth? For instance, public or community-owned housing units with low monthly fees may not represent private wealth for an individual, but are a tremendous source of economic stability and security. Should the wealth-creation vehicles have strings attached, with funds restricted to education, homeownership, and retirement? How should we recognize, in some financial way, the legacy of racial discrimination in wealth-building? How do we protect the ideas from being co-opted by neo-conservatives and avoid risking greater erosion of the welfare state? And what are the politically winnable forms of wealth taxation?

Wealth-building efforts need a revenue stream in order to have a real impact. Organizations working at the state and national levels to defend the estate tax, and progressive taxes more generally, need a positive, galvanizing policy agenda. In sum, wealth taxation and asset development need one another. Taxing concentrated wealth and linking the revenues to programs that will spread wealth in the next generation is the political heart of a winning strategy to expand wealth ownership and build a more equitable society.

From *Dollars & Sense* magazine, January/February 2004.

> *Closing the racial wealth divide will require that we not only take strong measures to spread wealth to the poor and middle class regardless of race, but that we also target and address the particular needs of historically disadvantaged groups. Only large-scale redistributive reforms can reduce persistent racial wealth disparities.*

CLOSING THE RACIAL WEALTH GAP FOR THE NEXT GENERATION

BY MEIZHU LUI

It was only after the civil rights movement opened up new opportunities for people of color that Judith Roderick, an African-American woman, landed a union job in the defense industry in Boston. She worked hard, and, for many years, earned high wages and enjoyed health and retirement benefits.

She saved her money and bought a home in a predominantly black neighborhood. When the local bank denied her a conventional loan to rehab the house, Judith resorted to taking a high-interest loan. She set to work on the home repairs and began making loan payments.

All of that changed in the early 1990s, when company managers, seeking to cut labor costs, laid her off.

As Judith struggled to find a job with a similar wage, the loan caused her to spiral into deeper debt. A few years later, the bank took her house.

As Judith's fortunes declined, the fortunes of many other Boston-area residents—people with advanced degrees, professional jobs, and stock investments—soared. For them, the 1990s economy was booming.

White professionals poured into her neighborhood (which, thanks to her own efforts and those of other local activists, had been fixed up and rid of crime)—sending her rent soaring to $2,000 a month. The bank sold her old house for more than four times what she had originally paid for it.

Judith, who had taken over the care of her grandson, received temporary transitional assistance from the state and managed to get medical benefits for the child. She also qualified for Section 8, a federal rental subsidy. Today, she struggles to pay her bills and keep a roof over her own and her grandson's head.

Unfortunately, Judith's story is not an unusual one among people of color. Better economic times bring small gains, thanks to immense organizing efforts and personal sacrifice. But when there's an economic downturn, racial and ethnic minorities are the first to be, well, turned down.

Whites and people of color move along different economic tracks. Because of past and present discrimination, people of color begin several paces behind the starting line and face more hurdles along the course.

Activists, scholars, and policymakers must bear this in mind as they work to address the national problem of wealth inequality. Policy strategies, whether universal (applying equally to all regardless of race or ethnicity), or targeted to disadvantaged groups, should be examined for their intended and unintended consequences for people of color.

Too often, nonwhites have been excluded from supposedly universal programs. For example, the federal government backed $120 billion in home loans through the Federal Housing Administration between 1934 and 1962, enabling millions of families to attain homeownership. But because of rules that tied mortgage eligibility to race, the vast majority of FHA-backed loans went to whites.

Strategies to close the wealth gap should ensure that minorities have equal access to program benefits, and that programs target not just the overall wealth gap, but the racial wealth gap specifically. Attaining parity will require some catch up.

What follows is a partial list of policies that, if implemented, would go a long way toward putting people of all ethnic and racial backgrounds on the same economic track.

1. HOMEOWNERSHIP

It is said that it is better to have loved and lost than to never have loved at all. The same doesn't hold for homeownership. It's worse to save and purchase a home, only to lose it.

Did Judith really have to lose her home? This question is legitimate given that the federal government props up and protects the nation's two largest mortgage lenders, the Federal National Mortgage Corporation and the Federal Home Loan Mortgage Corporation (better known as Fannie Mae and Freddie Mac). These for-profit corporations were chartered by the government specifically to provide affordable housing for low- and moderate-income people.

These corporations don't make loans directly to individuals; rather, they buy small and medium-sized mortgages from banks, package them together into tradeable securities, and sell these mortgage packages to pension funds and other investors. This arrangement encourages local banks to issue home mortgage loans in low-income communities (because they know they'll be able to resell the loan to these corporations).

Fannie Mae and Freddie Mac also work with community organizations to provide credit counseling and other information services in low-income neighborhoods.

The federal government heavily supports Fannie Mae and Freddie Mac with billion-dollar low-interest lines of credit from the Treasury, tax exemptions, and federal insurance, and the federal government could certainly require more of them.

To ensure that Fannie Mae and Freddie Mac reach their mandated quotas of services to low-income people, stronger enforcement mechanisms are needed. In addition, explicit quotas for assistance to people of color and immigrants should be introduced.

Too many immigrants still lack access to information about available housing programs. Many are unfamiliar with the process of purchasing a home, or for that matter, starting a business. This could be reversed if Fannie Mae and Freddie Mac worked with banks to target underserved immigrant communities with multilingual, culturally competent outreach programs. If financial institutions knew they would face repercussions for underserving non-English speaking households, they would design services to better meet their needs.

The 1977 Community Reinvestment Act (CRA) was a major victory for community members mobilized to combat discrimination in home financing. The law requires banks to offer low- and moderate-income people equal access to loans. However, almost 30 years after passage of the CRA, people of color remain less likely than comparable whites to be approved for home mortgages.

Because they buy so many mortgage loans, Fannie Mae and Freddie Mac wield great influence over home-lending practices nationwide. They could impose stricter anti-discrimination requirements on lenders and permit consumers who lack credit histories to submit alternative evidence of their capacity to save and pay bills on time.

Just as important, all regulated lenders should be required to take measures to protect low- and moderate-income borrowers from foreclosure through loan forgiveness programs, payment reductions, and payment waivers. For Judith, the foreclosure took away the asset she had saved to build and literally pushed her from the middle class back into poverty. Rather than profit from layoffs and other economic misfortunes that fall disproportionately on people of color, banks ought to make it their mission to build wealth in households of color and disadvantaged communities.

If Judith could have held on to her home for a few more years, she would have been able to sell the house herself when the market turned, regain her initial investment, and save enough to begin rebuilding her assets.

2. HIGHER EDUCATION

Today, higher education is more important than ever. The wage gap between those with a high school diploma and those with a college degree has continued to widen.

Yet the cost of tuition at public and private universities alike has skyrocketed over the last few decades, making college less affordable for those who most need the leg up it provides. At the same time, the mix of federally funded scholarships and loans has shifted: today, 77% of student aid is in loans, so that even those low- and moderate-income students who manage to complete college will start their work lives with tens of thousands of dollars of debt. What's more, aid has become less needs-based and more merit-based, disproportionately benefiting white and wealthier students.

In contrast to today's students, who are left to bear the cost of college largely on their own or with loans, a whole generation of white men in the post-World War II generation got help from the federal government. The 1944 GI Bill subsidized college education for white war veterans, enabling large numbers to move into professional jobs. While African-American and Latino veterans also had formal rights to GI Bill aid, discrimination by universities blocked many from actually using those benefits.

In the 1960s and 1970s, civil rights legislation and affirmative action finally opened college doors for nonwhites—but the rising cost of college, and court challenges to affirmative action, are putting those advances at risk.

We need a new education initiative on the scale of the GI Bill—a massive effort to make higher education affordable to all college-ready students. Short of that, more investment in publicly funded higher education, increased funding for Pell grants and need-based scholarships, and strengthened affirmative action programs would be a good start. Without this sort of educational assistance, Judith's grandson will be unable to pay for college and will likely find himself struggling to get by in a low-wage job.

3. NATIONAL HEALTH CARE

Almost half of all personal bankruptcy filings are due to a lack of adequate health insurance or other health-related expenses. People of color, who make up a third of the nonelderly population, comprise over half of the uninsured, according to the Kaiser Family Foundation. It's no wonder that one of the top policy priorities of the Black Congressional Caucus in 2004 is the provision of health insurance for all.

There is nothing magic about insurance—insurance is basically a system for sharing the risk of unexpected losses. It's an idea that grew from longstanding community practice. Before companies like Blue Cross were formed, extended families would pitch in when any family member had doctors' bills he couldn't pay. In other words, families shared each individual family member's risk of ill health. Today, we're going backwards—each individual is supposed to take care of his or her own costs. When one premature baby can require a half-million dollars of care, this makes no sense. A universal health program would create a huge risk pool comprised of everyone in the country. The more people who share the risk, the more efficient the program, and the more affordable the cost of care.

4. UNIONIZATION AND FAIR TRADE

Union members have higher wages and better benefits than nonunion workers. This is not because union members have better skills, but because they exert collective pressure on employers and thereby gain a greater share of the wealth created by their labor.

Heavy unionization in manufacturing industries like steel and autos gave some African-American workers a foothold of economic security in the middle of the last century, enabling them to earn decent wages, with benefits and pensions, and to begin to realize the American dream.

The decline of U.S. manufacturing began in the 1970s and is accelerating today as global free-trade agreements give corporations the "freedom" to search the world for those most desperate for work at any wage.

During the same period, employers have used increasingly militant tactics to crush the labor movement, with the help of a multibillion dollar industry of anti-union consulting firms. Today, just 13% of the workforce belongs to unions, down from a peak of 35% in the 1950s.

Strengthening workers' right to organize unions would help restart the stalled process of building an African-American middle class—and also benefit immigrant workers. Fair trade agreements guaranteeing worker rights worldwide would, over the long run, also protect workers' job security at home.

5. ASSET DEVELOPMENT POLICIES

Various proposals for asset "starter kits" have been floated in the United States and elsewhere. Independent Development Accounts (IDAs) were launched by a 1998 federal pilot program. Children's Savings Accounts (CSAs) have been established in the United Kingdom, but remain at the proposal stage in the United States.

IDAs are a form of matched savings account in which savings may be withdrawn only for asset-building investments (for example, to buy a home, start a business, or go to school). The matching funds come from the government or a nonprofit organization. IDAs are administered by community-based organizations in partnership with financial institutions that hold deposits. There are now over 500 IDA initiatives across the country, according to the Center for Social Development.

CSAs ensure that every child starts life with a trust fund. At a child's birth, an account is established for her with perhaps $500 to $1,000 of public funds. Parents are encouraged to add roughly that amount to the fund every year, matched by more public and private funds, for up to five years. When the child reaches 18, she would have around $40,000 to use for education, to start a business, or as a down payment on a home.

IDAs should be expanded and funded more heavily and CSAs made available. Both programs should have a progressive matching system to provide larger matching funds to lower-income people. This would enable someone like Judith, who has worked hard all her life but has no cushion of savings, to pass along a financial nest egg to her grandchild. (You never know—he could be an African-American Bill Gates!) Asset starter kits ensure all children, including poor children, have opportunities to develop their talents.

Asset-building programs like these must be designed with and for communities of color and immigrant communities. Many groups already form informal rotating savings and credit associations: individuals put in a certain amount of money every month, and then, in rotation, each has a turn at using all the money in the pot. These accounts have helped to start and expand many businesses, for example, in Korean communities. But "ROSCAs" face certain barriers. Most significantly, banks treat personal deposits as belonging to an individual or household, reporting any deposit of more than $10,000 to the Internal Revenue Service. Reforms should at minimum create a tax exemption for these collective savings pools, and, better still, bolster them with matching funds.

When Martin Luther King traveled to Washington, D.C., in 1963, he didn't go to tell people about a dream. He went to "cash a promissory note"—the Constitution's promise of life, liberty, and the pursuit of happiness for all. This promise cannot be kept without a government commitment to provide some measure of financial opportunity and security for all of us. For centuries, vast private wealth was created from a human rights disaster: the African slave trade. While this is an uncomfortable topic that most white Americans would just as well put under "file closed," slavery left a legacy that is still very much with us today. African Americans like Judith, whether descended from slaves or not, still suffer from the accumulated effects of the historical social and economic exclusion of their people, and the barriers to wealth creation that persist. If, as a society, we truly believe in equal opportunity for all, then we cannot claim there is a fair race being run when some people have not even approached the starting line. Call it reparations, or restitution, or a chance to catch up—or simply call it justice.

If, by the time Judith Roderick's grandchild is grown, he has access to a good education, health insurance, a financial nest egg, encouragement from an entire society cheering his success, and a guarantee that the color of his skin will not have any bearing on his future, then this nation will at last be on the road to closing the racial wealth gap.

The distribution of wealth in the United States is not likely to change dramatically unless the institutional framework for creating and distributing it is altered. A wide range of community economic development institutions, created by visionary activists and government officials across the country, is beginning to point the way.

COMMUNITY ECONOMIC DEVELOPMENT

An Alternative Vision for Creating and Distributing Wealth

BY THAD WILLIAMSON

nequalities of wealth in the United States result from an economic system that encourages individuals and corporations to accumulate private wealth for private ends. Corporations may rule the world today, but even within modern capitalist economies, there are counter-examples of public, quasi-public, and community-based institutions generating shared, common wealth and using it for shared, common ends. Although these institutions are minute relative to those of the mainstream economy, taken together they are beginning to achieve sufficient size and maturity so as to be able to suggest the outlines of an entirely different economic system.

The most obvious—and perhaps still the most important—example of publicly held wealth is the federal government itself, which owns over 3 billion square feet of building space and millions of acres of undeveloped land. Total federal assets, including land, buildings, infrastructure, and equipment, are estimated to exceed $1.4 trillion. The public also owns the airwaves, a priceless commodity. (Radio and TV networks are tenants of the airwaves, not owners.)

Recognizing just how much federally controlled wealth remains in the United States even today is important—not least because some conservatives and libertarians would like to see the government sell off (or give away) its vast assets. But these assets are of little or no direct value to the people on the wrong side of the wealth gap. The fact that the government owns vast tracts in Wyoming means little in low-income communities around the country where savings and steady work are scarce.

That's where local-scale, community-based economic institutions come in. Under the radar of mainstream media attention, an impressive array of alternative wealth-holding and job-creating institutions has evolved and matured in the past 30 years. While the mechanics of these institutions vary widely, all are built on the principle that profits accumulated through economic activity should be invested in the community or otherwise used to benefit all its members.

Perhaps the best known of these institutional innovations is the **community development corporation** (CDC). CDCs are nonprofit organizations governed by representatives from particular communities (neighborhoods, or entire cities or counties), charged with trying to stimulate economic development in depressed areas. Many CDCs focus on housing development; for example, they may buy abandoned or dilapidated properties, renovate them, then sell them to moderate-income families under special equity rules designed to keep the housing permanently affordable.

Other CDCs have branched out and established their own businesses. CDC-owned businesses both provide jobs to local residents and create a revenue stream that can be used to finance other activities (for example, anti-drug education, child care, or job training) that enhance the local quality of life.

Two CDCs that have been particularly successful in developing a portfolio of community-controlled businesses are the New Community Corporation in Newark, N.J., which employs 2,300 people and generates over $200 million a year in economic activity, and The East Los Angeles Community Union (TELACU), with assets of over $300 million. TELACU employs more than 700 people in businesses such as construction management, telecommunications, and roofing supply.

Closely related to the growth of CDCs are a range of **community development financial institutions** (CDFIs)—banks, credit unions, and microlenders that focus explicitly on assisting community development in depressed areas. Two of the best known examples are Shorebank, a network of financial institutions that invests over $150 million a year in low-income neighborhoods in Chicago, Cleveland, Michigan, and the Pacific Northwest; and Self-Help in Durham, N.C., which has provided over $3.5 billion in assistance to poor people since 1980 in the form of personal loans, business loans, and mortgages. Self-Help also played a critical role in helping pass landmark anti-predatory lending legislation in North Carolina in 1999.

In the 1990s, the federal government established the Community Development Financial Institutions Fund to provide badly needed capital support and technical assistance to fledgling CDFIs. The Bush administration has cut funding for the CDFI Fund; restoring and indeed dramatically expanding support for the fund should be a major policy priority.

Nonprofit-owned businesses are another promising model for broadening wealth. In the last decade, more and more nonprofits have sought to become financially independent by launching business activities. One is Pioneer Human Services in Seattle, a $55 million organization that employs over 1,000 people—most of whom are disadvantaged—in eight businesses, including a precision light-metal fabricator. Pioneer uses revenues from its enterprises to fund a wide range of social services for homeless people and addicts. Another example is Rubicon Programs in Richmond, Calif., which uses revenues from a bakery, a landscaping service, and a home care agency to fund about half of its $14 million budget. The funds are used to provide job training and other assistance to poor people.

Employee ownership is another powerful vehicle for broadening wealth. Over 11,000 firms in the United States are now at least partially employee-owned, and majority employee-owned firms have been successful in a range of sectors, from steel to supermarkets. Research conducted by Peter Kardas, Adria Scharf, and Jim Keogh shows that workers in majority employee-owned firms are better paid than workers in comparable traditional firms, and that these employees get nearly $20,000 more in pension benefits on average than their counterparts in conventional firms. Majority employee-owned firms where workers have full voting rights are unlikely to abandon local communities in search of a higher profit elsewhere; evidence suggests that employee-owned firms are also less likely to declare bankruptcy.

Local public enterprise is surprisingly widespread in the United States, and offers yet another way communities can create jobs and public wealth at the same time. The United States has a long tradition of publicly held electric utilities, which consistently offer lower rates and are generally credited with much more responsible and proactive environmental policies than private, for-profit utilities. The Sacramento Municipal Utility District, which employs more than 2,000 people, spends over $25 million a year on energy efficiency initiatives, discounts to low-income users, and other public programs.

The public utility approach now extends far beyond electricity. Glasgow, Ky., a small rural community, pioneered the concept of a publicly owned and operated telecommunications system. In 1988, the town's electric utility began constructing a citywide communications network to provide cable television, computer networking, and eventually high-speed Internet access. The town's citizens and businesses now enjoy high-speed Internet access and cable television service at a fraction of the rate charged by private providers: residents have saved an estimated $14 million in cable bills alone since 1989. Glasgow's investment in information-technology infrastructure has also attracted many new employers to the city.

By the year 2000, over 250 municipalities had plans in place to own and operate telecommunications systems. One of the largest is in Tacoma, Wash., which in the late 1990s created the Click! Network, part of the public utility Tacoma Power, to compete against AT&T Broadband and other private cable and high-speed Internet providers. By 2001, Click! began turning a profit and now helps bolster Tacoma Power's overall financial position. As in Glasgow, in addition to saving Tacoma residents money, the Click! network has benefited local businesses and helped bolster local economic development. Utility officials also plan to use detailed information transmitted by the network to improve energy management and encourage energy conservation by residents.

Telecommunications is not the only game in town for cities and states wishing to boost revenues and hold down tax rates by establishing public enterprises. Other cities, including Hartford, Seattle, and Oakland, run real estate businesses, using city-owned land to leverage other forms of local economic development. San Diego generates some $43 million a year in revenues from the over 400 properties it leases. Municipalities are also generating revenue through composting systems, methane recovery operations, and retail activities. In addition to the jobs for local residents and other social benefits of many of these ventures, the additional revenue they generate helps pay for vital city services.

Perhaps the most dramatic example of how a public entity can reshape the accumulation and distribution of wealth is the Alaska Permanent Fund. Revenues from oil extraction not only pay for almost the entire Alaska state government, they also fund an annual "dividend" payout to each Alaskan of roughly $1,000 to $2,000. The dividend checks are a major boost to working-class and lower-income Alaskans and are one of the largest sources of income in the state economy as a whole.

Alaska's situation is unique, but its experience points to broader possibilities for asserting public control over natural resources and other public goods in order to provide everyone a steady stream of income and—at least slightly—to level the wealth distribution. It is easy to imagine entrepreneurial cities establishing public control over downtown land and then using revenues from leasing the land to fund dividends for city residents and other public purposes. Or the federal government devoting fees from broadcasters' use of the public airwaves to particular public goods. (Reading programs funded by revenue from TV networks might be appropriate!)

Advocates for a more egalitarian society in which wealth is less concentrated have to do more than critique today's disturbing trends. They must consider alternative mechanisms for producing and distributing wealth that really do lift all boats. Community-based economic institutions have an important role to play: they provide tangible benefits to people right now, they offer models that can be replicated and expanded, and, more broadly, they highlight a new understanding of wealth as a public, shared good that can and should be used for public, shared purposes.

Predatory lenders who charge usurious rates, write loans full of pitfalls in fine print, and push homeowners into foreclosure are literally stripping the wealth out of poor communities and communities of color. Activist David Swanson shows how a grassroots campaign forced the nation's largest predatory lender to pay back the people it swindled and adopt permanent reforms.

FLAME-BROILED SHARK

BY DAVID SWANSON

I f someone told you that a number of low-income people, most of them African-American or Latino, most of them women, most of them elderly, had been robbed of much of their equity or of their entire homes by a predatory mortgage lender, you might not be surprised. But if you heard that these women and men had brought the nation's largest high-cost lender to its knees, forced it to sell out to a foreign company, and won back a half a billion dollars that had been taken from them, you'd probably ask what country this had happened in. Surely it couldn't have been in the United States, land of unbridled corporate power.

And yet it was. In 2001, these families, all members of the Association of Community Organizations for Reform Now (ACORN), launched a campaign against the nation's largest and most notorious predatory lender, Household International (also known as Household Finance or Beneficial). The 2003 settlement included a ban on talking about the damage Household had inflicted on borrowers and neighborhoods. That's one reason many people haven't heard this story—the families who defeated Household are in effect barred from publicly criticizing the corporation and teaching others the lessons they learned. (I was ACORN's communications coordinator during much of the Household campaign but left before it ended. No one asked me not to tell this story.)

In low-income minority neighborhoods in the United States, the little wealth that exists lies in home equity (see "Home Equity as a Percent of Net Worth"). People of color have made gains in home ownership during the past few decades, thanks in part to efforts by community groups like ACORN and National

HOME EQUITY AS A PERCENT OF NET WORTH, BY INCOME QUINTILE, 2000

	Lowest	Next-Lowest	Middle	Next-to-Highest	Highest
Non-Hispanic Whites	85.6	77.7	70.8	62.9	44.4
Hispanics	90.0	73.5	76.3	70.9	64.9
African Americans	NA	78.7	70.9	73.5	67.8

People's Action to force banks to make loans in communities of color (see "Minority Homeownership Is Growing"). Overall, these gains have been good for the new homeowners and good for their neighborhoods.

But low-income home ownership is fragile. Half of all extremely low-income homeowners pay more than half of their income for housing, according to the National Low Income Housing Coalition. Because low-income homeownership is not protected by additional savings, a temporary loss of income or a sudden large expense, such as a medical bill, can mean the loss of the home.

High-cost lenders—including large national operations like Household, Wells Fargo, and Citigroup, as well as small-time local sharks—strip away, rather than build up, equity in poor neighborhoods. Predatory high-cost lenders turn the usual logic of lending upside down. They make their money by intentionally issuing loans that borrowers will be unable to repay. Their loans invariably leave borrowers worse off, not better off.

Most high-cost (also called "subprime") loans are home-mortgage refinance loans. They carry excessive, and sometimes variable, interest rates and exorbitant fees. The more abusive lenders bundle bogus products like credit insurance into their loans, which accrue more interest and fees. Some lenders quietly omit taxes and insurance costs from monthly mortgage statements, causing crises when the yearly tax and insurance bills arrive. Others encourage borrowers to consolidate credit card and other debt within the mortgage, which further decreases home equity and places the home at greater risk. Loans may even exceed the value of the home, trapping people in debt they cannot refinance with a responsible lender. Hidden balloon payments force repeated refinancing (with fees each time). When borrowers find themselves unable to meet payments, the predatory lender refinances them repeatedly and ultimately seizes the house. Borrowers often have little recourse, as mandatory arbitration clauses written into their loan contracts prevent them from taking lenders to court.

High-cost loans are not made only to people with poor credit. Fannie Mae estimates that as many as half of all subprime borrowers could have qualified for a lower-cost mortgage. After British financial corporation HSBC bought Household International in March 2003, it announced that 46% of Household's real estate-backed loans had been made to borrowers with 'A' credit. But Household had made no 'A' (standard low-cost) loans. In fact, Household was a leading cause of the rows of vacant houses appearing in ACORN neighborhoods in the 1990s.

FIGHTING BACK

ACORN members didn't take this abuse lying down. Their grassroots effort against Household relied on numerous strategies, including shareholder activism, political advocacy, and the old stand-by of direct action. It offers a model for low-income communities seeking to challenge exploitative corporations.

In 2001, ACORN members launched the campaign with simultaneous protests inside Household offices in cities around the country, and then began work to pass anti-predatory lending legislation at local, state, and federal levels.

Later that year, ACORN, together with the advocacy group Coalition for Responsible Wealth, introduced a shareholder resolution that proposed to tie Household executives' compensation to the termination of the company's predatory lending practices. When Household held its annual meeting in a suburb of Tampa, Fla., a crowd of ACORN members arrived at the event wearing shark suits and holding shark balloons. The resolution won 5% of the shareholders' vote. In 2002, Household held its meeting an hour and a half from the nearest airport in rural Kentucky. ACORN members weren't deterred by the remote location—they came from all over the country by car. The protest may have been the biggest thing the town of London, Ky., had ever seen. This time, 30% of the shareholders supported the resolution.

ACORN also helped borrowers file a number of class-action suits against Household for practices that were clearly illegal under existing law, and it let Wall Street

MINORITY HOMEOWNERSHIP IS GROWING

Over the past decade, homeownership rates among minority households have risen more quickly than among other groups. In 1993, 42.6% of African-American and 40.0% of Latino households owned homes. In 2002, 48.9% and 47.4% of those groups owned homes, respectively. This reflects a more rapid rate of increase than for whites, whose homeownership grew from an already high 70.4% to 74.7%. Minorities, as a share of all first-time homebuyers, rose from 19.1% in 1993 to 30% in 1999. Indeed, minorities accounted for 41% of net growth in homeowners during that same period, according to Harvard University's Joint Center for Housing Studies.

analysts know what Household stood to lose from these lawsuits. ACORN urged state attorneys general and federal regulators to investigate the firm, and simultaneously put pressure on stores, including Best Buy, that issued Household credit cards. As a result of ACORN agitation, various local and state governments passed resolutions urging their pension funds to divest from the firm.

In the summer of 2002, ACORN members did something that really got the attention of Household executives and board members. On a beautiful day, thousands of Household borrowers poured out of buses onto the lawns of the company CEO and board members in the wealthy suburbs north of Chicago. They knocked on the officials' doors, speaking directly to the people whose policies had hurt them from a distance. When forced to leave, ACORN members plastered "Wanted" posters all over the neighborhood.

Through all of this, ACORN worked the media. It kept a database of borrowers' stories, and put reporters in touch with them, generating several hundred national print articles and television and radio spots. It also maintained an enormous website about Household (which has since been removed as part of the gag-order agreement).

Meanwhile, ACORN Housing Corporation, a nonprofit loan-counseling agency created by ACORN, helped many borrowers cancel rip-off services, such as credit insurance, that were built into their loans, and, when possible, refinance out of their Household loans altogether.

HOUSEHOLD'S CONCESSIONS

For more than two years, a small handful of ACORN staff organized thousands of members in an unrelenting effort, until Household International could no longer sustain the negative attention, shareholder discontent, and legal and regulatory pressures. In early 2003, the lender agreed to pay $489 million in restitution to borrowers through the 50 state attorneys general. The company later agreed to pay millions more to ACORN to fund new financial literacy programs. This was one of the largest consumer settlements in history, but it amounted to only a fraction of what Household had taken from people, and it could not undo all the damage done to families who had lost their homes. In addition to the payments, the company will:

- Ensure that new loans actually provide a benefit to consumers prior to issuing the loans.
- Reform and improve disclosures to consumers.
- Reimburse states to cover the costs of the investigations into Household's practices.
- Limit prepayment penalties to the first two years of a loan.
- Limit points and origination fees, upfront charges built into the loan, to 5%. (A "point" is one percentage point of the loan amount.)

ACORN members from 27 states protest Wells Fargo's predatory lending practices as part of the ACORN national convention in Los Angeles, 2004.

- Eliminate "piggyback" second mortgages. (When Household issued home loans, it would simultaneously issue a second, smaller, loan at an even higher rate. It often labeled these second loans "lines of credit" in order to avoid federal regulations that limit the rate that can be charged.)
- Implement a "Foreclosure Avoidance Program" to provide relief to borrowers who are at risk of losing their homes due to delinquent payments (for example, reducing interest rates, waiving unpaid late charges, deferring interest, and reducing the principal).

ACORN-led efforts won legislative and corporate reforms as well. Several cities and states (including Arkansas, California, New Mexico, New Jersey, and New York) have banned abusive practices that were once routine. One practice ACORN targeted aggressively was "single-premium credit insurance," a nearly useless and overpriced insurance policy that predatory lenders added to many loans (often falsely describing it as a requirement or failing to tell borrowers it had been included). In 2002, Household and other major lenders announced they would drop the product. This was one of several corporate reforms ACORN won during the course of the campaign.

This campaign demonstrates that a well-organized grassroots effort can combat corporate exploitation and extract significant concessions. By pursuing different strategies at once, ACORN repeatedly hit Household with the unexpected, and put it on the defensive. The outcome is good news for low-income neighborhoods, and bad news for Wells Fargo, the predatory lender who is next on ACORN's list.

From *Dollars & Sense* magazine, July/August 2004.

UNIONS AND THE WEALTH DIVIDE

An Interview with Bill Fletcher

BY MEIZHU LUI

Meizhu Lui: When we think of unions, we think about their role in increasing wages. Have they also played a role in increasing the wealth of union members?

Bill Fletcher: If it were up to employers, they would pay subsistence wages, only enough to keep workers alive and able to reproduce the workforce. Unions for the most part succeeded in winning wages above the subsistence level, so that workers could save money, buy homes, and achieve "middle-class" lifestyles. Unfortunately, many unions explicitly excluded people of color in their constitutions—some up until the 1950s—and this exclusion contributed to the racial economic and wealth gap. Later, as people of color not only were allowed to join unions but infused new energy into the labor movement—African Americans joining public sector unions in the 1960s and '70s as part of the civil rights movement, and new immigrants today—they also were able to begin to build up some savings. Union women as a group have also benefited.

ML: Are there other more explicit wealth-creation activities that unions engaged in? For example, when did they start thinking about the need for pensions—assets for retirement?

BF: The pension idea dates all the way back to Samuel Gompers, who was the first president of the American Federation of Labor (from 1886 to 1924). In the 1800s, early unions and guilds provided burial funds for their members, since burial required more savings than some workers could probably muster. In the early 20th

211

century, this old practice went in two new directions. One led toward health insurance, the other toward pensions. Instead of just negotiating wages for actual work hours, labor leaders began to ask employers to create pension funds so that wages would continue into retirement. This kind of asset is important, so that retired workers don't have to spend down their savings, but can still count on income, and can pass along their savings to their children. Pensions allow for the accumulation of family assets over generations.

ML: Originally, unions negotiated "defined benefit" pension plans, where employers committed to pay workers a certain percentage of their income in retirement for the rest of their lives, regardless of the number of years they might live. Workers could calculate their yearly retirement incomes. More recently, the majority of employer pension plans are 401(k)s, or "defined contribution" plans, where employers contribute a certain percent of their workers' wages into investment plans. Workers are at the mercy of the stock market; if stocks go down, their retirement incomes go down as well. What has the unions' role been in this change?

BF: This change began to occur in the 1980s, when Reagan launched an all-out attack on organized labor. Labor did fight back, but lost this battle. It is important to note that nonunion workers were the real losers as unions' power weakened. Today, guaranteed benefit plans are rare; and defined contribution plans compromise economic security for older people. This lesson came home during the Enron scandal.

ML: You mention health insurance as the other "line" coming out of the old burial fund idea. Health insurance paid for by employers was important for workers' economic security; as we know today, most people who lose all their assets do so because they are uninsured and a health crisis occurs in their family.

BF: Yes. For many, this is the most important benefit in their union contracts, especially as health costs rise. Going back to the early labor movement, Gompers felt that every economic benefit should come through the union. Other unions, particularly those in the CIO (Congress of Industrial Organizations), which organized not by craft but by entire workplaces and industries, took up the fight for employers to pay for health insurance. The Gompers notion can work when there are multiple employers and union density is high. But it misses the point that it is a legitimate role of government to provide health care security for its people—that is, national health insurance. Gompers would have been well liked by some of our anti-government, free-market apologists today!

ML: Interesting image—Grover Norquist and Sam Gompers, hand in hand!

BF: If labor had used its clout to bring about a national health plan as happened in a number of European countries, and the uninsured didn't have to spend all their assets for inevitable health crises, then workers as a whole would hold more wealth.

ML: There was an interesting example in Boston where the Hotel Employees and Restaurant Employees union (HERE) won a housing benefit for its workers. How did that happen?

BF: Local 26 in Boston had to change the National Labor Relations Act in order to have the right to bargain around creating an employer-union housing benefit plan. In 1988, they negotiated the first collectively bargained housing trust fund with Boston hotel owners. They then proceeded to take on the federal government, and won the right to bargain such an agreement in 1990—the cart pushing the horse! With union membership as an organizing base and with the support of other community activists, they were able to kick Fleet Bank's butt around its predatory lending practices through research reports and court suits, and by embarrassing the CEO wherever he went. Predatory lending involves charging exorbitant interest rates with the intention of stealing the homes of long-term lower-income homeowners who are property-rich but cash-poor. The settlement of the case against Fleet not only brought a huge amount of money into their loan fund, but set up the Neighborhood Assistance Corporation of America (NACA) to administer the funds. Today, NACA has over $10 billion and provides mortgages with no down payment, no closing costs, no fees, and a below-market interest rate.

Working-class people far beyond Boston are benefiting from the efforts of one union's feisty and far-sighted membership. Since Local 26 has a membership of many people of color and immigrants, they also confronted racial wealth inequality. First, they stopped many discriminatory lending practices which had targeted people of color, for example, by charging them disproportionate interest rates for bank mortgages. Second, they were successful in building wealth for their members, even those who were at the lowest ends of the income and asset scales, who do not have parents who can "gift" them the down payment money. Owning a home became a real possibility for many who would not have been able to do so without this union benefit.

ML: Given the significance of this win, are other unions also using the NLRA to bargain for housing benefits?

BF: Strangely enough, I have not heard of this model spreading to other places. But it is there for unions to take advantage of; the groundwork has been done.

ML: As pension funds have grown into huge pools of dollars, some unions have been using those funds to increase assets for community people. I believe that a construction trade union used pension funds to build affordable housing.

BF: Yes. The Bricklayers Union was one that did build a number of units of housing in Boston. This was great—a way to bridge community and union—but it was on a small scale. A question for labor might be how to bring this kind of project to scale.

An interesting initiative begun a few years ago is the "labor/community strategic partnerships" initiative of the AFL-CIO. The program is called HIT, the Housing Investment Trust, and it uses the clout of union pension fund dollars to be a catalyst for building affordable housing. By bringing investment dollars to the table, and getting matches from local governments and businesses, they have built over 60,000 units of new affordable housing. The projects also have provided 50,000 jobs in the construction industry, and of course, the workers have to be union! But in any case, the AFL-CIO is definitely getting beyond the Gompers model, and thinking about how to provide benefits for more working people than just their own members.

ML: Those pension funds are a potential source of a lot of power!

BF: Yes. Unions have in the last 20 years or so started to develop strategies that use their massive pension funds for investments that can affect corporate behavior and for social change. One of the main architects of this is Randy Barber from the Center for Economic Organizing in Washington, D.C.; he's a real visionary. Pension funds represent the collective wealth of many workers. If used creatively, there is great potential for unions to use this wealth—just as the rich use their dollars—to gain power. Hopefully, unions can use their own wealth to influence the redistribution of wealth in this country, including to close the racial wealth divide. That's a stretch today but hey, keep hope alive!

Pension wealth is one of the most powerful and underused weapons of working people. Most pension wealth is invested by the financial industry with no concern for the impact on working people or their communities. But among union and public-employee pension trustees, there's a growing movement to direct a portion of workers' pension wealth toward worker-friendly investments that bolster the labor movement, save jobs, and build affordable housing.

LABOR'S CAPITAL

Putting Pension Wealth to Work for Workers

BY ADRIA SCHARF

Pension fund assets are the largest single source of investment capital in the country. Of the roughly $17 trillion in private equity in the U.S. economy, $6 to 7 trillion is held in employee pensions. About $1.3 trillion is in union pension plans (jointly trusteed labor-management plans or collectively bargained company-sponsored plans) and $2.1 trillion is in public employee pension plans. Several trillion more are in defined contribution plans and company-sponsored defined benefit plans with no union representation. These vast sums were generated by—and belong to—workers; they're really workers' deferred wages.

Workers' retirement dollars course through Wall Street, but most of the capital owned *by* working people is invested with no regard *for* working people or their communities. Pension dollars finance sweatshops overseas, hold shares of public companies that conduct mass layoffs, and underwrite myriad anti-union low-road corporate practices. In one emblematic example, the Florida public pension system bought out the Edison Corporation, the for-profit school operator, in November 2003, with the deferred wages of Florida government employees—including public school teachers. (With just three appointed trustees, one of whom is Governor Jeb Bush, Florida is one of the few states with no worker representation on the board of its state-employee retirement fund.)

The custodians of workers' pensions—plan trustees and investment managers—argue that they are bound by their "fiduciary responsibility" to consider only narrow financial factors when making investment decisions. They maintain they have a singular obligation to maximize financial returns and minimize financial risk for beneficiaries—with no regard for broader concerns. But from the perspective of the teachers whose dollars funded an enterprise that aims to privatize their jobs, investing in Edison, however promising the expected return (and given Edison's track record, it wasn't very promising!), makes no sense.

A legal concept enshrined in the 1974 Employee Retirement Income Security Act (ERISA) and other statutes, "fiduciary responsibility" does constrain the decision-making of those charged with taking care of other people's money. It obligates fiduciaries (e.g., trustees and fund managers) to invest retirement assets for the exclusive benefit of the pension beneficiaries. According to ERISA, fiduciaries must act with the care, skill, prudence, and diligence that a "prudent man" would use. Exactly what that means, though, is contested.

The law does *not* say that plan trustees must maximize short-term return. It does, in fact, give fiduciaries some leeway to direct pension assets to worker- and community-friendly projects. In 1994, the U.S. Department of Labor issued rule clarifications that expressly permit fiduciaries to make "economically targeted investments" (ETIs), or investments that take into account collateral benefits like good jobs, housing, improved social service facilities, alternative energy, strengthened infrastructure, and economic development. Trustees and fund managers are free to consider a double bottom line, prioritizing investments that have a social pay-off so long as their expected risk-adjusted financial returns are equal to other, similar, investments. Despite a backlash against ETIs from Newt Gingrich conservatives in the 1990s, Clinton's Labor Department rules still hold.

Nevertheless, the dominant mentality among the asset management professionals who make a living off what United Steelworkers president Leo Gerard calls "the deferred-wage food table" staunchly resists considering any factors apart from financial risk and return.

This is beginning to change in some corners of the pension fund world, principally (no surprise) where workers and beneficiaries have some control over their pension capital. In jointly managed union defined-benefit (known as "Taft-Hartley") plans and public-employee pension plans, the ETI movement is gaining ground. "Taft-Hartley pension trustees have grown more comfortable with economically targeted investments as a result of a variety of influences, one being the Labor Department itself," says Robert Pleasure of the Center for Working Capital, an independent capital stewardship-educational institute started by the AFL-CIO. Concurrently, more public pension fund trustees have begun adopting ETIs that promote housing and economic development within state borders. Most union and public pension trustees now understand that, as long as they follow a careful process and protect returns, ETIs do not breach their fiduciary duty, and may in certain cases actually be sounder investments than over-inflated Wall Street stocks.

SAVING JOBS: HEARTLAND LABOR CAPITAL NETWORK

During the run-up of Wall Street share prices in the 1990s, investment funds virtually redlined basic industries, preferring to direct dollars into hot public technology stocks and emerging foreign markets, which despite the rhetoric of fiduciary responsibility were often speculative, unsound, investments. Even most collectively bargained funds put their assets exclusively in Wall Street stocks, in part because some pension trustees feared that if they didn't, they could be held liable. (During an earlier period, the Labor Department aggressively pursued union pension trustees for breaches of fiduciary duty. In rare cases where trustees were found liable, their personal finances and possessions were at risk.) But in the past five years, more union pension funds and labor-friendly fund managers have begun directing assets into investments that bolster the "heartland" economy: worker-friendly private equity, and, wherever possible, unionized industries and companies that offer "card-check" and "neutrality." ("Card-check" requires automatic union recognition if a majority of employees present signed authorization cards; "neutrality" means employers agree to remain neutral during organizing campaigns.)

The Heartland Labor Capital Network is at the center of this movement. The network's Tom Croft says he and his allies want to "make sure there's an economy still around in the future to which working people will be able to contribute." Croft estimates that about $3 to $4 billion in new dollars have been directed to worker-friendly private equity since 1999—including venture capital, buyout funds, and "special situations" funds that invest in financially distressed companies, saving jobs and preventing closures. Several work closely with unions to direct capital into labor-friendly investments.

One such fund, New York-based KPS Special Situations, has saved over 10,000 unionized manufacturing jobs through its two funds, KPS Special Situations I and II, according to a company representative. In 2003, St. Louis-based Wire Rope Corporation, the nation's leading producer of high carbon wire and wire rope products, was in bankruptcy with nearly 1,000 unionized steelworker jobs in jeopardy. KPS bought the company and restructured it in collaboration with the United Steelworkers International. Approximately 20% of KPS's committed capital is from Taft-Hartley pension dollars; as a result, the Wire Rope transaction included some union pension assets.

The Heartland Labor Capital Network and its union partners want to expand this sort of strategic deployment of capital by building a national capital pool of "Heartland Funds" financed by union pension assets and other sources. These funds have already begun to make direct investments in smaller worker-friendly manufacturing and related enterprises; labor representatives participate alongside investment experts on their advisory boards.

"It's simple. Workers' assets should be invested in enterprises and construction projects that will help to build their cities, rebuild their schools, and rebuild America's infrastructure," says Croft.

"CAPITAL STEWARDSHIP": THE AFL-CIO

For the AFL-CIO, ETIs are nothing new. Its Housing Investment Trust (HIT), formed in 1964, is the largest labor-sponsored investment vehicle in the country that produces collateral benefits for workers and their neighborhoods. Hundreds of union pension funds invest in the $2 billion trust, which leverages public financing to build housing, including low-income and affordable units, using union labor. HIT, together with its sister fund the Building Investment Trust (BIT), recently announced a new investment program that is expected to generate up to $1 billion in investment in apartment development and rehabilitation by 2005 in targeted cities including New York, Chicago, and Philadelphia. The initiative will finance thousands of units of housing and millions of hours of union construction work. HIT and BIT require owners of many of the projects they help finance to agree to card-check recognition and neutrality for their employees.

HIT and BIT are two examples of union-owned investment vehicles. There are many others—including the LongView ULTRA Construction Loan Fund, which finances projects that use 100% union labor; the Boilermakers' Co-Generation and Infrastructure Fund; and the United Food and Commercial Workers' Shopping Center Mortgage Loan Program—and their ranks are growing.

Since 1997, the AFL-CIO and its member unions have redoubled their efforts to increase labor's control over its capital through a variety of means. The AFL-CIO's Capital Stewardship Program promotes corporate governance reform, investment manager accountability, pro-worker investment strategies, international pension fund cooperation, and trustee education. It also evaluates worker-friendly pension funds on how well they actually advance workers' rights, among other criteria. The Center for Working Capital provides education and training to hundreds of union and public pension fund trustees each year, organizes conferences, and sponsors research on capital stewardship issues including ETIs.

PUBLIC PENSION PLANS JOIN IN

At least 29 states have ETI policies directing a portion of their funds, usually less than 5%, to economic development within state borders. The combined public pension assets in ETI programs amount to about $55 billion, according to a recent report commissioned by the Vermont state treasurer. The vast majority of these ETIs are in residential housing and other real estate.

The California Public Employees' Retirement System (CalPERS) is an ETI pioneer among state pension funds. The single largest pension fund in the country, it has $153.8 billion in assets and provides retirement benefits to over 1.4 million members. In the mid-1990s, when financing for housing construction dried up in California, CalPERS invested hundreds of millions of dollars to finance about 4% of the state's single-family housing market. Its ETI policy is expansive. While it requires economically targeted investments earn maximum returns for their level of risk and fall within geographic and asset-diversification guidelines, CalPERS also considers the investments' benefits to its members and to state residents, their job creation potential, and the economic and social needs of different groups in the state's population. CalPERS directs about 2% of its assets—about $20 billion as of May 2001—to investments that provide collateral social benefits. It also requires construction and maintenance contractors to provide decent wages and benefits.

Other state pension funds have followed CalPERs' lead. In 2003, the Massachusetts treasury expanded its ETI program, which is funded by the state's $32 billion pension. Treasurer Timothy Cahill expects to do "two dozen or more" ETI investments in 2004, up from the single investment made in 2003, according to the *Boston Business Journal*. "It doesn't hurt our bottom line, and it helps locally," Cahill explained. The immediate priority will be job creation. Washington, Wisconsin, and New York also have strong ETI programs.

In their current form and at their current scale, economically targeted investments in the United States are not a panacea. Pension law does impose constraints. Many consultants and lawyers admonish trustees to limit ETIs to a small portion of an overall pension investment portfolio. And union trustees must pursue ETIs carefully, following a checklist of "prudence" procedures, to protect themselves from liability. The most significant constraint is simply that these investments must generate risk-adjusted returns equal to alternative investments—this means that many deserving not-for-profit efforts and experiments in economic democracy are automatically ruled out. Still, there's more wiggle room in the law than has been broadly recognized. And when deployed strategically to bolster the labor movement, support employee buyouts, generate good jobs, or build affordable housing, economically targeted investments are a form of worker direction over capital whose potential has only begun to be realized. And (until the day that capital is abolished altogether) that represents an important foothold.

As early as the mid-1970s, business expert Peter Drucker warned in *Unseen Revolution* of a coming era of "pension-fund socialism" in which the ownership of massive amounts of capital by pension funds would bring about profound changes to the social and economic power structure. Today, workers' pensions prop up the U.S.

economy. They're a point of leverage like no other. Union and public pension funds are the most promising means for working people to shape the deployment of capital on a large scale, while directing assets to investments with collateral benefits. If workers and the trustees of their pension wealth recognize the power they hold, they could alter the contours of capitalism.

From *Dollars & Sense* magazine, September/October 2005.

Are communities powerless against mega-corporations? Adam Sacks describes a struggle between corporate agribusiness and small towns in rural Pennsylvania, in which citizens have organized to protect their environment, their economy, and the social fabric of their community against factory pig farms and the politicians who love them.

RIGHTS FIGHT

BY ADAM SACKS

> They hang the man and flog the woman,
> Who steals the goose from off the common,
> Yet let the greater villain loose,
> That steals the common from the goose.
> —*17th-century English protest rhyme*

In the late 1990s, life was getting tough for agribusiness in North Carolina. Over the previous decade or so, the state had risen from the number 15 hog producer in the country to number two. With more hogs than people, North Carolina's largely African-American Duplin and Sampson counties were the two largest pork-producing counties in the nation. By 1997, pollution, public health, and environmental justice problems were causing such widespread outcry that the state imposed a moratorium on all new pig farms that would last for almost six years. Soon factory farm corporations went on the prowl for greener pastures, so to speak.

Central Pennsylvania looked like an attractive target. It has an excellent system of roadways and accessible distribution centers. Land is relatively cheap. Many small farmers were, as usual, struggling. The Pennsylvania Farm Bureau, nominally a farmer advocacy organization, is firmly in the pocket of big agribusiness and highly influential in the state legislature. The central part of the state is rural, with township populations ranging from several hundred to a few thousand. This means there were no zoning regulations—the townships didn't think they needed them—to get in the way of large-scale hog farming. Rural township governments had no idea how to deal with powerful businesses. In short, the townships between Philadelphia in the east and Pittsburgh in the west were sitting ducks. Or so the ag boys thought.

ONSLAUGHT

The phone was ringing off the hook in the office of Thomas Linzey, a young attorney at the nonprofit organization he founded, the Community Environmental Legal Defense Fund (CELDF). Three years out of law school, Linzey was one of a rare breed of lawyer dedicated full time to public interest law. Idealistic and determined, he had set up a regulatory practice to help communities appeal permits issued to businesses they didn't want in their backyards. And he was good at it. In hearing after hearing, he pointed out defects in permit applications and convinced regulators and judges that these irresponsible corporate entities shouldn't be allowed to ply their noxious trades. Permits were rescinded, communities celebrated victories, Linzey and CELDF won prizes and kudos and were invited to Environment Day at the White House as guests of Vice President Al Gore. But there was a problem.

A few months after a community victory, the heretofore unpermitted corporation would return, permit in hand, ready to do business. What had happened? The only relevant issue in the regulatory appeal, whether all the bureaucratic dotted i's and crossed t's were in place, was resolved: the community had unearthed the problems with the permit, and the corporation proceeded to fix them. By challenging the permit and exposing the defects, the community had unwittingly done the corporation's work for free. Since townships of a few thousand people generally don't stand much of a chance against corporate legal budgets, practically speaking there was no further recourse.

Linzey had been puzzling over the battles won and wars lost in his first three years when the factory farm onslaught began. Local township officials, farmers, and concerned citizens were calling him, desperate, saying, "They're telling us that all we can do is regulate manure odor—but we don't want these toxic and destructive factory farms in our community *at all!* Please help us figure this out."

Factory pig farm operations produce tons of manure a day, which ends up in lakes, rivers, and drinking water. They not only seriously damage the environment—they also wreak havoc on the local economy and put independent family farmers out of business. Struggling farmers enter into one-sided output contracts with agribusiness corporations, agreeing to sell only to them. On their face, these contracts appear to be a way of guaranteeing a small farmer a market. But farmers soon find themselves trapped. The contracts hook them into expensive capital improvements that can cost hundreds of thousands of dollars, often paid for with loans issued by the corporations themselves. The contracts give the corporation ownership over all of the farm's animals—unless some die, in which case responsibility for the carcasses reverts to the farmers for disposal. And they allow the corporations to evade responsibility for environmental damage, since the giant firms don't technically own the property.

The result is an unequal arrangement in which the farmers own their land, but are so in hock to their corporate buyers, and utterly dependent on them, that they

TAKING THE CONSTITUTION AWAY FROM CORPORATIONS

In 2002, Licking and Porter Townships in Clarion County, Pa., passed ordinances that strip corporations of their constitutional rights. The ordinances arose from residents' concern about a corporation suing them over their right to regulate sewage sludge. By abolishing corporate constitutional rights, the township eliminated the corporation's right to go to court against it, in effect returning the corporation to its status in the late 18th and early 19th centuries, before the courts began granting corporations the constitutional rights of people.

The ordinance reads, in part:

An Ordinance by the Second Class Township of _____, _____ County, Pennsylvania, Eliminating Legal Personhood Privileges from Corporations Doing Business Within _____ Township to Vindicate Democratic Rights

Section 5. Statement of Law. Corporations shall not be considered to be "persons" protected by the Constitution of the United States or the Constitution of the Commonwealth of Pennsylvania within the Second Class Township of _____, _____ County, Pennsylvania.

effectively lose control of their operations. The corporate party can unilaterally terminate the contract at any time, leaving the farmers to bail themselves out if they can. Most lose everything.

Like the township officials, Linzey was at a loss at first, but figured it was worth looking around to see what the possibilities were. He discovered that nine states, from Oklahoma in 1907 to South Dakota in 1998, had passed laws or constitutional amendments against corporate ownership or control of farms. Some of these laws contained exceptions for incorporated farms that were family owned and operated on a daily basis by one or more family members. That is, they didn't affect real farmers—people who wake up before sunrise, mingle with cows and pigs, and get their hands and boots dirty—but did cover the farms owned by corporate executives. Linzey converted text from these existing laws into a "Farm Ownership Ordinance" that many townships considered, and some passed. The ordinance template stated: "No corporation or syndicate may acquire, or otherwise obtain an interest, whether legal, beneficial, or otherwise, in any real estate used for farming in this Township, or engage in farming."

WHAT HAPPENED TO OUR LOCAL DEMOCRACY?

Although the citizens of rural Pennsylvania townships would be the last to call themselves activists or revolutionaries, their battles to preserve the health and integrity of their lives and homes against corporate assault have the makings of a sociopolitical earthquake. These mostly conservative Republican communities found themselves asking what had happened to their democracy.

How did it come to pass that a small handful of corporate directors a thousand miles away got to decide what takes place in their backyards? Why does the democratic decision of hundreds or thousands of citizens to keep out dangerous and destructive activity get trumped by distant interests whose only concern is how much of the community's wealth they can run away with, regardless of the collateral damage to the environment, economy, and social fabric of the community? As one town supervisor put it, "What the hell are rights of corporations?"

In short, the townspeople began having conversations about what it means to be a sovereign people, with inalienable rights, whose government operates only with their consent—conversations that hadn't been heard in the town commons or around kitchen tables for a long, long time. Organized by community leaders among friends and neighbors who had never before been active in civic affairs, their meetings took various forms. There were formal county-wide gatherings of hundreds of people, small conclaves in living rooms, and backyard barbecue chats. Armed with copies of the Constitution and Declaration of Independence, they asked and tried to answer basic questions, such as: What is a democracy? What are the people's rights, responsibilities, and privileges? What is the law? Who makes it and who enforces it? What are the courts? Whose side are they on?

Citizens realized that the issue was not really the factory farm or the sludged field. The issue was who has the right to decide what happens in our communities: we the people, or the corporations that have taken over our economy and our government for the benefit of the very few to the detriment of the rest of us. Farms are just one of a thousand different fronts to fight harms from pollution to corruption to war. But after all, in a democracy—and perhaps in human society in general—there's only one fundamental issue, from which all governing process derives: the right to decide.

People in many central Pennsylvania townships had these conversations. They began shunning the regulatory system and instead passed ordinances to control both factory farms and another threat that appeared at around the same time: land-applied sewage sludge (which had caused the tragic deaths of two teenagers in 1995). Seventy townships passed antisludge ordinances, which imposed a fee to render land application of sewage sludge unprofitable. They remain sludge-free. Eleven townships passed factory farm ordinances, which outlawed nonfamily corporate ownership and control of farming operations. None has a factory farm to date. Two townships, Licking and Porter, even passed ordinances stripping corporations of their constitutional rights outright. Within their towns, corporations would no longer have the status of "persons" (see "Taking the Constitution Away from Corporations").

All of this exercise of local control began to cause some serious discomfort among agribusiness interests. Of course, corporations could go ahead and sue the townships, which they did, claiming that their constitutional rights as legal persons had been abrogated. Such outrageous but judicially and legislatively supported claims infuriated the people in targeted communities: citizen response to the corporate claim of personhood became a crucial component in the subsequent organizing. But soon corporations were pursuing a more efficient tactic than lawsuits. It involved having elected officials do their heavy lifting.

POLITICAL BLOWBACK

On May 2, 2001, Pennsylvania Senate Bill 826 was filed with the Agriculture and Rural Affairs Committee. Couched as an amendment to a 1982 act protecting agricultural operations from nuisance suits and ordinances under certain circumstances, the bill aimed to crack down on township efforts. The amendment further limited the ability of localities to pass ordinances, and it wasn't the least bit subtle, reading: "No municipality shall adopt or enact a frivolous ordinance that would prohibit, restrict, or regulate an agricultural operation." What counts as "frivolous"? Any attempt to "regulate the type of business that may own or conduct an agricultural operation." Just to drive home the point and punish any township that tried to protect itself, the bill entitles the aggrieved party to recover costs and attorney fees from lawsuits they file to challenge the ordinances.

When Linzey heard about 826, he set out to rally the people. An unprecedented coalition formed to oppose this assault on local democracy. The Sierra Club, the United Mine Workers of America, Common Cause, the Pennsylvania Farmers Union, the Pennsylvania Association for Sustainable Agriculture, and 400 rural township governments all joined to defeat 826. Groups that ordinarily wouldn't be talking to each other found common ground not because they were fighting sewage sludge or factory farms or some other single issue, but because they could all agree that the state was out of bounds in usurping basic democratic rights. Senate Bill 826 never made it out of committee.

But it wasn't over yet.

In one of those dark backrooms of the statehouse where corporate politics thrive, the bill was renumbered, and on May 2, 2002, it was slipped back into the Senate, where it passed 48 to 2. A leaked Pennsylvania Farm Bureau memorandum said that the renumbering was necessary to avoid any bad publicity. People told Linzey, "Nice try—but you'll never win against a vote like that." Undaunted, the coalition stormed into action, and threatened enough legislators with loss of a job that the bill never came to a vote in the House.

And it still wasn't over—illustrating the Jeffersonian wisdom that the price of liberty is constant vigilance.

This time, in 2003, the agribusiness forces attached the substance of the bill to an anti-sexual predator law on the last day of the legislative session. They figured that in an election year no legislator would want to be vulnerable to charges of favoring molesting children (although the freshman sponsor of that bill withdrew her sponsorship, saying that the bill was intended to protect children, not corporations). As soon as the bill landed on the desk of Democratic Governor Ed Rendell, the local democracy forces barraged him. He backed down and didn't sign the bill, but explained that this was only because better top-down regulatory protection was in order. With better state rules, he implied, it would be okay to strip municipalities of their rights.

In 2004, Rendell unveiled his ACRE initiative (Agriculture, Communities, and Rural Environment), under which an appointed political board would have the authority to overturn local laws. In other words, laws passed democratically by a majority of citizens in a community could be struck down by an unelected collection of corporate appointees. The coalition has beat that one back too for now—it will likely come up again in the next legislative session.

So the vigilance continues. Each time the state government attempts such pro-business shenanigans, it increasingly reveals on whose behalf it is working. And each time, more people see with growing clarity how relentlessly their lives and rights are sold and legislated away, and begin to understand how the failure of democracy leads to very real harms in their communities.

There is broader significance to such fights to save the sustainable family farm. It's about the underlying political power structure and its links to economic power. It's about who decides the fate of communities, and in whose interest those decisions are made. Just as past empires established colonies—including those that rebelled to form our nation—for the purposes of expropriating resources to feed and entertain the nobility and the rising merchant class, so today do corporate-driven governments sustain a culture of expropriation of the commons, with a blindness and ferocity that threatens to render the earth unlivable.

Saving the sustainable family farm is also about uniting all of us who are fighting important single-issue battles. As long as we are divided and scattering our energies in a thousand different directions, we will continue to lose. When we finally unite on the common terra firma of local control over sustainability, health, well-being, and democracy, we will be in a position to create an irresistible force.

From *Dollars & Sense* magazine, July/August 2005. A version of this article was published by Food First/Institute for Food and Development Policy (www.foodfirst.org) in April 2005.

For most poor farmers in South Africa, the end of the apartheid era has not produced many tangible economic benefits. But in the South African wine industry, a small but growing number of worker-owned vineyards have helped to promote land redistribution, more egalitarian labor arrangements, and black empowerment. William Mosely looks at three worker co-owned vineyards, and how their efforts are helping to make a better life for the working poor.

POST-APARTHEID VINEYARDS

BY WILLIAM MOSELY

As I walked through the rows of grape vines with a representative of one of South Africa's few worker co-owned vineyards, I could tell that he was proud of what his group had accomplished. Nearly all of the 60 members of the Bouwland partnership trust are coloured or black farm workers. They own a controlling share of the Bouwland vineyard and wine label, producing 17,000 bottles of wine per year, with exports to Europe and Canada. By all accounts, this is an amazing achievement for an effort that is only three years old. But the group is also nervous. They are still heavily dependent on the expertise and equipment of their white partners, and they must repay a substantial commercial bank loan. This project and others like it represent a small but growing number of worker-owned vineyards in post-Apartheid South Africa. These efforts embody the hopes, dreams, and challenges of those who aspire to make the new South Africa a reality for the working poor.

In 1994, the African National Congress (ANC) took power in South Africa under the leadership of Nelson Mandela, formally ending decades of state-sponsored discrimination. Among a wide range of exclusionary policies during the Apartheid era were restrictions on the ownership of farmland by non-whites outside of the homelands or Bantustans—a policy that left only 13% of the country's land for the entire majority black population. This led to complete white domination of commercial agriculture, particularly in the Western Cape Province, an area often thought of as the historical hearth of white farming. Of all of South Africa's provinces, agriculture in the Western Cape is the most commercialized and export-oriented. Wine exports in particular have skyrocketed since Apartheid ended and the international community lifted sanctions. While South African wines were once unheard-of in North American and European supermarkets, they now compete with wines from their southern hemisphere counterparts, mainly Chile and Australia, for a share of the "good value" wine market (i.e., reasonable-quality wines of low to moderate price). In fact, South Africa's wine production nearly quadrupled between 1994 and 2004, and the country is now the eighth or ninth largest wine producer in the world. But what has this growth meant for South Africa's historically disadvantaged groups, particularly the farm workers who comprise one of the poorest segments of the country's population? What is the ANC government doing, if anything, to ensure that the wealth from growing wine exports trickles down to the poorest workers?

While many North Americans are familiar with the struggle against Apartheid and the subsequent political opening in the 1990s, fewer may be aware of efforts to transform South Africa's economy. The ANC has promised to redress the legacy of discriminatory land ownership policies in the farming sector through a land reform program that facilitates the transfer of land from whites to blacks (a generic term in South Africa that encompasses people of African, mixed race and Indian origin). In fact, the government has pledged to redistribute 30% of the country's agricultural land by 2014. Land reform is part of a broader transformation strategy for South Africa's agricultural sector aimed at increasing black participation in decision-making. The wine industry in the Western Cape is one instance where the effects of that strategy are visible, and this is significant given its economic importance to the province, its growing export potential, and the history of white dominance.

THE COLOURED FARM WORKER POPULATION AND THE SOUTH AFRICAN WINE INDUSTRY

Wine production in South Africa's Western Cape Province dates back to the 17th century, when the Dutch established an outpost at Cape Town to provision ships sailing from Europe to the Far East. Because the area's local Khoisan population was sparse and unaccustomed to agricultural labor, the Dutch brought slaves from East Africa, Madagascar, and the East Indies to work their farms. The farm laborer population evolved into a mixed race or mulatto group, locally referred to as coloureds, who now comprise 60% of the Western Cape's population.

Even though slavery was abolished in 1834, conditions on farms remained difficult and wages were low. The historic relationship between white farmers and farm workers has often been described in terms of paternalism and dependency. Permanent farm workers (as opposed to seasonal laborers) lived on the farms, often for multiple generations. In addition to meager wages, permanent workers typically received housing, food, and wine. Many farm workers bought goods on credit at the company stores their bosses owned and fell into the classic debt-bondage cycle. The provision of cheap wine to workers as a component of compensation, known as the "tot or dop" system, was used to attract and retain workers in a low-wage industry (and the poorest white farmers were often the greatest abusers of this practice). While this practice has been illegal since the 1960s, and more strictly monitored in the post-Apartheid era, alcoholism continues to be a major problem among farm workers.

Raising grapes required a tremendous amount of labor, so those farms with larger areas in grape production often employed 30 to 60 permanent workers who lived on the farm with their families. Spouses and children would then join the work-force at key moments in the agricultural season. Until the end of Apartheid, wine production remained limited because international sanctions blocked exports. Fur-thermore, other than the dreg wine reserved for the coloured farm workers in the Western Cape, wine consumption was reserved largely for whites—blacks in other parts of the country were encouraged to drink beer.

POST-APARTHEID AGRICULTURE

Since the end of Apartheid, shifts in the international political economy, as well as a number of policies and programs at the national level, have had a profound impact on commercial agriculture and on the wine industry in particular. At the interna-tional level, the biggest change was the end of sanctions on products that were clearly South African. This change had little impact on exports whose origin was ambiguous, such as table fruit, whose sale continued unabated in Europe during the Apartheid era. But as origin and label are extremely important for all but the cheapest wines, the end of sanctions represented a huge opening of markets for the South African wine industry. As a result, South African wine production went from 38.9 million liters in 1994 to 153.4 million liters in 2004. Today, there are some 4,400 farming units that produce wine grapes in South Africa. Almost all are in the Western Cape because the Mediterranean climate in this region favors their production (see map). The livelihoods of over 108,000 South Africans depend on the wine industry.

Once Apartheid ended, international financial institutions such as the World Bank and the IMF pressed South Africa to adopt neoliberal economic policies that encouraged export orientation and free trade. Key donors, including the United States, pushed the ANC government to focus narrowly on establishing a procedural democracy, rather than pursuing a broader vision of democracy involving economic justice. The ANC would also come under pressure from the World Bank to adopt a policy of negotiated land reform based on the principle of willing seller/willing buyer, rather than a more radical alternative.

Within this international context, the formerly Marxist ANC government devel-oped five sets of policies that would affect wine farming: 1) liberalizing agricultural trade and deregulating the marketing of agricultural products; 2) abolishing certain tax concessions and reducing direct subsidies to farmers; 3) introducing a minimum wage and other protections for farm workers; 4) implementing land reform policies and programs; and 5) setting broad goals for black empowerment and transformation in the agricultural sector.

In order to ensure food self-sufficiency at the national level, and to cater to an important constituency of the conservative National Party, Apartheid-era governments provided white commercial farms with a range of subsidies and tariff protections. The ANC government subsequently moved toward a dramatic liberalization of South African agricultural policy. This shift was motivated not only by external pressures, but also by the need to redirect resources away from agricultural subsidy programs to other areas, and by little sympathy in the new government for the situation of white commercial farmers. The increasingly competitive commercial agriculture sector has led to the loss of smaller and more marginal farms. With farms going out of business—and with commercial farmers seeking to avoid offering newly required legal protections to workers—the number of permanent farm laborer positions has dropped.

LAND REDISTRIBUTION AND TRANSFORMATION IN THE AGRICULTURAL SECTOR

Since the late 1990s, land redistribution programs have provided government grants to help blacks and coloureds acquire land when they are not in a position to benefit from land restitution. This program provides approximately $3,080 per eligible individual for the purchase of farmland (or more if the beneficiary contributes additional capital). In the Western Cape, the majority of land redistribution beneficiaries are current or former farm workers. Because farmland is relatively expensive in the province (especially vineyard appropriate land), large groups of beneficiaries, often 50 to 100 people, must pool their grants in order to buy a farm. In some instances, farms are purchased outright at market prices from willing sellers and then run independently by the land redistribution beneficiaries. In other instances, people use their grants to buy a portion of an existing farm, going into partnership with a white farmer. This second approach, known as a share equity scheme, is the only approach used to date with vineyards.

The reasons why vineyards have not been purchased outright number at least two: the purchase price of most vineyards is so high that it would take a vast number of grantees to purchase one; and there are certain advantages to going into partnership with an established wine grape farmer who presumably already has the know-how and contacts needed to run a successful vineyard. As of early 2005, there were 101 government land redistribution projects in the Western Cape, and of these nine were share equity schemes producing wine grapes. To put this in perspective, there are 7,185 commercial farms in the Western Cape, of which roughly 2,372 produce 100 tons or more of grapes annually. As such, land redistribution projects only constitute 1.4% of all farms in the Western Cape, and projects focused on the produc-

A SAMPLING OF SOUTH AFRICA'S WORKER CO-OWNED VINEYARDS AND WINERIES

Bouwland

Description: Formed in 2003, this farm outside of Stellenbosch is 74% owned by farm workers.

Contact Information: Tel: +27 21 865-2135; Fax: +27 21 865-2683; Email: bouwland@adept.co.za; Website: www.bouwland.co.za. Address: P.O. Box 62, Koelenhof 7605 South Africa

Wines: Chenin Blanc, Cabernet-Sauvignon-Merlot

Export destinations: U.K., the Netherlands, Belgium, Denmark, Germany and Canada. They are working with their Canadian distributor to expand exports to the United States.

New Beginnings

Description: The oldest and most celebrated worker co-owned vineyard in South Africa, this project began in 1997 when the owner of Nelson's Creek winery and vineyard gave 9.5 hectares of land to 18 of his workers as an expression of thanks for their efforts on his farm.

Contact Information: Tel: +27 21 869-8453; Fax: +27 21 869-8424; Email: newbeginnings@nelsonscreek.co.za. Website: www.nelsonscreek.co.za/new_beginnings/new_beginnings.htm. Address: P.O. Box 2009, Windmeul, 7630 Paarl, South Africa

Wines: Chardonnay, Cabernet Sauvignon, Pinotage

Export Destinations: Germany and the Netherlands. Export opportunities to the United States are being explored.

Thandi

Description: This is the label under which Nuutbegin and three other worker co-owned vineyards sell their wine. Thandi became the first wine brand in the world to achieve fair trade status.

Contact information: Tel: +27 21 886 6458; Fax: +27 21 886 6589; Email: rydal@thandi.com; Website: www.thandi.com/. Address: R310, Lynedoch, P.O. Box 465, Stellenbosch 7613, South Africa

Wines: Pinot Noir, Cabernet Sauvignon, Chardonnay, Sauvignon Blanc-Semillon, Merlot-Cabernet

Export Destinations: U.K., the Netherlands, Belgium, Germany, and Japan. The label will be introduced to the United States, Canada and Scandinavia shortly.

tion of wine grapes make up less than half of one percent of all farms in this category. However, in addition to the nine government supported share equity schemes, there are also a number of worker co-owned vineyards that have been privately financed by progressive commercial farmers, international donors, foundations, and local wine industry groups.

South Africa's land redistribution program has been criticized from both right and left. Many conservative white South Africans believe that black or coloured farmers are incapable of effectively managing commercial farms. They see land redistribution as a waste of the government's money at best and, at worst, a program that could lead to collapse of the agricultural sector. Current problems with neighboring Zimbabwe's land reform process, including a series of disputed farm occupations by black war veterans, have only further fueled these fears.

Critics of the program from the political left, and even center, have focused on several issues. First, the pace at which the program is redistributing land has been exceptionally slow. By mid-2005, a little less than 3% of the formerly white-owned land had been redistributed to black or coloured South Africans, a long way from the 30% targeted for redistribution by 2014. Second, critics are questioning the "willing seller/willing buyer" principle that relies on the voluntary sale of commercial farms at market value, as the government does not have anything close to the level of resources needed to purchase 30% of white-owned farmland at market prices by 2014. Third, whether the large-scale, commercial orientation of the land redistribution program is appropriate has come into question at a time when so many commercial farms are going under. Finally, there are some specific concerns about share equity schemes because this mechanism may be manipulated by white farmers to obtain capital without actually relinquishing control. Furthermore, some have questioned how realistic it is to go into partnership with someone who may previously have been the autocratic "boss."

In addition to land redistribution, the South African government has a broader plan for transformation in the agricultural sector. This includes setting targets to increase the representation of blacks in management positions, to increase black ownership of agro-enterprises, and to increase the supply of produce to supermarkets by black-owned farms. Increasing black participation in the management of farms is key because farm workers have been excluded for years from the business and management side of farming. While farm workers are highly skilled in certain tasks, such as the pruning of grape vines, under Apartheid few blacks and coloureds were able to develop the managerial and business skills needed to run commercial farms. Moving farm workers into management positions will develop a cadre of black people who could go on to run successful commercial farms of their own.

While encouraging ownership of wineries and wine labels by black business interests is important for economic equality in South Africa, this is not the same as ownership by farm workers. Farm ownership by the emerging black upper class of business entrepreneurs does not automatically help the poor; worker-owned wineries and vineyards have a better chance of doing so.

THREE WORKER CO-OWNED VINEYARDS

The Bouwland partnership trust, the Nelson's Creek New Beginnings project and the Nuutbegin trust represent three different models of worker co-owned vineyards (see map). The Bouwland partnership trust came into being in 2003, when 60 land redistribution beneficiaries (of whom 55 are farm workers from the nearby Beyerskloof and Kanonkop vineyards) bought a 76% share of the 56-hectare Bouwland vineyard from Beyerskloof outside of Stellenbosch (of which 40 hectares is planted in Pinotage, Cabernet Sauvignon, and Merlot grapes). The trust's membership is roughly half male and half female (see photo), a split that is not only required by the government to receive grants, but that reflects the significant presence of women as farm workers in the South African wine industry. The group went into partnership with the winemaker for Beyerskloof and Kanonkop and with the owner of a London-based wine distribution firm. Using land redistribution grants from the government, and a commercial bank loan, they purchased both a majority share of the vineyard and a stake in the established Bouwland wine label.

The Bouwland trust operates with a somewhat complicated labor arrangement. Rather than working on their land during off hours, the trust shares the cost of a team of workers with Beyerskloof (which includes many trust members) that spends 40% of its time on the Bouwland land. The Bouwland property has no infrastructure, but rather relies on Beyerskloof for the use of its equipment and tasting room. With the exception of one full time employee who is involved in marketing and management, nearly of all of the group's shareholders have kept their day jobs as farm laborers on the nearby Beyerskloof and Kanonkop vineyards. The group currently produces and sells 17,000 cases of wine annually but is just breaking even, largely because they are paying off a loan. Their wine is sold in local supermarkets and exported to the UK, the Netherlands, Belgium, Denmark, Germany, and Canada. They currently are working with their Canadian distributor to expand exports to the United States. This is a solid project with a bright future, but the group is wrestling with the fact that it has yet to turn a profit, as well as some concerns about its dependence on Beyerskloof.

The Nelson's Creek New Beginnings Project is the oldest and most celebrated worker-owned vineyard in South Africa. This project began in 1997 when the owner of Nelson's Creek winery and vineyard gave 9.5 hectares of land to 18 of his workers as an expression of thanks for their efforts on his farm. The vineyard has subsequently grown to 13.5 hectares (the additional land was purchased from Nelson's Creek), producing Chardonnay, Cabernet Sauvignon and Merlot grapes. The group has its own wine label, New Beginnings, and sells wines to local supermarkets, along with exports to Germany and the Netherlands. Export opportunities to the United States are being explored. The group is reliant on Nelson's Creek for equipment, management, and winemaking expertise. The New Beginnings project is turning a profit and its members are using the money to buy food and consumer goods and pay their children's school fees.

The Nuutbegin trust began in 2000 when 99 farm workers from the Waterskloof and Fransmanskloof vineyards obtained land redistribution grants to purchase a 50% share of a long-term lease from the municipality for 25 hectares of prime vineyard land (see photo). The other two partners, the owners of the Waterskloof and Fransmanskloof vineyards, each have a 25% stake in the project. The group produces Merlot, Shiraz, and Cabernet Sauvignon grapes which are sold to the Thandi winery, in which the Nuutbegin trust has a 7% stake. Thandi produces a variety of wines, sourcing its grapes from four different worker co-owned vineyards in the area. Significantly, this is the first wine label to be fair-trade accredited in the world. While this accreditation should allow Thandi to fetch a small premium on the global market, Nuutbegin's 7% share in the label means that its returns from this end of the business are more limited. All of the shareholders have maintained their day jobs as farm workers, and they coordinate with the owners of Waterskloof and Fransmanskloof to schedule time to work the vines at Nuutbegin. Like Bouwland, this group has yet to turn a profit, and they are somewhat concerned about their continuing dependence on their white partners.

THE WAY FORWARD

As these case studies make clear, land redistribution and black empowerment in the wine industry are extremely challenging. High land prices and capital costs, not to mention the need for sophisticated business and wine-making expertise, mean that worker co-owned vineyards and wine labels are few in number, slow to start, and often dependent on the good graces of white employers and partners. It is important to note that the real money to be made in viticulture is in the selling of wine, not in the production of grapes. So vineyards with their own labels, such as the Bouwland and New Beginnings projects, have an advantage. Furthermore, because land, investment, and capital costs are so high, new projects must take on significant debt obligations that severely limit profits in the early years. Unlike Bouwland and Nuutbegin, New Beginnings did not incur significant debt; thus it can generate dividends for its membership more quickly and so benefit from a higher level of worker interest in the project.

The role of government land redistribution initiatives in the viticulture sector may always be minimal because the costs are so high. Interestingly, there has been more private support for black empowerment in viticulture than any other agricultural subsector, probably because the opportunity for new markets and profits is so high. This presents both an opportunity and a danger. On the positive side, private money means additional support for projects such as New Beginnings. But there is also a danger that private backers may see black empowerment and fair trade solely as means to earning greater profits rather than as paths toward economic justice. The key to lasting change will be having policy makers, academics, and consumers who are attuned to the difference between vineyards and wine labels that are truly co-owned by workers and those that are co-owned by black business interests with no or nominal participation of the workers.

Alas, what should North American and European wine consumers with a conscience do? I say seek out, and demand that your local wine market order, those South African labels that are co-owned and produced by farm workers (see "A Sampling of South Africa's Worker Co-Owned Vineyards and Wineries"). Yes, the South African land redistribution program is not perfect, but a growing market for worker-friendly wines will make existing ventures more profitable and encourage more white winemakers to go into partnership with their workers. This is more than just fair trade—it is about creating a marketplace that rewards those working for change and economic justice, a world where workers really benefit from the fruits of their labor.

Resources: 2006; Mather, C. 2002. "The Changing Face of Land Reform in Post-Apartheid South Africa." *Geography.* 87(4): 345-354; Scully, P. 1992. "Liquor and Labor in the Western Cape, 1870-1900." In: Crush, J. and C. Ambler (eds). *Liquor and Labor in Southern Africa.* Athens: Ohio University Press, 56-77; Williams, G. 2005. "Black Economic Empowerment in the South African Wine Industry." *Journal of Agrarian Change.* 5(4): 476-504; Zimmerman, F.J. 2000. "Barriers to Participation of the Poor in South Africa's Land Redistribution." *World Development.* 28(8): 1439-1460.

From *Dollars & Sense* magazine, January/February 2006.

The New York City restaurant industry is renowned for low pay and exploited workers, particularly immigrant labor. John Lawrence reports on a worker-owned, democratically-run restaurant that's breaking the mold.

COLORS: A WORKER COOPERATIVE RESTAURANT CHALLENGES THE INDUSTRY

BY JOHN LAWRENCE

In the fall of 2005, COLORS restaurant opened in the heart of Greenwich Village, in New York City. In an elegant setting with Bauhaus and Art Deco touches, COLORS offers a creative seasonal menu based on favorite family recipes of its staff, who hail from 22 countries.

More than an excellent restaurant, however, COLORS is one part of a labor struggle to revolutionize the New York restaurant industry (see "Immigrant Restaurant Workers Hope to Rock New York," *Dollars & Sense*, Jan/Feb 2004). The restaurant is a democratic worker cooperative, founded by former workers of the Windows on the World restaurant (located on the top floor of the World Trade Center until 9-11), with help from the Restaurant Opportunities Center (ROC-NY), a workers' center established in 2002.

New York's famed restaurant industry is built on exploited immigrant labor, according to a study commissioned by ROC-NY. Only 20% of restaurant jobs pay a livable wage of $13.47 an hour or higher. Ninety percent of workers have no employer-sponsored health coverage. Immigrants of color are usually in low-paying back house jobs like dishwasher, food preparer, and line cook. Thirty-three percent of those surveyed "reported experiencing verbal abuse on the basis of race, immigration status, or language." Other illegal labor practices are common, such as work "off the clock," overtime, and minimum-wage violations, and health and safety code violations.

COLORS aims to be different. The minimum salary for back house worker-owners is $13.50 an hour. Front house worker-owners are paid minimum wage plus tips. Tips are split more equitably among the various occupations than the industry standard. In addition, every worker-owner has a benefits package that includes health insurance, paid vacation, and a pension.

Worker-owner Rosario Ceia, a 10-year veteran of the restaurant industry, says working at COLORS has been a radical change. Besides providing fair wages and benefits to worker-owners, COLORS is democratically organized into eight teams based on occupation—managers, line cooks, prep cooks, waiters, back waiters ("bus boys"), runners, dishwashers, and hosts. Each team has a representative on the board of directors. Rosario is not only a back waiter, but also treasurer of the board. Everyone participates in decision-making, Rosario emphasized, from adopting bylaws to choosing the restaurant's design.

Those in management, such as the executive chef, general manager, and wine director, play typical roles in providing needed expertise to the restaurant. In their day-to-day relationship with the other worker-owners, though, they are teammates, not bosses. As an additional safeguard against abusive hierarchy, all non-management worker-owners belong to the Hotel and Restaurant Employees Union (HERE).

Rosario believes COLORS will benefit all restaurant workers—not only by providing a successful model of "high road" business practices, but by actively advocating for workers in restaurant owners' association meetings. COLORS also extends its values down the supply chain by supporting fair trade, sustainable agriculture, and local producers.

The venture is also revitalizing an old labor organizing strategy of developing democratic worker cooperatives. The first union in the United States, Knights of Labor, wanted "to establish cooperative institutions such as will tend to supersede the wage-system, by the introduction of a cooperative industrial system." Perhaps, in addition to challenging an industry, COLORS is modeling a "new" organizing strategy for the 21st-century U.S. labor movement.

From *Dollars & Sense* magazine, July/August 2006.

Many small farmers have lost their land to big developers. Conservation land trusts provide an option for tenant farmers to take more control over their land, resist corporate consolidation of agricultural production, and help to protect communities and the environment.

THE LAND TRUST SOLUTION

BY MICHELLE SHEEHAN

I t was back in the early 1970s that Steven and Gloria Decater of Covelo, Calif., first started farming an unused plot of land belonging to a neighbor. Over many years, they turned the fallow plot into fertile farmland that yielded a bounty of organic vegetables. They named it "Live Power Community Farm" and launched California's first successful community supported agriculture (CSA) program there in 1988. But the Decaters' hold on the land was vulnerable. Without ownership rights, they risked losing the farm to encroaching development. The couple wanted to buy the property but could not afford the land into which they had poured their lives.

The Decaters found a solution to their land-tenure challenge that gave them ownership rights *and* ensured the land would remain an active organic farm. Their solution creates an important precedent—and a possible path for other small tenant farmers.

With the help of Equity Trust Inc., a Massachusetts-based organization that promotes property ownership reform, the Decaters gained ownership rights to the land in 1995—without having to pay the full value themselves. The couple purchased just its "agricultural use value," while Equity Trust, acting as a conservation land trust (a nonprofit institution that controls land for the benefit of current and future generations), purchased "easements," or deed restrictions, that were equal in value to the land's development rights. Together, the two payments amounted to the original asking price.

Agricultural easements are a good way for small farmers to gain ownership control over land when they're not looking to develop or sell it anyway, because they limit the property's market price to its working agricultural value, making it more affordable—while conserving it.

In transferring development rights to the conservation land trust, the Decaters forever forfeited their rights to subdivide or develop the land for anything other than farming; the terms cannot be changed unless both parties agree through a court process. The transaction unpacked the bundle of property rights associated with land ownership, dividing ownership between two entities and placing deliberate restrictions on how the land could be used in the future.

RAMPED UP LAND-USE RULES

This approach made sense for the Decaters, because they were interested in more than just owning the farm for themselves. "We wanted to have some sort of relationship where it wasn't merely privatized ownership," Gloria explains, "but a socially and economically responsible form of land tenure." They also wanted to make certain that the land would continue to be cultivated by resident farmers with sustainable methods well into the future.

Their vision for the farm was secured by designing easement provisions that went beyond any existing precedent. For example, most easements on farmland define agriculture rather loosely. As Equity Trust's Ellie Kastanopoulos notes, "anyone willing to put a few cows on their property and call it a farm" could exploit many agricultural easements. The Decaters and Equity Trust built in a "ramped up" agriculture requirement: Live Power Community Farm must be farmed continually by resident farmers and remain organic or "biodynamic" (a farming philosophy that treats the

FIGURE 1

Average Real Estate Value of U.S. Farms

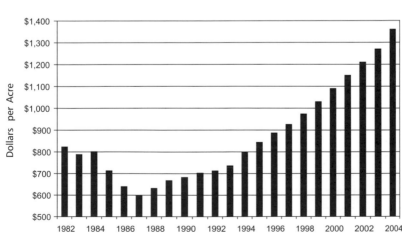

Source: U.S. Department of Agriculture National Agricultural Statistics Service <www.usda.gov/nass>

FIGURE 2

Number of Land Trusts Whose Primary Purpose is to Protect this Land Type*

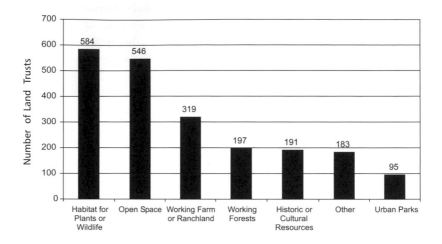

*One land trust may choose more than one primary land type.

Source: "National Land Trust Census," Land Trust Alliance, 2004

land as a balanced and sustainable unit and uses the rhythms of nature to maintain the health of the farm).

The Decaters' other major concern was the affordability of their land for future farmers. They see a lot of young farmers for whom "one of the biggest stumbling blocks is getting access to land," Gloria says. While traditional conservation easements ban developers, they do not curb the upward pressure on the price of the land from individual home or estate buyers. Steve worried that when he and Gloria were ready to pass on the land, market forces could "spike the cost of the land so high that any farmer would be bid clear out of the picture." To prevent this, the Decaters and Equity Trust crafted limitations on the resale price of the land into the easement.

Today, Live Power is an active 40-acre horse-powered community supported agriculture (CSA) farm, thriving amidst encroaching development and the huge corporate farms that dominate California agriculture. Not only do the Decateown their land, but their unique conservation easement ensures that it will permanently remain an affordable, active, and ecologically sustainable farm. The Decaters are true stewards of the land, and the land trust's easement provisions reflect their commitment.

WHAT ARE CONSERVATION LAND TRUSTS?

Conservation land trusts are nonprofit organizations designed to protect ecologically fragile environments, open space, or small farms. According to the 2003 National Land Trust Census, there are 1,537 local and national conservation land trusts in operation nationwide, protecting approximately 9 million acres of land, an area four times the size of Yellowstone National Park. This is twice the acreage protected by conservation land trusts just five years ago. New conservation land trusts are formed at the rate of two per week, according to the Land Trust Alliance. They exist in every state; California leads with 173 land trusts, followed by Massachusetts (154) and Connecticut (125). While land trusts protect land in a variety of ways, two of the most common approaches are acquiring land and acquiring conservation easements, legal agreements that permanently restrict the use of land, shielding it from development to ensure its conservation.

For more information on land trusts, see: Land Trust Alliance <www.lta.org>, Equity Trust, Inc. <www.equitytrust.org>, and Vermont Land Trust <www.vlt.org>.

NEW WAYS OF LOOKING AT LAND OWNERSHIP

In addition to conservation land trusts, Equity Trust and others have implemented a second land trust model. So-called "community land trusts" usually focus on low-income housing in urban areas (see "Burlington Bursts the Affordable Housing Debate," p.244), but have in some cases included agricultural interests. They operate by purchasing tracts of land and then leasing them on a long-term basis to tenants who agree to a detailed land-use agreement. Although a farmer who enters into such a relationship would not own the land, he or she would have agricultural control and would own any improvements made to the land. In the tenant contract, the land trust would retain a purchase option for those improvements so that when the farmer was ready to move on, the land trust could ensure the lands remained affordable for new farmers. The land-use agreement could also include provisions to ensure the land remains in production. This option works well in areas where land is exorbitantly expensive, prohibiting the farmer from purchasing even restricted land, or when easements are not available.

In both land trust models, Equity Trust stresses, there is flexibility in how the relationship between the land trust and farmer is defined. Key to the definition is the land use agreement, which can be tailored for the particular situation according to either party's wishes. Kastanopolous notes that these are complex arrangements and "there is no black and white way of doing things." Indeed, one of Equity Trust's missions is to "change the way people think about and hold property." Their goal is to provide models that can be replicated and adapted to varied situations.

These partnerships and new ways of looking at land ownership acknowledge that there are diverse interests in a piece of land. The farmers, the community, the environment, and future users are all considered. Steven Decater is excited by the prospect of agricultural land trusts catching on. "We'll have permanent farms," he says, "and they're going to be needed." He's right about that. Farm real estate values have risen by 70% in the last 20 years (see figure). Across the country, massive mechanized and chemically sustained corporate-controlled farms are rapidly replacing small-time farmers.

The most vulnerable small farmers are ones who sink tremendous energy and resources into improving their soil but are unable to afford the market value of the land they work. Their lack of ownership control puts their land, and their investment, in jeopardy. This is a particularly common experience for operators of CSA farms, in which producers sell "shares" directly to consumers who receive regular harvest portions during the growing season. According to an informal survey conducted by Equity Trust in the late 1990s, 70% of CSA farms operated on rented land.

Land trusts allow small tenant farms to access land, resist rising property values, and conserve small agricultural tracts. They provide an alternative to unchecked development and farm consolidation, while helping to preserve communities, shield the environment from development, and protect the livelihoods of small farmers. But they are underutilized—in part because the strategy poses certain challenges. It requires:

- resources to purchase the agricultural value of the land,
- willingness by current landowners to sell or donate the land to a land trust,
- technical expertise, and
- in the conservation land trust model, the presence of a conservation land trust with enough resources to pay for easements—which has become more difficult with skyrocketing property values.

Yet thanks to the hard work of the Decaters, Equity Trust, and other organizations including the Vermont Land Trust (VLT) and the Institute of Community Economics (ICE), this innovative approach to land ownership has taken hold in several parts of the country (see "What Are Conservation Land Trusts?"). The VLT oversees many similar transactions every year; it has worked with more than 1,000 landowners and conserved more than 400 farms. Although the group has not quite figured out how to meet the high demand for affordable land as demand pressure drives land prices up across the state, it is nevertheless successfully managing to preserve large areas of farmland in Vermont—and writing affordability restrictions into their easements wherever possible.

Steve Getz, a dairy farmer assisted by the VLT through an easement purchase, says, "We would not have been able to afford the land without the VLT." He and his wife Karen say they respect how the land trust model challenges the "it's my land and I'll do whatever I please with it" mantra that reflects the dominant conception of private land ownership in this country. They now own a successful pasture-based dairy farm in Bridport that will be forever preserved.

From *Dollars & Sense* magazine, March/April 2005.

High real estate prices prevent renters from saving enough money to buy their own homes. Community land trusts are one strategy to help people transition from renting to home ownership. By removing properties from the speculative market, the trust model aims to stop the concentration of ownership. Daniel Fireside describes an innovative land trust program in Burlington, Vermont.

BURLINGTON BUSTS THE AFFORDABLE HOUSING DEBATE

BY DANIEL FIRESIDE

"Housing used to be an opportunity ladder in our country. You started out in a rental and began to save. Then you bought a small home, and eventually you moved up. Today, housing prices are so high that if you're renting an apartment, you can't possibly save," says Brenda Torpy, executive director of the Burlington Community Land Trust.

With housing prices skyrocketing beyond the means of the average worker, rents eating up a greater share of household income, and HUD funding on the chopping block, local governments have few tools at their disposal to create affordable housing. Too often, mayors are reduced to offering tax breaks to big developers in exchange for a few token "below market rate" apartments. In the old debate between supply-siders and government interventionists, it's clear who has the momentum.

Undaunted by these grim trends, community leaders in Burlington, Vt., are continuing to carry out a 20-year experiment in affordable housing based on the radical precept that housing should not be treated as a market commodity. The Burlington Community Land Trust (BCLT) represents an altogether different approach to housing security—and one that holds important lessons for community organizers around the country.

BCLT IS BORN

In the early 1980s, wealthy out-of-town speculators began driving up the cost of housing in Burlington. Harried New York City yuppies saw the bucolic college town of 40,000 as an ideal place for their vacation homes, and longtime working class residents were being rapidly priced out of their own neighborhoods. Housing prices in Burlington were rising at twice the national rate.

Frustration over housing issues came to a boiling point when the political establishment cut a deal with big-time developers to put an upscale apartment complex on the city's scenic waterfront. Voter disgust with this plan to privatize public space led to an upset victory in the mayoral race by Socialist gadfly Bernie Sanders and his ragtag Progressive Coalition in 1981.

Sanders and the Progressive Coalition quickly sought to develop institutions and programs that would have a lasting impact on the community. The Progressives decided to make affordable housing a signature issue. Things got off to a rough start when their proposal for rent control was voted down after a coalition of property owners and establishment politicians hired a professional consultant to defeat it. With rent control off the table, and federal funding in short supply, the Progressives had to turn to more creative measures to address the housing crisis.

In 1983, they created the Community and Economic Development Office (CEDO), a permanent community-development office that would set development goals and initiate creative projects. CEDO initially focused on three areas of housing policy: protecting the vulnerable, preserving affordable housing, and producing affordable housing. While these goals sound typical of many municipal development authorities, CEDO's strategy was distinctive. It sought to decommodify residential property, ensure its housing projects would be permanently affordable, and actually empower residents. Its most important initiative, and the key to all of these goals, was the Burlington Community Land Trust.

RETHINKING PRIVATE PROPERTY

In the late 1970s, Vermont environmentalist Rick Carbin had formed the Vermont Land Trust (VLT) in an effort to preserve open space as developers bought up farms. Instead of buying and holding land, as some land trusts do, the VLT used its resources to buy undeveloped properties at the edge of urban areas and resell them, often at a profit, but with strict conservation easements that prohibited future development. The VLT's successful track record paved the way for Burlington's housing land trust program.

The Institute for Community Economics, a thinktank based in Springfield, Mass., approached CEDO planners with a proposal to use the land trust model as a tool to address Burlington's housing crisis. Much as the VLT program "unbundled" the ownership of property from its function in the future, the housing land trust separated the ownership of a house from the land it sits on. As Brenda Torpy summarizes, "Conservation land trusts take land out of the market to protect the natural environment. Community land trusts take land out of market to protect the urban environment including the people who live there."

CEDO established the Burlington Community Land Trust as an independent nonprofit corporation in 1984, with official backing from the Burlington City Council and $200,000 in seed money. The trust was viewed as an integral part of the city's affordable housing program. Even traditional politicians came to see the land trust model as an acceptable compromise between a flawed free market approach and heavy-handed government intervention, especially as it promoted the popular concept of home ownership. Democratic and Republican politicians have found it difficult to oppose a program that offered life-long renters a "piece of the American Dream."

At its founding, the BCLT was the first municipally funded community land trust in the country. Today it is the nation's largest community land trust, with over 2,500 members.

HOUSING TRUST 101

Buying land through a housing trust involves several steps. To start, the trust acquires a parcel of land through purchase, foreclosure, tax abatements, or donation, and then arranges for a housing unit to be built on the parcel if one does not yet exist. The trust sells the building but retains ownership of the land underneath. It leases the land to the homeowner for a nominal sum (e.g., $25 per month), generally for 99 years or until the house is sold again.

This model supports affordable housing in several ways. First, homebuyers have to meet low-income requirements. Second, the buying price of the home is reduced because it does not include the price of the land. Third, the trust works with lenders to reduce the cost of the mortgage by using the equity of the land as part of the mortgage calculation. This reduces the size of the down payment and other closing costs and eliminates the need for private mortgage insurance. In all, the trust can cut the cost of home ownership by at least 25%.

For longtime BCLT member Bob Robbins, purchasing a home through the trust "was the only affordable option. We did not have access to money for a down payment on a regular home, and at our income level, we wouldn't have qualified for a mortgage. Through the BCLT, we were able to purchase a $99,000 home with just $2,500 down."

Unlike federal programs that only help the initial buyer, the BCLT keeps the property affordable in perpetuity by imposing restrictions on the resale of the house. Specifically, the contract restricts the profit buyers are able to take when they later sell the house. According to the terms of the BCLT leases, homeowners get back all of their equity from their mortgage plus the market value of any capital improvements they made. However, they only get 25% of any increase in the value of the house (which constitutes 75% of the total value of the property), and none of the increase in the value of the land.

Since buyers keep a portion of the housing value appreciation, families do accumulate some wealth through BCLT homeownership. And as time passes, if the surrounding housing prices continue to rise, the trust prices become even more affordable relative to market housing, and the trust captures more wealth on behalf of the community.

When the homeowner sells, the new buyer must agree to the same terms. If no buyers are interested or the owners default on the mortgage, the BCLT retains the option to buy the property.

This model gives the buyer the benefits of homeownership (including the tax deduction for mortgage interest, wealth accumulation through equity, and stable housing costs) that would otherwise be beyond her means. In return, she gives up the potential of windfall profits if the market keeps rising. BCLT recently published a study of the first 100 trust homes that were sold to a second generation. "The implications were very powerful," says Brenda Torpy. "The initial homebuyers realized a net gain of 29% on the money they had invested. Our homeowners were taking an average of $6,000 with them. These aren't the sky-high returns that some people have come to expect from the housing market, but these were people who would never have entered it in the first place." That's because most BCLT homeowners "would never have been able to buy homes otherwise, even with existing federal and state programs," explains Torpy. "For many, we are a stepping stone between renting and homeownership."

Urban land is not a normal economic good because it exists in a fixed quantity. (They're not making any more of it, as realtors say.) Since the supply cannot rise to meet growing demand, the price is subject to speculative forces. The housing supply can be increased by building in greater density, but this does not happen quickly. When a normal home is offered for sale on the usual terms, it does virtually nothing to make the overall housing market more affordable. A land trust home, by contrast, creates a permanently affordable property because the land it sits on is removed from the speculative market. Most of the appreciation is retained by the housing trust (and by extension, the community), rather than the individual. In this way the trust model creates a bridge between purely public and purely private property. "We're trying to stop the concentration of land in the hands of a wealthy minority," says Torpy.

The land trust program was designed to outlast any change in city hall. This was an important strategy in the Progressive Coalition's early years. As it turned out, the Progressives hung on to control, with the exception of a single Republican administration in the mid-1990s. As a result, they have been able to expand on the aims of their original programs and establish a broad base of support for their housing agenda.

The BCLT has become an important force in Burlington's housing market. After 20 years, the trust controls almost 650 housing units, including over 270 rental apartments and 370 shared-appreciation single-family homes and condominiums—about 4% of Burlington's total housing stock. The process is "buyer initiated"; the buyer picks out the house and asks the trust to incorporate it. Therefore the units are dotted all over the city. The trust has also built a wide variety of homes in various styles to fit into particular neighborhoods. "Most of them are modest," says Torpy. "We've found that condos are good starter homes. They're something new but are still affordable. But we're also building modular homes and 2- and 3-bedroom homes." The BCLT's programs also include tenant-owned cooperatives, a family shelter, a transitional shelter, and housing for homeless youth, the mentally ill, and people with HIV/AIDS.

The BCLT is remarkable not only for its size, but as an organizing structure that promotes community empowerment. Tenants and owners of BCLT units vote for and serve on its governing board, along with government officials and other residents with technical expertise, such as architects and urban planners. The system is designed so that the BCLT doesn't play the role of landlord to tenants and homeowners. Rather, all interested parties have a voice and a vote. In this way it's also an experiment in democratic self-governance.

By looking at housing as a fundamental human right rather than a market good that goes to the highest bidder, and with shrewd political organizing in a hostile environment, housing advocates in Burlington have created a sustainable model for affordable housing that deserves to be emulated across the country. Others are catching on. Since the BCLT published its study, the Fannie Mae Corporation, other city planning offices, and state financing offices have all contacted the BCLT for information about how to use housing trusts in an environment of shrinking funds. Today there are 130 community land trusts in more than 30 states, including in large cities like Atlanta and Cincinnati. The largest growth has been in California and the Pacific Northwest. BCLT itself is expanding into the surrounding counties.

BCLT homeowner Bob Robbins says, "I think every community should have a land trust—not just as a fringe option but as the dominant model to keep housing affordable.

From *Dollars & Sense* magazine, March/April 2005.

Looking Forward

The roots of wealth inequality lie in economic institutions: the corporation and the financial system. Reform movements are already underway in both venues, and, according to William Greider, the transformation of capitalist institutions is not only possible but likely.

TRANSFORMING THE ENGINES OF INEQUALITY

BY WILLIAM GREIDER

American politics has always involved a struggle between "organized money" and "organized people." It's a neglected truth that has resurfaced with ironic vengeance in our own time—ironic because the 20th century produced so much progress toward political equality among citizens, and because the emergence of a prosperous and well-educated middle class was expected to neutralize the overbearing political power of concentrated wealth. Instead, Americans are reminded, almost any time they read a newspaper, that the rich do indeed get richer and that our political system is, as Greg Palast put it, "the best democracy money can buy."

What should we make of this retrogressive turn—a nation of considerable abundance still ruled by gilded-age privilege? A cynic would say it was ever thus, end of story. Political commentators argue it's a sign of the country's maturation that its citizens now accept what they once resisted—gross and growing inequalities of wealth. And many economists simply avert their gaze from the troubling consequences of maldistribution for economic progress and the well-being of society.

I stake out a contrary claim: The United States remains an unfinished nation—stunted in its proclaimed values—so long as it fails to confront the enduring contradictions between wealth and democracy. That is not a utopian lament for radical change, but simply an observation of what our own era has taught us.

Inequality retains its crippling force over society and politics and the lives of citizens, despite the broader distribution of material comforts. We are not the nation of 80 or 100 years ago, when most Americans struggled in very modest circumstances, often severe deprivation. Yet, despite the nation's wealth (perhaps also because of it), the influence of concentrated economic power has grown stronger and more intimate in our lives. Today the social contract is determined more by the needs and demands of corporations and finance than by government or the consensual will of the people.

The federal government and several generations of liberal and labor reformers did achieve great, life-improving gains during the last century. But those reforms and redistributive programs did not succeed in altering the root sources of economic inequality, much less taming them. On the contrary, the U.S. economic system recreates and even expands the maldistribution of incomes and wealth in each new generation.

The root sources of inequality are located within the institutions of advanced capitalism—in the corporation and financial system—with their narrow operating values and the peculiar arrangements that consign enormous decision-making power to a remarkably small number of people. The problem of inequality is essentially a problem of malformed power relationships: Advanced capitalism deprives most people of voice and influence, while it concentrates top-down authority among the insiders of finance and business. Ameliorative interventions by government (for example, through regulation, taxation, and reform) have never succeeded in overcoming the tendency within capitalism toward increased concentrations of economic power.

The drive for greater equality must involve governmental actions, of course, but it cannot succeed unless it also confronts the engines of inequality within the private realm and forces deep changes in how American capitalism functions. The challenge is nothing less than to rearrange power relationships within the corporation and finance capital.

Who has the power to restructure capitalist institutions? In my view, ordinary people do—at least potentially—acting collectively as workers, investors, consumers, managers or owners and, above all, as citizens, to force change. Many are, in small and different ways, already at work on the task of reinventing capitalism.

TRANSFORMING THE WORKPLACE

The workplace is perhaps the most effective engine of inequality, since it teaches citizens resignation and subservience, while it also maldistributes the returns of enterprise. For most Americans, the employment system functions on the archaic terms of the master-servant relationship inherited from feudalism. The feudal lord commanded the lives and livelihoods of serfs on his land and expelled those who disobeyed. The corporate employer has remarkably similar powers, restrained only by the limited prohibitions in law or perhaps by the terms of a union contract. Elaine Bernard, director of Harvard's trade union studies program, described the blunt reality:

As power is presently distributed, workplaces are factories of authoritarianism polluting our democracy. Citizens cannot spend eight hours a day obeying orders and being shut out of important decisions affecting them, and then be expected to engage in a robust, critical dialogue about the structure of our society.

Where did people learn to accept their powerlessness? They learned it at work. Nor is this stunted condition confined to assembly lines and working-class occupations. The degradation of work now extends very far up the job ladder, including even well-educated professionals whose expert judgments have been usurped by distant management systems.

In most firms, only the insiders at the top of a very steep command-and- control pyramid will determine how the economic returns are distributed among the participants. Not surprisingly, the executives value their own work quite generously while regarding most of the employees below as mere commodities or easily interchangeable parts. More importantly, these insiders will harvest the new wealth generated by an enterprise, while most workers will not. In the long run, this arrangement of power guarantees the permanence of wealth inequalities.

Joseph Cabral, CEO of Chatsworth Products Inc., a successful employee-owned computer systems manufacturer in California, is an accountant, not a political philosopher, but he understands the wealth effects of closely held control in private businesses. "The wealth that's created ends up in too few hands," he said. "The entrepreneur who's fortunate enough to be there at the start ends up really receiving a disproportionate amount of wealth. And the working folks who enabled that success to take place share in little of that wealth. At some point, capitalism is going to burst because we haven't done right for the folks who have actually created that wealth."

But there are other, more democratic, ways to structure the work environment. At Chatsworth, where the workers collectively purchased the enterprise, "Everyone is sharing in the wealth they're creating. ... We're not just doing this for some outside shareholder. We're doing it because we are the shareholders."

Employee ownership, worker-management, and other systems of worker self-organization provide a plausible route toward reforming workplace power relations and spreading financial wealth among the many instead of the few.

TRANSFORMING FINANCE CAPITAL

The top-down structure of how Wall Street manages "other people's money" ensures the maldistribution of financial returns. As wealthy people know, those who bring major money to the table are given direct influence over their investments and a greater return on their risk-taking. The rank-and-file investors—because their savings are modest and they lack trustworthy intermediaries to speak for them—are regarded as passive and uninformed, treated more or less like "widows and orphans," and blocked from exerting any influence over how their wealth is invested. To put the point more crudely, the stock market is a casino, and the herd of hapless investors is always the "mark."

Nevertheless, finance capital is, I predict, the realm of capitalism most vulnerable to reform pressures. That's mainly because it operates with other people's money, and most of that money belongs not to the wealthiest families but to the broad ranks of ordinary working people. A historic shift in the center of gravity has occurred in U.S. finance over the past decade: Fiduciary institutions like pension funds and mutual funds have eclipsed individual wealth as the largest owner of financial assets. Their collectivized assets now include 60% of the largest 1,000 corporations. Because these funds invest across the broad stock market, they literally own the economy.

Public pension funds, union-managed pension funds, and shareholder activists are already working to forge an engaged voice for the individuals whose wealth is in play, and to force the fiduciary institutions to take responsibility for the social and environmental effects of how these trillions in savings are invested. The collapse of the stock-market bubble and subsequent corporate scandals have accelerated these reform efforts.

Some of the largest public-employee pension funds including the California Public Employees' Retirement System and the New York State public employees fund, joined by state officials who sit on supervisory boards, are aggressively leading the fight for corporate-governance reform and for stricter social accountability on urgent matters like workers' rights and global warming. The labor movement is organizing proxy battles to press for corporate reforms at individual companies including the Disney Corporation and Royal Dutch Shell, while the AFL's Office of Investment won a victory for mutual-fund investors in early 2003 when it persuaded the Securities and Exchange Commission to require mutual funds to disclose their proxy votes in corporate-governance shareholder fights. (The mutual fund industry is working to resist the measure, and for good reason. Investment firms regularly vote against the interests of their own rank-and-file investors in order to curry favor with the corporations that hire them to manage corporate-run pension funds and 401(k) plans.)

The major banks and brokerages cannot brush aside these new critics as easily as corporate directors often do. Wall Street will respond to fiduciary concerns because it must. It needs the rank-and-file's capital to operate. When six or seven major funds, collectively holding nearly $1 trillion, speak to Wall Street, things do change. Their unspoken threat to scorn companies or financial firms that ignore larger social obligations and shift their money elsewhere sends broad shockwaves across both financial markets and corporate boardrooms.

The more profound tasks are to challenge fraudulent economic valuations (think Enron) and to account for (and internalize) the true costs of products and production processes. Both steps would refocus capital investing toward creating real, long-term value and away from the transient thrill of quarterly returns. The fiduciary funds have the potential power to enforce this new economic perspective, though it is not yet widely understood or accepted by them. As universal owners of the economy, their own portfolios are the losers when individual corporations throw off externalities in order to boost their bottom lines. The costs will be borne by every other firm, by the economy as a whole, or by taxpayers who have to clean up the mess. The compelling logic of this new economic argument is this: what is bad for society cannot be good for future retirees or for their communities and their families.

Citizens, in other words, have more power than they imagine. If they assert influence over these intermediaries, they have the power to punish rogue corporations for anti-social behavior and block the low-road practices that have become so popular in business circles. In coalition with organized labor, environmentalists, and other engaged citizens, they have the capacity to design—and enforce—a new social contract that encourages, among other things, participatory management systems and worker ownership, loyalty to community, and respect for our deeper social values.

While none of this promises a utopian outcome of perfect equality, the redistribution of power within capitalism is certainly a predicate for the creation of a more equitable society.

My conviction is that we are on the brink of a broad new reform era, in which reorganizing capitalism becomes the principal objective. What I foresee is a long, steady mobilization of people attempting to do things differently, often in small and local settings, trying out new arrangements, sometimes failing, then trying again. As these inventive departures succeed, others will emulate them. In time, an alternative social reality will emerge with different values, alongside the archaic and destructive system that now exists. When that begins to happen and gains sufficient visibility, the politics is sure to follow. If all this sounds too remote to the present facts, too patient for our frenetic age, remember that this is how deep change has always occurred across American history.

This article is adapted with permission from *The Soul of Capitalism* (Simon & Schuster, 2005).

Taxing wealth is a sure way to address the growing wealth gap: it can prvide revenue to meet pressing social needs and at the same time slow or reverse the trend toward wealth concentration. But conventional political wisdom says sinificant wealth taxes simply won't fly in American politics. Political ecoomist Gar Alperovitz takes on the conventional wisdom and explains why he is optimistic about the prospects for a new program of taxing large concentrations of wealth.

THE COMING ERA OF WEALTH TAXATION

BY GAR ALPEROVITZ

Americans concerned with inequality commonly point to huge disparities in the distribution of income, but the ownership of wealth is far, far more concentrated. This fact is certain to bring the question of wealth taxation to the top of the nation's political agenda as the country's fiscal crisis deepens and, with it, the deterioration of public institutions and the pain of all those who rely on them.

Broadly, in any one year the top 20% garners for itself roughly 50% of all income, while the bottom 80% must make due with the rest. The top 1% regularly takes home more income than the bottom 100 million Americans combined.

When it comes to wealth, these numbers appear almost egalitarian. The richest 1% of households owns half of all outstanding stock, financial securities, trust equity, and business equity! A mere 5% at the very top owns more than two-thirds of the wealth in America's gigantic corporate economy, known as financial wealth—mainly stocks and bonds.

This is a medieval concentration of economic power. The only real question is when its scale and implications will surface as a powerful political issue. A wealth tax is "by definition, the most progressive way to raise revenue, since it hits only the very pinnacle of the income distribution," notes economist Robert Kuttner. But conventional wisdom says that it is impossible to deal with wealth head-on. The battle over repeal of the estate tax, in this view, demonstrated that even the most traditional of "wealth taxes" are no longer politically feasible.

Perhaps. However, a longer perspective reminds us that times can change—as, indeed, they often have when economic circumstances demanded it.

EMERGING SIGNS OF CHANGE

Indeed, times are already beginning to change. One sign: Although many Democrats were nervous about challenging George W. Bush in the first year after he took office, by early 2004 all the Democrats running for president had come to demand a repeal in some form of his tax giveaways to the elite.

It is instructive to trace the process of change. At the outset, only a few liberals challenged the president. The late Paul Wellstone, for instance, proposed freezing future income tax reductions for the top 1% and retaining the corporate Alternative Minimum Tax (AMT), for an estimated $134 billion in additional revenue over 10 years. Ted Kennedy proposed delaying tax cuts for families with incomes over $130,000 and keeping the estate tax (while gradually raising the value of exempted estates from a then-current $1 million to $4 million by 2010). Kennedy estimated this would generate $350 billion over 10 years.

By May 2002, even centrist Democrat Joseph Lieberman urged postponing both the full repeal of the estate tax and reductions in the top income-tax rates. Lieberman estimated his plan would save a trillion dollars over 20 years. The Bush tax cuts were simply unfair, he said, "giving the biggest benefit to those who needed it the least."

The Democrats failed to stop Bush's 2001 and 2003 rounds of tax cuts. But there are reasons to believe that politicians will ultimately come to accept the validity of maintaining and raising taxes on the wealthiest Americans. Just as many Democrats changed their stand on the Bush tax cuts, a similar progression is likely with regard to wealth taxation more generally over the next few years—and for two very good reasons. First, there is an extraordinary fiscal crisis brewing; and second, wealth taxes—like taxes on very high-income recipients—put 95% to 98% of the people on one side of the line and only 2% to 5% or so on the other.

GO WHERE THE MONEY IS

The hard truth is that it is now all but impossible to significantly raise taxes on the middle class. This reality flows in part from the ongoing decline of organized labor's political power, and in part from the Republicans' takeover of the South—another long and unpleasant political story. At any rate, it means that the only place to look for significant resources is where the remaining real money is—in the holdings of corporations and the elites who overwhelmingly own them. Put another way: Raising taxes first on the income and ultimately on the wealth of the very top groups is likely to become all but inevitable as, over time, it becomes clear that there is no way to get much more in taxes from the middle-class suburbs.

Moreover, as Democratic politicians have come increasingly to realize, the "logic of small versus large numbers" could potentially neutralize a good part of the suburbs politically, painting conservatives into a corner where they're forced to defend the very unreasonable privileges of the very rich.

The knee-jerk reaction that taxing wealth is impossible is based upon the kind of thinking about politics that "remembers the future"—in other words, thinking that assumes the future is likely to be just like the past, whether accurately remembered or not. Since wealth has not been taxed, it cannot be taxed now, goes the argument (or rather, assumption).

Of course, taxation of wealth has long been central to the American tax system for the kind of wealth most Americans own—their homes. Real estate taxes, moreover, are based on the market value of the home—not the value of a homeowner's equity: An owner of a $200,000 home will be taxed on the full value of the asset, even if her actual ownership position, with a mortgage debt of, say, $190,000, is only a small fraction of this amount. A new, more equitable form of wealth taxation would simply extend this very well established tradition and—at long last!—bring the elites who own most of the nation's financial wealth into the picture.

Many Americans once thought it impossible to tax even income—until the 1913 passage, after long debate and political agitation, of the 16th Amendment to the U.S. Constitution. Note, however, that for many years, the amendment in practice meant targeting elites: Significant income taxation was largely restricted to roughly the top 2% to 4% until World War II.

Even more important is a rarely discussed truth at the heart of the modern history of taxation. For a very long time now the federal income tax has, in fact, targeted elites—even in the Bush era, and even in a society preoccupied with terrorism and war. In 2000, the top 1% of households paid 36.5% of federal income taxes. The top 5% paid 56.2%. Although detailed calculations are not yet available, the massive Bush tax cuts are not expected to alter the order of magnitude of these figures. Estimates suggest that, ultimately, the tax reductions may modify the figures by no more than two or perhaps three percentage points.

In significant part this results from the rapidly growing incomes of the wealthiest: even at lower rates, they'll still be paying nearly the same share of total income tax. The simple fact is, however, that the record demonstrates it is not impossible to target elites. We need to take this political point seriously and act on it aggressively in the coming period.

FISCAL CRUNCH AHEAD

What makes wealth taxes even more likely in the coming period is the extraordinary dimension of the fiscal crisis, which will force government at all levels to adopt new strategies for producing additional resources. Projections for the coming decade alone suggest a combined federal fiscal deficit of more than $5 trillion—$7.5 trillion if Social Security Trust Fund reserves are left aside.

A worsening fiscal squeeze is coming—and it is not likely to be reversed any time soon. Critically, spending on Social Security benefits and Medicare will continue to rise as the baby-boom generation retires. So will spending on Medicaid. Recent studies project that by 2080 these three programs alone will consume a larger share of GDP than all of the money the federal government collects in taxes. And, of course, the ongoing occupation of Iraq will continue to demand large-scale financial support.

Nor are the trends likely to be altered without dramatic change: The truth is that the Bush tax and spending strategies, though particularly egregious, are by no means unique. Long before the Bush-era reductions, domestic discretionary spending by the federal government was trending down—from 4.7% of GDP a quarter century ago to 3.5% now, a drop during this period alone of roughly 25%.

A radically new context is thus taking shape which will force very difficult choices. Either there will be no solution to many of the nation's problems, or politicians and the public will have to try something new. Suburban middle-class voters, who rely on good schools, affordable health care, assistance for elderly parents, and public infrastructure of all kinds, will begin to feel the effects if the "beast" of government is truly starved. This pain is likely to redirect their politics back toward support for a strong public sector—one which is underwritten by taxes on the wealthiest. Quite simply, it is the only place to go.

TIME TO TAX WEALTH

Ideological conservatives like to argue that all Americans want to get rich and so oppose higher taxes on the upper-income groups they hope to join. In his recent history of taxation, *New York Times* reporter Steven Weisman has shown that this may or may not be so in normal times, but that when social and economic pain increase, politicians and the public have repeatedly moved to tax those who can afford it most. Bill Clinton, for one, raised rates on the top groups when necessity dictated. So did the current president's father! Now, several states—including even conservative Virginia—have seen pragmatic Republicans take the lead in proposing new elite taxation as the local fiscal crisis has deepened.

The likelihood of a political shift on this issue is also suggested by the growing number of people who have proposed direct wealth taxation. A large group of multimillionaires has launched a campaign opposing elimination of taxes on inherited wealth—paid only by the top 2%—as "bad for our democracy, our economy, and our society." Yale law professors Bruce Ackerman and Anne Alstott in their book **The Stakeholder Society** have proposed an annual 2% wealth tax (after exempting the first $80,000). Colgate economist Thomas Michl has urged a net-worth tax, and Hofstra law professor Leon Friedman has proposed a 1% tax on wealth owned by the top 1%. Even Donald Trump has proposed a one time 14.25% net-worth tax on Americans with more than $10 million in assets.

Wealth taxation is common in Europe. Most European wealth taxes have an exemption for low and moderate levels of wealth (especially the value of pensions and annuities). Economist Edward Wolff, who has studied these precedents carefully, suggests that America might begin with a wealth tax based on the very modest Swiss effort, with marginal rates between 0.05% and 0.3% after exempting roughly the first $100,000 of assets for married couples. He estimates that if this were done, only millionaires would pay an additional 1% or more of their income in taxes.

Europe also offers examples of much more aggressive approaches. Wealth taxation rates in 10 other European countries are much higher than Switzerland's—between 1% and 3%—and would yield considerable revenues if applied here. Wolff calculated that a 3% Swedish-style wealth tax in the United States would have produced $545 billion in revenue in 1998. Although an updated estimate is not available, nominal GDP increased about 19% between 1998 and 2002, and wealth taxes would likely produce revenues that roughly tracked that increase.

Some writers have held that wealth taxes are prohibited by the U.S. Constitution. There appear to be two answers to this. The first is legal: Ackerman, a noted constitutional expert, has argued at length in the Columbia Law Review that wealth taxes are not only constitutional, but represent the heart of both original and contemporary legal doctrine on taxation.

The second answer is political. We know that courts have a way of bending to the winds of political-economic reality over time. As the pain deepens, the courts are likely one day to recognize the validity of the legal arguments in favor of wealth taxation. Alternatively, political pressure may ultimately mandate further constitutional change, just as it did in 1913 with regard to income taxation.

There is no way of knowing for sure. But as with all important political change, the real answer will be found only if and when pressure builds up both intellectually and politically for a new course of action. The challenge, as always, is not simply to propose, but to act.

From *Dollars & Sense* magazine, July/August 2004.

Americans are constantly exhorted to save—but also to spend! Social Securty alone is not enough to fund even a modestly comfortable retirement—but many families cannot save enough to fill the gap or meet a financial setback. How should the nation understand and address these dilemmas? Here, economist Ellen Frank looks at how we can both meet individuals' need for economic security and maintain the stability of a modern market economy. Her answer: forget about legislating ever more vehicles for tax-advantaged individual savings, and instead expand the institutions of social wealth.

NO MORE SAVINGS!

The Case for Social Wealth

BY ELLEN FRANK

Pundits from the political left and right don't agree about war in Iraq, gay marriage, national energy policy, tax breaks, free trade, or much else. But they do agree on one thing: Americans don't save enough. The reasons are hotly disputed. Right-wingers contend that the tax code rewards spenders and punishes savers. Liberals argue that working families earn too little to save. Environmentalists complain of a work-spend rat race fueled by relentless advertising. But the bottom line seems beyond dispute.

Data on wealth-holding reveal that few Americans possess adequate wealth to finance a comfortable retirement. Virtually none have cash sufficient to survive an extended bout of unemployment. Only a handful of very affluent households could pay for health care if their insurance lapsed, cover nursing costs if they became disabled, or see their children through college without piling up student loans. Wealth is so heavily concentrated at the very top of the income distribution that even upper-middle class households are dangerously exposed to the vagaries of life and the economy.

With low savings and inadequate personal wealth identified as the problem, the solutions seem so clear as to rally wide bipartisan support: Provide tax credits for savings. Encourage employers to establish workplace savings plans. Educate people about family budgeting and financial investing. Promote home ownership so people can build home equity. Develop tax-favored plans to pay for college, retirement, and medical needs. More leftish proposals urge the government to redistribute wealth through federally sponsored "children's development accounts" or "American stakeholder accounts," so that Americans at all income levels can, as the Demos-USA website puts it, "enjoy the security and benefits that come with owning assets."

But such policies fail to address the paradoxical role savings play in market economies. Furthermore, looking at economic security solely through the lens of personal finance deflects focus away from a better, more direct, and far more reliable way to ensure Americans' well-being: promoting social wealth.

THE PARADOX OF THRIFT

Savings is most usefully envisaged as a physical concept. Each year, businesses turn out automobiles, computers, lumber, and steel. Households (or consumers) buy much, but not all, of this output. The goods and services they leave behind represent the economy's savings.

Economics students are encouraged to visualize the economy as a metaphorical plumbing system through which goods and money flow. Firms produce goods, which flow through the marketplace and are sold for money. The money flows into peoples' pockets as income, which flows back into the marketplace as demand for goods. Savings represent a leak in the economic plumbing. If other purchasers don't step up and buy the output that thrifty consumers shun, firms lay off workers and curb production, for there is no profit in making goods that people don't want to buy.

On the other hand, whatever consumers don't buy is available for businesses to purchase in order to expand their capacity. When banks buy computers or developers buy lumber and steel, then the excess goods find a market and production continues apace. Economists refer to business purchases of new plant and equipment as "investment." In the plumbing metaphor, investment is an injection—an additional flow of spending into the economy to offset the leaks caused by household saving.

During the industrial revolution, intense competition meant that whatever goods households did not buy or could not afford would be snatched up by emerging businesses, at least much of the time. By the turn of the 20th century, however, low-paid consumers had become a drag on economic growth. Small entrepreneurial businesses gave way to immense monopolistic firms like U.S. Steel and Standard Oil whose profits vastly exceeded what they could spend on expansion. Indeed expansion often looked pointless since, given the low level of household spending, the only buyers for their output were other businesses, who themselves faced the same dilemma.

As market economies matured, savings became a source of economic stagnation. Even the conspicuous consumption of Gilded Age business owners couldn't provide enough demand for the goods churned out of large industrial factories. Henry Ford was the first American corporate leader to deliberately pay his workers above-market wages, reasoning correctly that a better-paid work force would provide the only reliable market for his automobiles.

Today, thanks to democratic suffrage, labor unions, social welfare programs, and a generally more egalitarian culture, wages are far higher in industrialized economies than they were a century ago; wage and salary earners now secure nearly four-fifths of national income. And thrift seems a quaint virtue of our benighted grandparents. In the United States, the personal savings rate—the percentage of income flowing to households that they did not spend—fell to 1% in the late 1990s. Today, with a stagnant economy making consumers more cautious, the personal savings rate has risen—but only to around 4%.

Because working households consume virtually every penny they earn, goods and services produced are very likely to find buyers and continue to be produced. This is an important reason why the United States and Europe no longer experience the devastating depressions that beset industrialized countries prior to World War II.

Yet there is a surprisingly broad consensus that these low savings are a bad thing. Americans are often chastised for their lack of thrift, their failure to provide for themselves financially, their rash and excessive borrowing. Politicians and economists constantly exhort Americans to save more and devise endless schemes to induce them to do so.

At the same time, Americans also face relentless pressure to spend. After September 11, President Bush told the public they could best serve their country by continuing to shop. In the media, economic experts bemoan declines in "consumer confidence" and applaud reports of buoyant retail or auto sales. The U.S. economy, we are told, is a consumer economy—our spendthrift ways and shop-til-you-drop culture the motor that propels it. Free-spending consumers armed with multiple credit cards keep the stores hopping, the restaurants full, and the factories humming.

Our schizophrenic outlook on saving and spending has two roots. First, the idea of saving meshes seamlessly with a conservative ideological outlook. In what author George Lakoff calls the "strict-father morality" that informs conservative Republican politics, abstinence, thrift, self-reliance, and competitive individualism are moral virtues. Institutions that discourage saving—like Social Security, unemployment insurance, government health programs, state-funded student aid—are by definition socialistic and result in an immoral reliance on others. Former Treasury Secretary Paul O'Neill bluntly expressed this idea to a reporter for the *Financial Times* in 2001. "Able-bodied adults," O'Neill opined, "should save enough on a regular basis so that they can provide for their own retirement and for that matter for their health and medical needs." Otherwise, he continued, elderly people are just "dumping their problems on the broader society."

This ideological position, which is widely but not deeply shared among U.S. voters, receives financial and political support from the finance industry. Financial firms have funded most of the research, lobbying, and public relations for the campaign to "privatize" Social Security, replacing the current system of guaranteed, publicly-funded pensions with individual investment accounts. The finance industry and its wealthy clients also advocate "consumption taxes"—levying taxes on income spent, but not on income saved—so as to "encourage saving" and "reward thrift." Not co-incidentally, the finance industry specializes in committing accumulated pools of money to the purchase of stocks, bonds and other paper assets, for which it receives generous fees and commissions.

Our entire economic system requires that people spend freely. Yet political rhetoric combined with pressure from the financial services industry urges individuals to save, or at least to try to save. This rhetoric finds a receptive audience in ordinary house-holds anxious over their own finances and among many progressive public-interest groups alarmed by the threadbare balance sheets of so many American households.

So here is the paradox. People need protection against adversity, and an ample savings account provides such protection. But if ordinary households try to save and protect themselves against hard times, the unused factories, barren malls, and empty restaurants would bring those hard times upon them.

SOCIAL WEALTH

The only way to address the paradox is to reconcile individuals' need for economic security with the public need for a stable economy. The solution therefore lies not in personal thrift or individual wealth, but in social insurance and public wealth.

When a country promotes economic security with dependable public invest-ments and insurance programs, individuals have less need to amass private savings. Social Security, for example, provides the elderly with a direct claim on the nation's economic output after they retire. This guarantees that retirees keep spending and reduces the incentive for working adults to save. By restraining personal savings, Social Security improves the chances that income earned will translate into income spent, making the overall economy more stable.

Of course, Americans still need to save up for old age; Social Security benefits re-place, on average, only one-third of prior earnings. This argues not for more saving, however, but for more generous Social Security benefits. In Europe, public pensions replace from 50% to 70% of prior earnings.

Programs like Social Security and unemployment insurance align private motiva-tion with the public interest in a high level of economic activity. Moreover, social in-surance programs reduce people's exposure to volatile financial markets. Proponents of private asset-building seem to overlook the lesson of the late 1990s stock market boom: that the personal wealth of small-scale savers is perilously vulnerable to stock market downswings, price manipulation, and fraud by corporate insiders.

It is commonplace to disparage social insurance programs as "big government" intrusions that burden the public with onerous taxes. But the case for a robust public sector is at least as much an economic as a moral one. Ordinary individuals and households fare better when they are assured some secure political claim on the economy's output, not only because of the payouts they receive as individuals, but because social claims on the economy render the economy itself more stable.

Well-funded public programs, for one thing, create reliable income streams and employment. Universal public schooling, for example, means that a sizable portion of our nation's income is devoted to building, equipping, staffing, and maintaining schools. This spending is less susceptible than private-sector spending to business cycles, price fluctuations, and job losses.

Programs that build social wealth also substantially ameliorate the sting of joblessness and minimize the broader economic fallout of unemployment when downturns do occur. Public schools, colleges, parks, libraries, hospitals, and transportation systems, as well as social insurance programs like unemployment compensation and disability coverage, all ensure that the unemployed continue to consume at least a minimal level of goods and services. Their children can still attend school and visit the playground. If there were no social supports, the unemployed would be forced to withdraw altogether from the economy, dragging wages down and setting off destabilizing depressions.

In a series of articles on the first Bush tax cut in 2001, the New York Times profiled Dr. Robert Cline, an Austin, Texas, surgeon whose $300,000 annual income still left him worried about financing college educations for his six children. Dr. Cline himself attended the University of Texas, at a cost of $250 per semester ($650 for medical school), but figured that "his own children's education will likely cost tens of thousands of dollars each." Dr. Cline supported the 2001 tax cut, the Times reported. Ironically, though, that cut contributed to an environment in which institutions like the University of Texas raise tuitions, restrict enrollments, and drive Dr. Cline and others to attempt to amass enough personal wealth to pay for their children's education.

Unlike Dr. Cline, most people will never accumulate sufficient hoards of wealth to afford expensive high-quality services like education or to indemnify themselves against the myriad risks of old age, poor health, and unemployment. Even when middle-income households do manage to stockpile savings, they have little control over the rate at which their assets can be converted to cash.

Virtually all people—certainly the 93% of U.S. households earning less than $150,000—would fare better collectively than they could individually. Programs that provide direct access to important goods and services—publicly financed education, recreation, health care, and pensions—reduce the inequities that follow inevitably from an entirely individualized economy. The vast majority of people are better off with the high probability of a secure income and guaranteed access to key services such as health care than with the low-probability prospect of becoming rich.

The next time a political candidate recommends some tax-exempt individual asset building scheme, progressively minded people should ask her these questions. If consumers indeed save more and the government thus collects less tax revenue, who will buy the goods these thrifty consumers now forgo? Who will employ the workers who used to manufacture those goods? Who will build the public assets that lower tax revenues render unaffordable? And how exactly does creating millions of little pots of gold substitute for a collective commitment to social welfare?

From *Dollars & Sense* magazine, May/June 2004.

The inheritance tax has been under fire from conservatives, who mockinly call it the "death tax." But they obscure the fact that only the wealthiest 1% of estates is taxed. Chuck Collins explains how Washington state voters recognized the value of their state's inheritance tax and voted to preserve it.

WASHINGTON STATE RECYCLES SOCIAL WEALTH

BY CHUCK COLLINS

In fall 2006, anti-tax organizations in Washington state sponsored an initiative, I-920, to abolish the state's estate tax. Given Washington's history of voting overwhelmingly for tax cuts, it looked as if the estate tax was a goner—especially as initial polls showed over half the state's voters believed they would have to pay the tax if it remained in place.

In reality, the tax is only paid on 200 to 250 estates a year, those worth over $2 million ($4 million for a couple). More than 99% of the state's taxpayers are exempt. Revenue from the tax is dedicated to the Education Legacy Trust Account, used to reduce class size in K-12 education statewide and provide scholarships and additional financial aid to nearly 18,000 low- and moderate-income college students.

In the end, the repeal effort was roundly defeated by a margin of 62-38. Majorities in all but 3 of the state's 39 counties, even in conservative western and southeastern Washington, voted against repeal.

Organizers say the main thing they had going for them was the linkage to education. "It would have been more difficult if we had not been able to tell people exactly where their money was going," said Sandeep Kaushik, communications director for the No on 920 campaign. "In every community, we knew how many students benefited."

Hundreds of students, educators, and parents were engaged in the effort to defeat the measure. The Washington Education Association, the statewide teachers union, put substantial resources into the campaign. And some of the state's multimillionaires were outspoken opponents of repeal as well, claiming that the tax is appropriate as a way to pay back the gift of education so that others can benefit as they did.

One of them, Bill Gates, Sr., father of the richest man on earth, argued in the *Seattle Post Intelligencer* that Washington's estate tax was an "opportunity recycling program." Gates's op-ed bears quoting at length:

Washington state has provided fertile ground for some very successful enterprises in the last generation. These individuals have made good use of their "American inheritance," including our accumulated scientific heritage and natural bounty. They have harvested plenty from our society's investments in technology and our remarkable system of property laws and regulated markets. Without this inheritance, they frankly wouldn't have succeeded in quite the same way.

If we abolish the state's inheritance tax we stop the opportunity recycling program. We allow the common wealth to stop flowing and concentrate it in the hands of a few. And worse, we slow the investments in opportunity that aim to provide every young person a chance, whether they were born in South Seattle or Mercer Island.

At the federal level, the estate tax is due to be ended for one year, 2010, then come back the following year at its 2006 levels. Partisans on all sides agree this is bad policy, an example of congressional sausage-making at its worst; Congress must act before 2010 to fix it. Total repeal of the tax is unlikely now, with a Democratic majority in Congress. This opens up all sorts of real opportunities for positive reform.

The fight to keep the federal estate tax could benefit from analyzing the Washington state experience. Why not suggest an estate tax reform that tracks the Washington state law: a $2 million exemption, along with a progressive rate structure? And why not set aside the revenue from the tax for a Children's Opportunity Trust Fund, to provide educational and wealth-creation opportunities?

While earmarking is not great public policy, in this instance it may be the best way to help the public build an enduring understanding that the estate tax represents an intergenerational transfer, a way to ensure that cultural and educational resources flow to the young. It may be the key to long term preservation of the inheritance tax.

Resources: William Gates Sr., "I-920: No, it's a small levy, so help recycle investment in the wealthy," *Seattle Post-Intelligencer*, 10/15/06, seattlepi.nwsource.com/opinion/288629_noestatetax15.html; www.washingtondefense.org; Washington Secretary of State, "2006 General Election Results," 64.146.248.152/?a=920#map.

From *Dollars & Sense* magazine, January/February 2007.

Most proposals to address today's yawning wealth gap aim to rechannel more of the world's privately held wealth into the hands of people who now have little or none of it. That is necessary. But in this visionary article, Working Assets founder Peter Barnes reminds us that there is another, vast source of wealth that people are barely aware of and that institutions neglect and abuse: the commons. And in it, he sees the potential to restore a modicum of both equity and ecological sanity to modern capitalist economies.

SHARING THE WEALTH OF THE COMMONS

BY PETER BARNES

We're all familiar with private wealth, even if we don't have much. Economists and the media celebrate it every day. But there's another trove of wealth we barely notice: our common wealth.

Each of us is the beneficiary of a vast inheritance. This common wealth includes our air and water, habitats and ecosystems, languages and cultures, science and technologies, political and monetary systems, and quite a bit more. To say we share this inheritance doesn't mean we can call a broker and sell our shares tomorrow. It *does* mean we're responsible for the commons and entitled to any income it generates. Both the responsibility and the entitlement are ours by birth. They're part of the obligation each generation owes to the next, and each living human owes to other beings.

At present, however, our economic system scarcely recognizes the commons. This omission causes two major tragedies: ceaseless destruction of nature and widening inequality among humans. Nature gets destroyed because no one's unequivocally responsible for protecting it. Inequality widens because private wealth concentrates while common wealth shrinks.

The great challenges for the 21st century are, first of all, to make the commons visible; second, to give it proper reverence; and third, to translate that reverence into property rights and legal institutions that are on a par with those supporting private property. If we do this, we can avert the twin tragedies currently built into our market-driven system.

DEFINING THE COMMONS

What exactly is the commons? Here is a workable definition: *The commons includes all the assets we inherit together and are morally obligated to pass on, undiminished, to future generations.*

This definition is a practical one. It designates a set of assets that have three specific characteristics: they're (1) inherited, (2) shared, and (3) worthy of long-term preservation. Usually it's obvious whether an asset has these characteristics or not.

At the same time, the definition is broad. It encompasses assets that are natural as well as social, intangible as well as tangible, small as well as large. It also introduces a moral factor that is absent from other economic definitions: it requires us to consider whether an asset is worthy of long-term preservation. At present, capitalism has no interest in this question. If an asset is likely to yield a competitive return to capital, it's kept alive; if not, it's destroyed or allowed to run down. Assets in the commons, by contrast, are meant to be preserved regardless of their return.

This definition sorts all economic assets into two baskets, the market and the commons. In the market basket are those assets we want to own privately and manage for profit. In the commons basket are the assets we want to hold in common and manage for long-term preservation. These baskets then are, or ought to be, the yin and yang of economic activity; each should enhance and contain the other. The role of the state should be to maintain a healthy balance between them.

THE VALUE OF THE COMMONS

For most of human existence, the commons supplied everyone's food, water, fuel, and medicines. People hunted, fished, gathered fruits and herbs, collected firewood and building materials, and grazed their animals in common lands and waters. In other words, the commons was the source of basic sustenance. This is still true today in many parts of the world, and even in San Francisco, where I live, cash-poor people fish in the bay not for sport, but for food.

Though sustenance in the industrialized world now flows mostly through markets, the commons remains hugely valuable. It's the source of all natural resources and nature's many replenishing services. Water, air, DNA, seeds, topsoil, minerals, the protective ozone layer, the atmosphere's climate regulation, and much more, are gifts of nature to us all.

Just as crucially, the commons is our ultimate waste sink. It recycles water, oxygen, carbon, and everything else we excrete, exhale, or throw away. It's the place we store, or try to store, the residues of our industrial system.

The commons also holds humanity's vast accumulation of knowledge, art, and thought. As Isaac Newton said, "If I have seen further it is by standing on the shoulders of giants." So, too, the legal, political, and economic institutions we inherit—even the market itself—were built by the efforts of millions. Without these gifts we'd be hugely poorer than we are today.

To be sure, thinking of these natural and social inheritances primarily as economic assets is a limited way of viewing them. I deeply believe they are much more than that. But if treating portions of the commons as economic assets can help us conserve them, it's surely worth doing so.

How much might the commons be worth in monetary terms? It's relatively easy to put a dollar value on private assets. Accountants and appraisers do it every day, aided by the fact that private assets are regularly traded for money.

This isn't the case with most shared assets. How much is clean air, an intact wetlands, or Darwin's theory of evolution worth in dollar terms? Clearly, many shared inheritances are simply priceless. Others are potentially quantifiable, but there's no current market for them. Fortunately, economists have developed methods to quantify the value of things that aren't traded, so it's possible to estimate the value of the "priceable" part of the commons within an order of magnitude. The surprising conclusion that emerges from numerous studies is that *the wealth we share is worth more than the wealth we own privately.*

This fact bears repeating. Even though much of the commons can't be valued in monetary terms, the parts that *can* be valued are worth more than all private assets combined.

It's worth noting that these estimates understate the gap between common and private assets because a significant portion of the value attributed to private wealth is in fact an appropriation of common wealth. If this mislabeled portion was subtracted from private wealth and added to common wealth, the gap between the two would widen further.

Two examples will make this point clear. Suppose you buy a house for $200,000 and, without improving it, sell it a few years later for $300,000. You pay off the mortgage and walk away with a pile of cash. But what caused the house to rise in value? It wasn't anything you did. Rather, it was the fact that your neighborhood became more popular, likely a result of the efforts of community members, improvements in public services, and similar factors.

Or consider another fount of private wealth, the social invention and public expansion of the stock market. Suppose you start a business that goes "public" through an offering of stock. Within a few years, you're able to sell your stock for a spectacular capital gain.

Much of this gain is a social creation, the result of centuries of monetary-system evolution, laws and regulations, and whole industries devoted to accounting, sharing information, and trading stocks. What's more, there's a direct correlation between the scale and quality of the stock market as an institution and the size of the private gain. You'll fetch a higher price if you sell into a market of millions

**APPROXIMATE VALUE OF NATURAL, PRIVATE, AND STATE ASSETS, 2001
(TRILLIONS OF U.S. DOLLARS)**

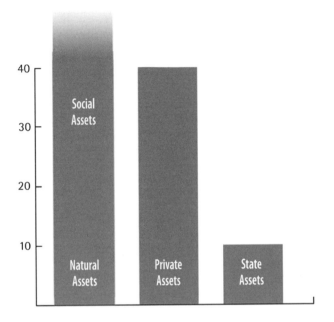

than into a market of two. Similarly, you'll gain more if transaction costs are low and trust in public information is high. Thus, stock that's traded on a regulated exchange sells for a higher multiple of earnings than unlisted stock. This socially created premium can account for 30% of the stock's value. If you're the lucky seller, you'll reap that extra cash—in no way thanks to anything you did as an individual.

Real estate gains and the stock market's social premium are just two instances of common assets contributing to private gain. Still, most rich people would like us to think it's their extraordinary talent, hard work, and risk-taking that create their well-deserved wealth. That's like saying a flower's beauty is due solely to its own efforts, owing nothing to nutrients in the soil, energy from the sun, water from the aquifer, or the activity of bees.

THE GREAT COMMONS GIVEAWAY
That we inherit a trove of common wealth is the good news. The bad news, alas, is that our inheritance is being grossly mismanaged. As a recent report by the advocacy

group Friends of the Commons concludes, "Maintenance of the commons is terrible, theft is rampant, and rents often aren't collected. To put it bluntly, our common wealth—and our children's—is being squandered. We are all poorer as a result."

Examples of commons mismanagement include the handout of broadcast spectrum to media conglomerates, the giveaway of pollution rights to polluters, the extension of copyrights to entertainment companies, the patenting of seeds and genes, the privatization of water, and the relentless destruction of habitat, wildlife, and ecosystems.

This mismanagement, though currently extreme, is not new. For over 200 years, the market has been devouring the commons in two ways. With one hand, the market takes valuable stuff from the commons and privatizes it. This is called "enclosure." With the other hand, the market dumps bad stuff into the commons and says, "It's your problem." This is called "externalizing." Much that is called economic growth today is actually a form of cannibalization in which the market diminishes the commons that ultimately sustains it.

Enclosure—the taking of good stuff from the commons—at first meant privatization of land by the gentry. Today it means privatization of many common assets by corporations. Either way, it means that what once belonged to everyone now belongs to a few.

Enclosure is usually justified in the name of efficiency. And sometimes, though not always, it does result in efficiency gains. But what also results from enclosure is the impoverishment of those who lose access to the commons, and the enrichment of those who take title to it. In other words, enclosure widens the gap between those with income-producing property and those without.

THE MARKET ASSAULT ON THE COMMONS

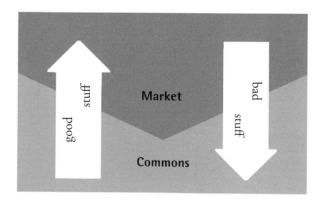

Externalizing—the dumping of bad stuff into the commons—is an automatic behavior pattern of profit-maximizing corporations: if they can avoid any out-of-pocket costs, they will. If workers, taxpayers, anyone downwind, future generations, or nature have to absorb added costs, so be it.

For decades, economists have agreed we'd be better served if businesses "internalized" their externalities—that is, paid in real time the costs they now shift to the commons. The reason this doesn't happen is that there's no one to set prices and collect them. Unlike private wealth, the commons lacks property rights and institutions to represent it in the marketplace.

The seeds of such institutions, however, are starting to emerge. Consider one of the environmental protection tools the U.S. currently uses, pollution trading. So-called cap-and-trade programs put a cap on total pollution, then grant portions of the total, via permits, to each polluting firm. Companies may buy other firms' permits if they want to pollute more than their allotment allows, or sell unused permits if they manage to pollute less. Such programs are generally supported by business because they allow polluters to find the cheapest ways to reduce pollution.

Public discussion of cap-and-trade programs has focused exclusively on their trading features. What's been overlooked is how they give away common wealth to polluters.

To date, all cap-and-trade programs have begun by giving pollution rights to existing polluters for free. This treats polluters as if they own our sky and rivers. It means that future polluters will have to pay old polluters for the scarce—hence valuable—right to dump wastes into nature. Imagine that: because a corporation polluted in the past, it gets free income forever! And, because ultimately we'll all pay for limited pollution via higher prices, this amounts to an enormous transfer of wealth—trillions of dollars—to shareholders of historically polluting corporations.

In theory, though, there is no reason that the initial pollution rights should not reside with the public. Clean air and the atmosphere's capacity to absorb pollutants are "wealth" that belongs to everyone. Hence, when polluters use up these parts of the commons, they should pay the public—not the other way around.

TAKING THE COMMONS BACK

How can we correct the system omission that permits, and indeed promotes, destruction of nature and ever-widening inequality among humans? The answer lies in building a new sector of the economy whose clear legal mission is to preserve shared inheritances for everyone. Just as the market is populated by profit-maximizing corporations, so this new sector would be populated by asset-preserving trusts.

Here a brief description of trusts may be helpful. The trust is a private institution that's even older than the corporation. The essence of a trust is a fiduciary relationship. A trust holds and manages property for another person or for many other people. A simple example is a trust set up by a grandparent to pay for a grandchild's education. Other trusts include pension funds, charitable foundations and university endowments. There are also hundreds of trusts in America, like the Nature Conservancy and the Trust for Public Land, that own land or conservation easements in perpetuity.

If we were to design an institution to protect pieces of the commons, we couldn't do much better than a trust. The goal of commons management, after all, is to preserve assets and deliver benefits to broad classes of beneficiaries. That's what trusts do, and it's not rocket science.

Over centuries, several principles of trust management have evolved. These include:

- Trustees have a fiduciary responsibility to beneficiaries. If a trustee fails in this obligation, he or she can be removed and penalized.
- Trustees must preserve the original asset. It's okay to spend income, but don't invade the principal.
- Trustees must assure transparency. Information about money flows should be readily available to beneficiaries.

Trusts in the new commons sector would be endowed with rights comparable to those of corporations. Their trustees would take binding oaths of office and, like judges, serve long terms. Though protecting common assets would be their primary job, they would also distribute income from those assets to beneficiaries. These beneficiaries would include all citizens within a jurisdiction, large classes of citizens (children, the elderly), and/or agencies serving common purposes such as public transit or ecological restoration. When distributing income to individuals, the allocation formula would be one person, one share. The right to receive commons income would be a nontransferable birthright, not a property right that could be traded.

Fortuitously, a working model of such a trust already exists: the Alaska Permanent Fund. When oil drilling on the North Slope began in the 1970s, Gov. Jay Hammond, a Republican, proposed that 25% of the state's royalties be placed in a mutual fund to be invested on behalf of Alaska's citizens. Voters approved in a referendum. Since then, the Alaska Permanent Fund has grown to over $28 billion, and Alaskans have received roughly $22,000 apiece in dividends. In 2003 the per capita dividend was $1,107; a family of four received $4,428.

What Alaska did with its oil can be replicated for other gifts of nature. For example, we could create a nationwide Sky Trust to stabilize the climate for future generations. The trust would restrict emissions of heat-trapping gases and sell a declining number of emission permits to polluters. The income would be returned to U.S. residents in equal yearly dividends, thus reversing the wealth transfer built into current cap-and-trade programs. Instead of everyone paying historic polluters, polluters would pay all of us.

Just as a Sky Trust could represent our equity in the natural commons, a Public Stock Trust could embody our equity in the social commons. Such a trust would capture some of the socially created stock-market premium that currently flows only to shareholders and their investment bankers. As noted earlier, this premium is sizeable—roughly 30% of the value of publicly traded stock. A simple way to share it would be to create a giant mutual fund—call it the American Permanent Fund—that would hold, say, 10% of the shares of publicly traded companies. This mutual fund, in turn, would be owned by all Americans on a one share per person basis (perhaps linked to their Social Security accounts).

To build up the fund without precipitating a fall in share prices, companies would contribute shares at the rate of, say, 1% per year. The contributions would be the price companies pay for the benefits they derive from a commons asset, the large, trusted market for stock—a small price, indeed, for the hefty benefits. Over time, the mutual fund would assure that when the economy grows, everyone benefits. The top 5% would still own more than the bottom 90%, but at least every American would have *some* property income, and a slightly larger slice of our economic pie.

SHARING THE WEALTH

The perpetuation of inequality is built into the current design of capitalism. Because of the skewed distribution of private wealth, a small self- perpetuating minority receives a disproportionate share of America's nonlabor income.

Tom Paine had something to say about this. In his essay "Agrarian Justice," written in 1790, he argued that, because enclosure of the commons had separated so many people from their primary source of sustenance, it was necessary to create a functional equivalent of the commons in the form of a National Fund. Here is how he put it:

> There are two kinds of property. Firstly, natural property, or that which comes to us from the Creator of the universe—such as the earth, air, water. Secondly, artificial or acquired property—the invention of men. In the latter, equality is impossible; for to distribute it equally, it would be necessary that all should have contributed in the same proportion, which can never be the case. ... Equality of natural property is different. Every individual in the world is born with legitimate claims on this property, or its equivalent.

Enclosure of the commons, he went on, was necessary to improve the efficiency of cultivation. But:

The landed monopoly that began with [enclosure] has produced the greatest evil. It has dispossessed more than half the inhabitants of every nation of their natural inheritance, without providing for them, as ought to have been done, an indemnification for that loss, and has thereby created a species of poverty and wretchedness that did not exist before.

The appropriate compensation for loss of the commons, Paine said, was a national fund financed by rents paid by land owners. Out of this fund, every person reaching age 21 would get 15 pounds a year, and every person over 50 would receive an additional 10 pounds. (Think of Social Security, financed by commons rents instead of payroll taxes.)

A PROGRESSIVE OFFENSIVE

Paine's vision, allowing for inflation and new forms of enclosure, could not be more timely today. Surely from our vast common inheritance—not just the land, but the atmosphere, the broadcast spectrum, our mineral resources, our threatened habitats and water supplies—enough rent can be collected to pay every American over age 21 a modest annual dividend, and every person reaching 21 a small start-up inheritance.

Such a proposal may seem utopian. In today's political climate, perhaps it is. But consider this. About 20 years ago, right-wing think tanks laid out a bold agenda. They called for lowering taxes on private wealth, privatizing much of government, and deregulating industry. Amazingly, this radical agenda has largely been achieved.

It's time for progressives to mount an equally bold offensive. The old shibboleths—let's gin up the economy, create jobs, and expand government programs—no longer excite. We need to talk about *fixing* the economy, not just growing it; about *income* for everyone, not just jobs; about nurturing *ecosystems, cultures,* and *communities,* not just our individual selves. More broadly, we need to celebrate the commons as an essential counterpoise to the market.

Unfortunately, many progressives have viewed the state as the only possible counterpoise to the market. The trouble is, the state has been captured by corporations. This capture isn't accidental or temporary; it's structural and long-term.

This doesn't mean progressives can't occasionally recapture the state. We've done so before and will do so again. It does mean that progressive control of the state is the exception, not the norm; in due course, corporate capture will resume. It follows that if we want lasting fixes to capitalism's tragic flaws, we must use our brief moments of political ascendancy to build institutions that endure.

Programs that rely on taxes, appropriations, or regulations are inherently transitory; they get weakened or repealed when political power shifts. By contrast, institutions that are self-perpetuating and have broad constituencies are likely to last. (It also helps if they mail out checks periodically.) This was the genius of Social

Security, which has survived—indeed grown—through numerous Republican administrations.

If progressives are smart, we'll use our next New Deal to create common property trusts that include all Americans as beneficiaries. These trusts will then be to the 21st century what social insurance was to the 20th: sturdy pillars of shared responsibility and entitlement. Through them, the commons will be a source of sustenance for all, as it was before enclosure. Life-long income will be linked to generations-long ecological health. Isn't that a future most Americans would welcome?

From *Dollars & Sense* magazine, November/December 2004.

APPENDIX

WEALTH-BUILDING STRATEGIES

Here is a partial list of promising strategies for asset building—national and local, private and public, large-scale and small.

COMMUNITY DEVELOPMENT FINANCIAL INSTITUTIONS (CDFIs)

CDFIs are nonprofit organizations that provide credit, capital, and financial services to communities neglected by commercial lenders. These "alternative" financial institutions include community development banks, community development loan funds, community development credit unions, micro-credit programs, community development corporations that loan or invest, and community development venture funds. CDFIs have various structures, but all channel resources (from individuals, foundations, religious organizations, unions, and the government) into community-determined development in order to meet the needs of low-income and low-wealth individuals and neighborhoods.

Over 1,000 CDFIs are in operation in the United States, ranging in size from small neighborhood credit unions to institutions with hundreds of millions of dollars in assets. Perhaps the largest CDFI, Self-Help Credit Union, is a national lender that has provided more than $3.5 billion in financing to over 40,000 home buyers, small business people, and nonprofits.

Modern CDFIs grew out of struggles against racial discrimination, gentrification, and community disinvestment in the 1960s and 1970s. Their impact on community development has been enormous, but many communities still lack CDFIs, many community members do not know about their services, and the CDFI sector remains under-capitalized.

For more information:

Coalition of Community Development Financial Institutions **www.cdfi.org**
Community Development Financial Institutions (CDFI) Fund,
     U.S. Department of the Treasury **www.cdfifund.gov**
National Community Capital Association **www.communitycapital.org**
Nat'l Federation of Community Development Credit Unions **www.natfed.org**

ROTATING SAVINGS AND CREDIT ASSOCIATIONS (ROSCAs)

Common in immigrant communities, ROSCAs are collective borrowing pools formed among family members or friends. Each person pays in a monthly sum and then has a turn at borrowing the entire pool with no interest. These informal arrangements are adapted from cultural practices indigenous to East Asia, Latin America, the Caribbean, the Near East, and Africa. Though widespread in the United States, they remain below the public radar. Participants are recruited on the basis of trust and are held accountable through community sanctions. In general, the pools of capital are small, although in some cases (for example, in Korean communities) sums large enough to finance small businesses have been collected.

For more information:
Global Development Research Center   **www.gdrc.org**

INDEPENDENT DEVELOPMENT ACCOUNTS (IDAs)

IDAs are matched savings accounts designed to help low-income families accumulate financial assets. An individual participant sets aside savings and receives matching dollars if and only if he or she uses the account for specific wealth-building purposes, for example, to buy a home, pay for college tuition, or start a small business. The match (typically two or three times the amount saved by the individual) comes from public sources or foundations and is capped in order to control program costs. A 1998 federal pilot program launched the first large-scale IDA demonstration projects. Today, about 250 neighborhoods have IDA programs.

So far, the results have been modest. A recent study found that participants saved an average of just $19 a month, producing total assets of about $700 per year, including the match. Many cash-strapped participants have been unable to save at all, or have had to withdraw their savings for nondesignated purposes (with no match).

Nevertheless, if brought to scale and fully funded as a federal program, IDAs would be a useful tool to help low-income families build assets. Washington University's Michael Sherradan and others argue that the existing model should be greatly expanded, making matched savings accounts available to all.

For more information:
Center for Social Development   **www.gwbweb.wustl.edu/csd**
Corporation for Enterprise Development   **www.cfed.org**
Welfare Information Network   **www.financeprojectinfo.org/win/individu.asp**

CHILDREN'S SAVINGS ACCOUNTS

In 2003, the United Kingdom established the Child Trust Fund in order to encourage saving and asset ownership. Each child receives a modest deposit of government funds (known as "baby bonds") at birth and at his or her seventh birthday, with children from lower-income households receiving additional government payments. Family and friends may also contribute to the child's account, which is controlled by the parents until the child reaches 18, at which time the funds may be withdrawn for any purpose. "The CTF account will help to strengthen the savings habit of future generations, spread the benefits of asset ownership to all, educate people in the need for savings, and give young people a basic understanding of financial products," according to the government.

U.S. Senator Robert Kerrey proposed a similar program in 1998. Under the "KidSave" initiative, children would have received $1,000 at birth, plus $500 a year from ages one to five, to invest. If a child's parents matched the government's $500 yearly contribution, he or she would have $40,000 at age 18. The legislation has languished.

For more information:

The Aspen Institute Initiative on Financial Security   **www.aspeninstitute.org**
Child Trust Fund of Inland Revenue   **www.inlandrevenue.gov.uk/ctf**
United Kingdom Parliament   **www.parliament.the-stationery-office.co.uk**

HOMEOWNERSHIP

In 1944, the nation made a massive commitment to expand homeownership. The Serviceman's Readjustment Act, better known as the GI Bill, provided veterans easy access to low-interest, long-term mortgage loans that were insured by the Federal Housing Authority and the Veterans Administration. The program was instrumental in building the white middle class in the years after World War II.

Today, the federal government supports homeownership primarily through the tax structure, not direct spending or loan guarantees. The tax deduction for mortgage interest is by far the largest single housing subsidy in the country, and tax advantages for homeownership total $110.5 billion, exceeding direct outlays for housing programs by 236 to 1, according to the Corporation for Enterprise Development report "Hidden in Plain Sight: A Look at the $335 Billion Federal Asset-Building Budget." The problem is, these subsidies don't reach those (mostly lower-income) taxpayers who do not itemize deductions on their tax returns.

Federal homeownership programs include the Department of Housing and Urban Development's HOME program (a federal block grant to state and local governments designed to create affordable housing for low-income households), the Federal Home Loan Bank Affordable Housing Program (which subsidizes long-term financing for very low-, low-, and moderate-income families), certain Community Development Block Grants, and the U.S. Department of Agriculture's rural homebuyers' program. In addition to these programs, government-sponsored mortgage buyers such as Fannie Mae and Freddie Mac provide a secondary market for home mortgage loans by purchasing mortgages from financial institutions.

Major home buying initiatives subsidized by federal dollars, comparable in scale to the GI Bill, are needed to dramatically expand homeownership opportunities. In addition, the Community Reinvestment Act of 1977, which mandated lending in minority neighborhoods, needs to be strengthened in order to end continuing racial discrimination in lending and ensure that low-cost home mortgage loans reach low-income communities and households of color.

For more information:
PolicyLink   **www.policylink.org**
U.S. Department of Housing and Urban Development   **www.hud.gov**

PUBLIC TRUSTS WITH RESIDENT DIVIDENDS

The Alaska Permanent Fund (APF) is a $27.6 billion trust fund that pays approximately $1,100 in dividends (2003 dollars) per year to every Alaska resident. The fourth largest cash infusion into the Alaska economy, the dividend payments account for approximately 10% of annual income for rural Alaskans, which in turn fuels economic growth in the state. The Alaska fund is the largest single example of a type of collective wealth-building strategy in which a public trust generates dividend payments for residents. Under this sort of trust arrangement, profits from the sale or use of public resources are returned to residents though dividend payments (often drawn from the interest on large capital funds created with those profits). Individuals have a right to a stream of income by virtue of membership in the group. In the case of the Alaska Permanent Fund, all Alaska residents receive equal dividends from oil revenues—providing a greater boon to lower-income community members.

Although similar arrangements could theoretically be set up within any group that owns or generates a lucrative resource, only a few dividend-paying public trusts actually exist in the United States: the Alaska Permanent Fund (which began operations in 1976) and some Indian casinos (in which individual tribes distribute dividends to help guarantee equitable division of their casino wealth).

Author Peter Barnes has proposed setting up a national "Sky Trust," which would collect permit fees from carbon-spewing companies. A percentage of the permit revenue would go to Congress and the states, and the remainder would be distributed annually to all U.S. citizens on a one-person, one-share basis. In 2003, Senators Joseph Lieberman (D-Conn.) and John McCain (R-Ariz.) introduced legislation that included elements of the Sky Trust idea. If passed into law, the Sky Trust would be the largest dividend-yielding public trust yet.

For more information:
Alaska Permanent Fund Corporation   **www.apfc.org**
National Indian Gaming Association   **www.indiangaming.org/library/index**
U.S. Sky Trust   **www.usskytrust.org**

PENSIONS AND INDIVIDUAL RETIREMENT PLANS

The federal government gives tax advantages to two general types of retirement policies: employer-sponsored retirement plans and individual savings accounts. Employer-sponsored plans include "defined benefit" pensions, which guarantee retirees a predictable level of income for the rest of their lives, and "defined contribution" plans, favored by most businesses, in which employees or employers contribute a defined amount to the retirement account, then invest the account assets, subjecting future retirement income to market risk. Examples of defined contribution plans are 401(k)s, savings and thrift plans, and employee stock ownership plans.

Fewer than half of all workers are covered by an employer-sponsored pension or retirement plan of either kind at any given time, and fewer than one in five has a defined benefit pension. Coverage rates are even lower among employees of small businesses and lower-wage workers, and because many retirement plans require a waiting period, employees who move between jobs by choice or necessity are not well served by the current pension system.

Individual retirement plans, including Individual Retirement Accounts and Keogh plans (which are specifically for the self-employed), are initiated and controlled by an individual. Pensions and tax-preferred saving plans together provide one-fifth of the income of the elderly, with the bulk of that money going to higher-income people.

For more information:

Employee Benefit Research Institute	**www.ebri.org**
AFL-CIO	**www.aflcio.org**
Employee Benefits Security Administration	**www.dol.gov/ebsa**
Pension Rights Center	**www.pensionrights.org**

SOCIAL SECURITY

Social Security is viewed by most as a source of retirement income, not a form of wealth. But Social Security is very much a form of social, or socialized, wealth—it's the largest component of the nation's social safety net, and it operates much like a national pension and insurance plan. No other government program has had more impact on the lives of the elderly and the disabled.

All workers who pay Social Security taxes for at least 40 quarter-years are eligible for Social Security retirement income. A lesser earning spouse gets 50% of the higher earning spouse or her own benefit, whichever is higher. Money is collected from the paychecks of working people to pay current retirees, with each generation paying for the retirement of the older generation. Forty percent of the elderly rely on Social Security for 90% or more of their income.

In addition to retirement income, Social Security provides survivors' and disability benefits. Of the 44 million people receiving Social Security benefits, 30 million are retirees and their dependents. The rest are disabled workers and their dependents and survivors of deceased workers.

For more information:

AARP	**www.aarp.org/socialsecurity**
Social Security Administration	**www.ssa.gov**
Social Security Network	**www.socsec.org**

WORKER OWNERSHIP

A worker cooperative is a self-managed business in which workers share the fruits of their own labor and have democratic control over the enterprise. Members finance the firm and collectively hold the net worth of the business. They have equal voting rights (on a one-member, one-vote basis), much like citizens in a democratic community. In cooperatives, authority resides in the collectivity as a whole. This is in contrast to the "rule by the few" approach common in other forms of business (e.g., proprietorships, partnerships, and corporations). The number of cooperatives in the United States is estimated to be between 1,000 and 5,000.

Employee stock ownership is a more common form of employee ownership. Less an experiment in economic democracy than the worker cooperative, employee stock ownership nevertheless can be an effective way to spread corporate wealth to working people. By far the most common form of employee stock ownership is the employee stock ownership plan or ESOP, an indirect form of employee ownership in which the company sets up a trust that holds stock on behalf of employees. Trustees, rather than workers themselves, have voting rights over the shares. Studies of ESOP firms in Massachusetts and Washington state found that ESOPs provide employees a significant pool of wealth. The Washington state study found that the average Washington ESOP participant's account was worth $24,260 in 1995. The Massachusetts study found that the per participant wealth held for employees in Massachusetts ESOPs was $39,895 in 2000. The studies suggest that most companies provide ESOPs as a supplement to, rather than a replacement for, wages and other benefits. The average value of total retirement plan assets (for example, 401(k) plus ESOP assets) in ESOP companies is far higher than the average value in comparable non-ESOP companies.

For more information:

Grassroots Economic Organizing (GEO) Newsletter	**www.geonewsletter.org**
The ICA Group	**www.ica-group.org**
National Center for Employee Ownership	**www.nceo.org**
Ownership Associates	**www.ownershipassociates.com**
U.S. Federation of Worker Coops	**www.usworker.coop**

LAND TRUSTS

A community land trust is a nonprofit organization that acquires and holds land for the benefit of the community. These trusts usually provide affordable housing for residents who have been priced out of commercial housing markets. Because the land is held by the trust, not the individual, and is democratically controlled, land trusts enable communities to maintain control over economic development and keep property values affordable for future generations.

Another common type of land trust, sometimes called a conservation land trust, protects open or green spaces from development. Three of the largest urban conservation land trusts in the country were formed in New York in 2004. The Bronx Land Trust, the Brooklyn/Queens Land Trust, and the Manhattan Land Trust will preserve 62 community gardens that the city had planned to destroy. The racially, culturally, and economically diverse trust members will ensure the gardens remain protected neighborhood resources for public use, according to the Trust for Public Land.

For more information:

Institute for Community Economics	**www.iceclt.org**
Trust for Public Land	**www.tpl.org**
Champlain Housing Trust	**www.champlainhousingtrust.org**

THE TAX STRUCTURE

Over the past 20 years, the American tax system has shifted the burden of taxation off the rich and off corporations, and onto everyone else. According to David Cay Johnston, author of *Perfectly Legal: The Covert Campaign to Rig Our Tax System to Benefit the Super Rich—and Cheat Everybody Else,* between 1992 and 2000, when the federal income tax burden on most Americans *rose* by 18%, it *fell* for the top 400 taxpayers, whose incomes had skyrocketed, thanks to tax breaks for the rich passed in 1997. Additional tax cuts for the very rich were passed in 2001 and 2003, subsidized by taxes on the poor and the middle class. Under the current system, most concentrated financial wealth goes untaxed. A major overhaul of the current system of taxation is essential to reducing growing extremes of income and wealth inequality.

For more information:

Citizens for Tax Justice	**www.ctj.org**
Tax Policy Center	**www.taxpolicycenter.org**

REFERENCES

Ackerman, Bruce and Anne Alstott. *The Stakeholder Society.* New Haven: Yale University Press, 1999.

Ackerman, Bruce. "Taxation and the Constitution." *Columbia Law Review* 99(1):1–58 (January 1999).

Agarwal, Bina and Pradeep Panda. "Spousal Violence in India: Does Women's Property Status Make a Difference?" Paper presented at the Annual Conference of the International Association for Feminist Economics, June 2003.

Agarwal, Bina and Pradeep Panda. "Home and the world: Revisiting violence." *Indian Express,* August 7, 2003.

Aizcorbe, Ana M., Arthur B. Kennickell, and Kevin B. Moore, "Recent Changes in U.S. Family Finances: Evidence from the 1998 and 2001 Survey of Consumer Finances," *Federal Reserve Bulletin* 89 (January 2003).

Amott, Teresa L. and Julie Matthaei. *Race, Gender, and Work: A Multicultural Economic History of Women in the United States.* Boston: South End Press, 1996.

Auerbach, Alan J., William G. Gale, and Peter R. Orszag. "Reassessing the Fiscal Gap." *Tax Notes* (July 28, 2003).

Barnes, Peter. *Who Owns the Sky? Our Common Assets and the Future of Capitalism.* Washington, D.C.: Island Press, 2001.

Blaug, Mark. *Economic Theory in Retrospect.* New York: Richard D. Irwin, 1968.

Boldrin, Michele and David K. Levine. "Perfectly Competitive Innovation." CEPR Discussion Paper No. 3274, 2002. <http://ssrn.com/abstrct=308040>

Bollier, David. *Silent Theft: The Private Plunder of Our Common Wealth.* New York: Routledge, 2003.

Carnegie, Andrew. *The Gospel of Wealth.* 1889. <www.fordham.edu/halsall/mod/1889carnegie.html>

Carnoy, Martin. *Faded Dreams: The Politics and Economics of Race in America.* New York: Cambridge University Press, 1994.

Citizens for Tax Justice. "The Bush Tax Cuts: The Most Recent CTJ Data." December 17, 2003.

Citizens for Tax Justice. "White House Reveals Nation's Biggest Problems: The Very Rich Citizens Don't Have Enough Money & Workers Don't Pay Enough in Taxes." December 2002.

Claessens, Stijn, Simeon Djankov, and Larry H. P. Lang. "Who Controls East Asian Corporations—and the Implications for Legal Reform." Washington, D.C.: World Bank, September 1999.

Collins, Chuck, Mike Lapham, and Scott Klinger. "I Didn't Do It Alone: Society's Contribution to Individual Wealth and Success." Boston: Responsible Wealth, a project of United for a Fair Economy, June 2004.

Collins, Chuck and Dedrick Muhammad. "Tax Wealth to Broaden Wealth." *Dollars & Sense* 251: 22–25 (January/February 2004).

Collins, Chuck and Felice Yeskel with United for a Fair Economy. *Economic Apartheid in America: A Primer on Economic Inequality and Insecurity.* New York: The New Press, 2000.

Conley, Dalton. *Being Black, Living in the Red: Race, Wealth, and Social Policy in America.* Berkeley and Los Angeles, Calif.: University of California Press, 1999.

Congressional Budget Office. "Effective Federal Tax Rates, 1997 to 2001," Table B1-B, April 2004. <www.cbo.gov/ftpdoc.cfm?index=4514&type=1>

Congressional Budget Office. "CBO's Current Budget Projection." March 2004. <www.cbo. gov/showdoc.cfm?index=1944&sequence=0#table5>

Costanza, Robert et al. "The value of the world's ecosystem services and natural capital." *Nature* 387: 253–260 (1997).

Cummings, Sarah et al. *Gender Perspectives on Property and Inheritance: A Global Source Book.* Oxford, U.K.: Oxfam, 2001.

Dixon, John A. and Kirk Hamilton. "Expanding the Measure of Wealth." Washington, D.C.: World Bank, 1996.

Dutta Das, Manju. "Improving the Relevance and Effectiveness of Agricultural Extension Activities for Women Farmers." Rome: U.N. Food and Agriculture Organization, 1995.

Economic Policy Institute. *Snapshot,* February 11, 2004.

Feagin, Joe R. *Racist America: Roots, Current Realities, and Future Reparations.* New York: Routledge, 2001.

Frank, Ellen. "No More Savings!" *Dollars & Sense* 253: 18–20 (May/Jun 2004).

Frank, Robert H. *Luxury Fever.* Princeton: Princeton University Press, 2000.

Freyfogle, Eric. *The Land We Share: Private Property and the Common Good.* Washington, D.C.: Shearwater Books, 2003.

Friedman, Leon. "A Better Kind of Wealth Tax." *The American Prospect* 11(23) (November 6, 2000).

Friedman, Leon. "Trump's Wealth Tax." *The Nation* 269(19): 4–5 (December 6, 1999).

Friends of the Commons. *The State of the Commons 2003/04.*

Fuchs, Lawrence H. *The American Kaleidoscope: Race, Ethnicity, and the Civic Culture.* Middletown, Conn.: Wesleyan University Press, 1990.

Fung, Archon, Tessa Hebb, and Joel Rogers, eds. *Working Capital: The Power of Labor's Pensions.* Ithaca, N.Y.: ILR Press, 2001.

Gale, William G., Peter R. Orszag, and Isaac Shapiro. "The Ultimate Burden Of The Tax Cuts." Washington, D.C.: Center on Budget and Policy Priorities & Tax Policy Center, June 2, 2004.

Gates, Jeff. *The Ownership Solution.* Reading, Mass.: Addison-Wesley, 1998.

Gates, William H., Sr., and Chuck Collins. *Wealth and Our Commonwealth: Why America Should Tax Accumulated Fortunes.* Boston: Beacon Press, 2002.

George, Henry. *Progress and Poverty.* New York: Robert Schalkenbach Foundation, 1948.

Ghilarducci, Teresa. "Small Benefits, Big Pension Funds, and How Governance Reforms Can Close the Gap." In *Working Capital: The Power of Labor's Pensions,* Fung, Hebb, and Rogers, eds. Ithaca: ILR Press, 2001.

Glenn, Evelyn N. *Unequal Freedom: How Race and Gender Shaped American Citizenship and Labor.* Cambridge, Mass.: Harvard University Press, 2004.

Gonzalez, Juan. *Harvest of Empire: A History of Latinos in America.* New York: Penguin Books, 2001.

Gouskova, Elena and Frank Stafford. "Trends in household wealth dynamics, 1999–2001." Ann Arbor: Institute for Social Research, Univ. of Michigan, September 2002.

Greider, William. *The Soul of Capitalism: Opening Paths to a Moral Economy.* New York: Simon & Schuster, 2003.

Hartzok, Alanna. "Henry George's 'Single Tax'." *Econ-atrocity Bulletin,* Center for Popular Economics, April 2004. <www.fguide.org/Bulletin/SingleTax.htm>

Heilbroner, Robert L. *The Worldly Philosophers.* New York: Simon & Schuster, 1999.

Hertz, Thomas. "Rags, Riches and Race: The Intergenerational Economic Mobility of Black and White Families in the United States." In *Unequal Chances: Family Background and Economic Success,* Bowles, Gintis, and Osborne, eds. Princeton University Press and Russell Sage, forthcoming 2005.

Hogarth, Jeanne M. and Chris E. Anguelov. "Descriptive Statistics on Levels of Net Worth, Financial Assets, and Other Selected Characteristics." Paper prepared for the Women & Assets Summit, March-April 2003. <www.heller.brandeis.edu/womenandassets>

Horwitz, Morton. *The Transformation of American Law, 1870–1960: The Crisis of Legal Orthodoxy.* New York: Oxford University Press, 1992.

Internal Revenue Service. "Personal Exemptions and Individual Income Tax Rates, 1913–2002." SOI Bulletin, Data Release, December 10, 2003. <www.irs.gov/taxstats/article/0,,id=96679,00.htm>

"Investment Product Review: Private Capital 2002." Report of the Investment Product Review Working Group, AFL-CIO, November 2002.

Jackson, Kenneth T. *Crabgrass Frontier: The Suburbanization of the United States.* New York: Oxford University Press, 1985.

Johnson, James H., Jr., and Melvin L. Oliver. "Economic Restructuring and Black Male Joblessness in U.S. Metropolitan Areas." *Urban Geography* 12 (1991).

Johnson, Richard W. "The Gender Gap in Pension Wealth: Is Women's Progress in the Labor Market Equalizing Retirement Benefits?" Washington, D.C.: Urban Institute, March 1999.

Johnson, Richard W., Usha Sambamoorthi, and Stephen Crystal. "Gender Differences in Pension Wealth." Unpublished manuscript, quoted in Johnson, "The Gender Gap in Pension Wealth."

Johnston, David Cay. "Dozens of Rich Americans Join in Fight to Retain the Estate Tax." *The New York Times,* February 14, 2001.

Johnston, David Cay. *Perfectly Legal: The Secret Campaign to Rig Our Tax System to Benefit the Super Rich—And Cheat Everybody Else.* New York: Portfolio, 2003.

Keister, Lisa A. *Wealth in America: Trends in Wealth Inequality.* New York: Cambridge University Press, 2000.

Keister, Lisa A. and Alexis Yamokoski. "Single Females & Wealth: The Assets of Young Baby Boomers." Unpublished paper, April 2004.

Kennickell, Arthur B. "A Rolling Tide: Changes in the Distribution of Wealth in the U.S., 1989–2001." Jerome Levy Economics Institute, November 2003.

Keynes, John Maynard. *The General Theory of Employment, Interest, and Money.* New York: Harcourt Brace, 1964.

Kogan, Richard. "Deficit Picture Even Grimmer Than New CBO Projections Suggest." Washington, D.C.: Center on Budget and Policy Priorities, August 2003. <www.cbpp.org/8-26-03bud.htm>

Krehely, Jeff, Meaghan House, and Emily Kernan. "Axis of Ideology: Conservative Foundations and Public Policy." Washington, D.C.: National Committee for Responsive Philanthropy, 2004.

Kuttner, Robert. "Bully For Trump." *The Boston Globe,* November 14, 1999.

Landes, David. *The Wealth and Poverty of Nations.* New York: W.W. Norton, 1999.

Leondar-Wright, Betsy. "Black Job Loss Déjà Vu." *Dollars & Sense* 253: 17 (May/June 2004).

Lipsitz, George. *The Possessive Investment in Whiteness: How White People Profit from Identity Politics.* Philadelphia: Temple University Press, 1998.

Marx, Karl. *The Communist Manifesto.* New York: W. W. Norton, 1988.

Mason, Edward. "Cahill to Boost Pension Fund Investments." *Boston Business Journal,* May 3, 2004.

Massey, Douglas S., and Nancy A. Denton. *American Apartheid: Segregation and the Making of the Underclass.* Cambridge, Mass.: Harvard University Press, 1993.

McCulloch, Heather with Lisa Robinson. "Sharing the Wealth: Resident Ownership Mechanisms: A PolicyLink Report," Oakland, Calif.: PolicyLink, 2001.

Menchaca, Martha. *Recovering History, Constructing Race: The Indian, Black, and White Roots of Mexican Americans.* Austin, Texas: University of Texas Press, 2001.

Michl, Thomas. "Prefunding is Still the Answer," *Challenge* 45(3): 112–116 (May-June 2002).

Mill, John Stuart. *Principles of Political Economy.* London: Longmans Green, 1909.

Mishel, Lawrence, Jared Bernstein, and Heather Boushey. *State of Working America: 2002–03.* Ithaca, N.Y.: ILR Press, 2003.

Muhammad, Dedrick, Attieno Davis, Meizhu Lui, and Betsy Leondar-Wright. "The State of the Dream 2004: Enduring Disparities in Black and White." Boston: United for a Fair Economy, January 2004.

National Urban League, *The National Urban League's Jobs Report*, January 2004.

Office of Management and Budget. *Budget of the United States 2004: Historical Tables*. August 2003. <http://w3.access.gpo.gov/usbudget/fy2004/pdf/hist.pdf>

Oliver, Melvin L. and Tom Shapiro. *Black Wealth/White Wealth: New Perspectives on Racial Inequality*. New York: Routledge, 1995.

Orzechowski, Shawna and Peter Sepielli. "Net Worth and Asset Ownership of Households: 1998 and 2000." *Current Population Reports,* U.S. Census Bureau, May 2003.

Phillips, Kevin. *Wealth and Democracy*. New York: Broadway Books, 2002.

Piketty, Thomas and Emmanuel Saez. "Income Inequality in the United States, 1918–1998." NBER Working Paper #8467, September 2001.

Pizzigati, Sam. *Greed and Good: Understanding and Overcoming the Inequality That Limits Our Lives*. New York: Apex Press, 2004.

Robinson, Randall. *The Debt: What America Owes to Blacks*. New York: Plume Books, 2001.

Rodrik, Dani. "Development Strategies for the Next Century." Paper prepared for the Institute for Developing Economies, Japan External Trade Organization Conference, February 2002.

Roediger, David R. *The Wages of Whiteness: Race and the Making of the American Working Class*. London: Verso, 1999.

Scott, Janny. "Nearly Half of Black Men Found Jobless." *The New York Times,* February 28, 2004.

Seager, Joni. *The Penguin Atlas of Women in the World*. New York: Penguin, 2003.

Shapiro, Thomas M. *The Hidden Cost of Being African American: How Wealth Perpetuates Inequality*. New York: Oxford University Press, 2003.

Sklar, Holly, Laryssa Mykyta, and Susan Wefald. *Raise the Floor: Wages and Policies that Work for All of Us*. Boston: South End Press, 2002.

Squires, Gregory D. "Runaway Plants, Capital Mobility, and Black Economic Rights." In *Community and Capital in Conflict: Plant Closings and Job Loss*, John C. Raines et al., eds. Philadelphia: Temple Univ. Press, 1982.

Thorndike, Joseph J., and Dennis J. Ventry, Jr., eds. *Tax Justice: The Ongoing Debate*. Washington, D.C.: Urban Institute Press, 2002.

Ratner, Sidney. *American Taxation*. New York: W.W. Norton, 1942.

Uchitelle, Louis. "Blacks Lose Better Jobs Faster As Middle-Class Work Drops." *The New York Times,* July 12, 2003.

United Nations Development Programme. *Human Development Report 1995 – Gender and Human Development*.

United Nations Development Programme. *Human Development Report 2003 – Millennium Development Goals*.

United Nations Division for the Advancement of Women. "Women and the Economy." Fact Sheet based on "Review and Appraisal of the Implementation of the Beijing Platform for Action: Report of the Secretary-General," May 2000.

United Nations Food and Agriculture Organization. "FAO Focus: Women and Food Security," no date.

U.S. House Committee on Ways and Means. Tax Revision Compendium, *The Place of the Personal Exemptions in the Present-Day Income Tax,* report prepared by Lawrence Seltzer, 1st Volume, 1959, pp. 493–514.

U.S. Social Security Administration. "The 2004 OASDI [Social Security] Trustees Report," March 23, 2004.

Wagner, Y. and M. Strauss. "The Theoretical Foundations of the Communist Manifesto's Economic Program." In *The Communist Manifesto,* New York: W. W. Norton, 1988.

Williamson, Thad, David Imbroscio, and Gar Alperovitz. *Making a Place for Community.* New York: Routledge, 2002.

Wolff, Edward N. "Changes in Household Wealth in the 1980s and 1990s in the U.S." In *International Perspectives on Household Wealth.* Northampton, Mass.: Edward Elgar, forthcoming.

Wolff, Edward N. "Recent Trends in Wealth Ownership, 1983–1998." Jerome Levy Economics Institute, April 2000.

Wolff, Edward N. *Top Heavy: The Increasing Inequality of Wealth in America and What Can Be Done About It.* New York: The New Press, 2002.

"Women's Property and Inheritance Rights: Improving Lives in Changing Times." Washington, D.C.: Women in Development/WID, March 2003.

Woo, Lillian G., F. William Schweke, and David E. Buchholz. "Hidden in Plain Sight: A Look at the $335 Billion Federal Asset-Building Budget." Washington, D.C.: The Corporation for Enterprise Development, 2004.

Zanglein, Jayne Elizabeth. "Overcoming Institutional Barriers on the Economically Targeted Investment Superhighway." In *Working Capital: The Power of Labor's Pensions,* Fung, Hebb, and Rogers, eds. Ithaca: ILR Press, 2001.

CONTRIBUTORS

Gar Alperovitz is professor of political economy at the University of Maryland and president of the National Center for Economic and Security Alternatives.

Peter Barnes is a successful entrepeneur who co-founded Working Assets and has served on several business boards. He is a senior fellow at the Tomales Bay Insitute.

Chuck Collins is a senior scholar at the Institute for Policy Studies and co-author of *The Moral Measure of the Economy* (Orbis, 2007) and *Economic Apartheid in America* (New Press, 2005).

James M. Cypher is profesor-investigador, Programa de Doctorado en Estudios del Desarrollo, Universidad Autónoma de Zacatecas, Mexico, and a *Dollars & Sense* associate.

Attieno Davis is the co-author of United for a Fair Economy's 2004 report *The State of the Dream: Enduring Disparities in Black and White.*

Michael Engel is an emeritus professor of political science at Westfield State College in Massachusetts. He is the author of *The Struggle for Control of Public Education* (Temple University, 2000).

Daniel Fireside is the book editor at *Dollars & Sense.*

Ellen Frank is senior economic analyst at the Poverty Institute at Rhode Island College.

Amy Gluckman is co-editor of *Dollars & Sense.*

William Greider has been a political journalist for more than 35 years. He is currently the national affairs correspondent for the *Nation* magazine.

Kayty Himmelstein is a former *Dollars & Sense* intern.

Howard Karger is professor of social work at the University of Houston and the author of *Short-Changed: Life and Debt in the Fringe Economy* (Berret-Koehler, 2005).

Ichiro Kawachi is a professor of social epidemiology at the Harvard School of Public Health.

Marjorie Kelly is editor and publisher of *Business Ethics: Corporate Social Responsibility Report,* a 17-year-old publication. She is also the author of *The Divine Right of Capital* (Berret-Koehler, 2003).

Paul Krugman teaches economics at Princeton University and is a columnist for the *New York Times.*

Dena Libner is a former *Dollars & Sense* intern.

John Lawrence teaches psychology at SUNY's College of Staten Island and is a member of the Grassroots Economic Organizing collective.

Betsy Leondar-Wright is former communications director of United for a Fair Economy and co-author of *The Color of Wealth: The Story Behind the U.S. Racial Wealth Divide* (New Press, 2006).

Meizhu Lui is former executive director of United For a Fair Economy.

Arthur MacEwan teaches economics at the University of Massachusetts-Boston. His most recent book is *Neo-Liberalism or Democracy? Economic Strategy, Markets and Alternatives for the 21st Century* (Zed Books, 1999).

John Miller John Miller teaches economics at Wheaton College and is a member of the *Dollars & Sense* collective.

William Moseley is an assistant professor of geography and former coordinator of the African Studies program at Macalester College in Saint Paul, Minn.

Dedrick Muhammad is senior organizer and research fellow at the Institute for Policy Studies.

Vasuki Nesiah is a senior associate at the International Center for Transitional Justice and co-editor of *lines* magazine.

Rebecca Parrish is a former *Dollars & Sense* intern.

Kevin Phillips is the author of the books *American Theocracy: The Peril and Politics of Radical Religion, Oil, and Borrowed Money in the 21st Century* (Viking Adult, 2006) and *American Dynasty: Aristocracy, Fortune, and the Politics of Deceit in the House of Bush* (Viking Books, 2004)

Sam Pizzigati is the author of *Greed and Good: Understanding and Overcoming the Inequality That Limits Our Lives* (Apex Press, 20004) and the editor of *Too Much,* a newsletter dedicated to capping excessive income and wealth.

Adam Sacks is Executive Director of The Center for Democracy and the Constitution.

Adria Scharf is director of the Richmond Peace Education Center in Richmond, Va., and is a former co-editor of *Dollars & Sense.*

Michelle Sheehan is a member of the *Dollars & Sense* collective.

David Swanson is a board member of the Progressive Democrats of America and is the Washington director of democrats.com.

Alissa Thuotte is a Dollars & Sense intern.

Chris Tilly is an economist teaching at the University of Massachusetts-Lowell and a *Dollars & Sense* associate.

Jessica Weisberg is a former *Dollars & Sense* intern.

Thad Williamson is assistant professor at the Jepson School of Leadership Studies, University of Richmond.